JOURNAL FOR THE STUDY OF THE OLD TESTAMENT
SUPPLEMENT SERIES
340

Sheffield Academic Press
A Continuum imprint

Second Temple Studies III

Studies in Politics, Class and Material Culture

edited by

Philip R. Davies and John M. Halligan

Journal for the Study of the Old Testament
Supplement Series 340

Published by
Sheffield Academic Press Ltd
The Tower Building, 11 York Road, London SE1 7NX
370 Lexington Avenue, New York, NY 10017-6550

www.SheffieldAcademicPress.com
www.continuumbooks.com

British Library Cataloguing-in-Publication Data

A catalogue record for this book is available from the British Library

Typeset by Sheffield Academic Press
Printed on acid-free paper in Great Britain by Bookcraft Ltd, Midsomer Norton, Bath

ISBN 0-8264-6030-5

CONTENTS

ABBREVIATIONS

AAWG	Abhandlungen der Akademie der Wissenschaften in Göttingen
AB	Anchor Bible
ABD	David Noel Freedman (ed.), *The Anchor Bible Dictionary* (New York: Doubleday, 1992)
AGJU	Arbeiten zur Geschichte des antiken Judentums und des Urchristentums
ANET	James B. Pritchard (ed.), *Ancient Near Eastern Texts Relating to the Old Testament* (Princeton: Princeton University Press, 1950)
ASAO	Association for Social Anthropology in Oceania
ASTI	*Annual of the Swedish Theological Institute*
ATANT	Abhandlungen zur Theologie des Alten und Neuen Testaments
BA	*Biblical Archaeologist*
BASOR	*Bulletin of the American Schools of Oriental Research*
BETL	Bibliotheca ephemeridum theologicarum lovaniensium
Bib	*Biblica*
BJRL	*Bulletin of the John Rylands University Library of Manchester*
BJS	Brown Judaic Studies
BZ	*Biblische Zeitschrift*
BZAW	Beihefte zur *ZAW*
CBQ	*Catholic Biblical Quarterly*
CBQMS	*Catholic Biblical Quarterly*, Monograph Series
CRINT	Compendia rerum iudaicarum ad Novum Testamentum
CSSH	*Comparative Studies in History and Society*
EI	*Eretz-Israel*
EncJud	*Encyclopaedia Judaica*
ESHM	European Seminar in Historical Methodology
HSM	Harvard Semitic Monographs
HTR	*Harvard Theological Review*
HUCA	*Hebrew Union College Annual*
IEJ	*Israel Exploration Journal*
JA	*Journal asiatique*
JAR	*Journal of Anthropological Research*
JBL	*Journal of Biblical Literature*
JCS	*Journal of Cuneiform Studies*

JHS	*Journal of Hellenic Studies*
JJS	*Journal of Jewish Studies*
JNES	*Journal of Near Eastern Studies*
JR	*Journal of Religion*
JRS	*Journal of Roman Studies*
JSJ	*Journal for the Study of Judaism in the Persian, Hellenistic and Roman Period*
JSOT	*Journal for the Study of the Old Testament*
JSOTSup	*Journal for the Study of the Old Testament*, Supplement Series
JSPSup	*Journal for the Study of the Pseudepigrapha*, Supplement Series
JSSR	*Journal for the Scientific Study of Religion*
JTS	*Journal of Theological Studies*
LCL	Loeb Classical Library
LEC	Library of Early Christianity
NEB	*New English Bible*
NovT	*Novum Testamentum*
NovTSup	*Novum Testamentum*, Supplements
OTP	James Charlesworth (ed.), *Old Testament Pseudepigrapha*
PEQ	*Palestine Exploration Quarterly*
RB	*Revue biblique*
REJ	*Revue des études juives*
RevQ	*Revue de Qumran*
RSV	Revised Standard Version
SBLDS	SBL Dissertation Series
SEÅ	*Svensk exegetisk årsbok*
SJLA	Studies in Judaism in Late Antiquity
SJOT	*Scandinavian Journal of the Old Testament*
TSAJ	Texte und Studien zum antiken Judentum
YCS	*Yale Classical Studies*
ZA	*Zeitschrift für Assyriologie*
ZAW	*Zeitschrift für die alttestamentliche Wissenschaft*
ZDPV	*Zeitschrift des deutschen Palästina-Vereins*
ZPE	*Zeitschrift für Papyrologie und Epigraphik*

LIST OF CONTRIBUTORS

Philip R. Davies is Professor of Biblical Studies, University of Sheffield, England.

Robert Doran is the Samuel Williston Professor of Greek and Hebrew at the Department of Religion, Amherst College, Amherst, MA, USA.

Lester Grabbe is Professor of Hebrew Bible and Early Judaism and Director of the Graduate Research Institute at the University of Hull, England.

John M. Halligan is at the Department of Religious Studies, St John Fisher College, Rochester, NY, USA.

Kenneth Hoglund is at the Department of Religion, Wake Forest University, NC, USA.

Richard Horsley is at the Department of the Study of Religion, University of Massachusetts, Boston, MA, USA.

James Pasto is at the Department of Anthropology, University of Massachusetts, Boston, MA, USA.

Patrick Tiller is an independent scholar residing in Sharon, MA, USA.

John W. Wright is Professor of Religion, Point Loma Nazarene University, San Diego, CA, USA.

INTRODUCTION

Philip R. Davies

Since the first volume of *Second Temple Studies* (Davies 1991) appeared
—itself the outcome of several years of focused attention to this period
within the SBL Sociology of the Second Temple Group—the agenda has
moved from denoting a relatively unfavoured postscript to the 'biblical
period' to a mainstream component of biblical studies. The second volume
in the series (Eskenazi and Richards 1994), focusing on the relationship of
the temple and the community, directed this attention to one of the central
issues, one also highlighted by the translation of several of Joel Weinberg's essays on the 'Citizen–Temple community' (Weinberg 1992).

So far, then, *Second Temple Studies* volumes have concentrated on the
Persian period, and perhaps rightly, since in the foundations of Second
Temple Judean society lies the key to its later development. But one of the
main obstacles to such research is the paucity of information. The Achaemenid era, at least in Judah, has been relatively less attended to than the Iron
Age, and we know why. The archaeology of the Iron Age in Israel and
Palestine has been driven above all by the belief that *here* lies the 'biblical
period', and *here* the correlation of bible and archaeology will be investi-
gated. But many of those engaged in studies of the Second Temple period
indeed regard *it* as the true 'biblical period' on the grounds that here is to be
found the social context in which all the scriptural books achieved their
biblical form and when the majority were in fact composed, even if in many
cases from some (inaccessible) earlier source materials.

But the Second Temple period offers much more to the scholar. It
comprises a relatively well-attested history in which from the ruins of
older Palestinian kingdoms, under a series of imperial regimes, two major
religions developed—at least to the point where the definitive end of the
period, the destruction of the Temple itself, launched them each into
broader social and theological directions. It is the period of the formation
of pre-rabbinic Judaism, including early Christianity. And, like the crea-

tion of the scriptural writings, these matters need to be analysed over a sufficiently *longue durée*.

The SBL Sociology of the Second Temple Group always had as its agenda an exploration of every phase in this 600-year period, and the contents of this volume do some justice to these wider horizons. Since the phases were addressed in subsequent years, the present volume contains material written some years before this publication. But although revised in some respects where necessary, the contents have not been substantially rewritten and they remain original, thorough and even fundamental exercises in sociological analysis of an age and its literature. For that reason, some of them are necessarily preliminary; while others show the extent to which detailed work is possible when history, text and sociology are integrated.

One sense in which the present volume is still preliminary is in its diachronic structure. This was an inevitable restriction, but it was decided that initially such an approach was best. Yet continuities are also important, and it remains for those threads to be individually and collectively explored (a more thematic structure will be reflected in the next volume of *Second Temple Studies*). But an adequate history of Second Temple Judah/Judea still remains rather distant.

The revolution in the agenda of biblical and Early Jewish studies was not created solely by the Sociology of the Second Temple Group. But that group has played a major role in defining and promoting the agenda. Since its inception, several other groups dealing with related agendas have been born from it, or influenced by it, in recognition of the fact that the 'sociology of the Second Temple period' cannot now be realistically defined merely as a section of biblical scholarship but rather is now a major aspect of virtually all biblical exegesis.

The three sections of the present volume do not, unfortunately, contain papers given specifically on the Ptolemaic and Roman periods, though Grabbe's essay on Hengel does include the Ptolemaic, and they were also covered in the Group's agenda. However, there is a considerable emphasis on the periods of Hellenistic and Hasmonean government, and here there is indeed no shortage of literary or archaeological information (except for the Ptolemaic period in Palestine, poorly researched archaeologically). The work offered here by Horsley, Tiller and Pasto is quite detailed and represents an integration of sociological modelling and precise attention to textual detail. In most of the other essays is reflected either the need for posing fundamental questions, or revising fundamental assumptions.

In the first section, on the Achaemenid period, Kenneth Hoglund's programmatic essay rightly begins the entire collection, and sets the methodological tone by commenting that 'the "archaeological record" is silent until we approach it with a set of theoretical understandings and assumptions that allow it to be perceived as having something to say' (p. 14); he applies this principle to the two questions set to him: 'What was the extent of postexilic society?' and 'What constituted membership of postexilic society?' His conclusion is challenging, because it illustrates his resistance to the 'urban' agenda of the many scholars who focus on the centrality of Jerusalem and its temple (and community). Here he develops his substantial essay in *Second Temple Studies 1* (Hoglund 1991) that the reconstitution of Yehud was primarily agricultural, rural, and not engineered through an urban elite. Even if the distinction between 'urban' and 'rural' is in some respects challengeable, Hoglund's claim questions a Jerusalem-centred ideology of the origins of Second Temple society. Have we yet again to beware of taking a biblical story sketched by Jerusalem scribes of a later time writing themselves back into the origins of their society, as a blueprint for our modern critical history? Perhaps not. In Hoglund's own words:

> The overall portrait that emerges in the postexilic community is of a decentralized, ruralized population spread across the central Judean hill country. Such a pattern calls into serious question any reconstruction of the social constitution of the postexilic community that requires an urban aristocracy or an extensive integration of population (p. 18).

Often overlooked in studies of the Achaemenid period is the gap between the 'edict of Cyrus' (itself far from an assured historical datum) and the emergence of the biblical narratives about the 'Return'. The gap may be ideologically closed in Ezra–Nehemiah but a century, after all, elapses between the advent of Cyrus and the time in which Nehemiah's activities are dated, during which period the state (and status) of Jerusalem is hardly known (we have only the curious books of Haggai and Zechariah). When (and why and how?) did the city of Jerusalem begin to develop into the prosperous temple-city implied, perhaps, already in Chronicles, but to become greater in the first century BCE and even more so in the first century CE? And meanwhile, what was the character of 'rural Judaism'? What, even, if Deuteronomy is to be dated to the fifth century after all, and should be read in the context of Jerusalem's reassertion of hegemony over Judah?

John Wright's essay deals with the urban phenomenon, yet conforms to

Hoglund's call for a methodological framework, as signalled by the opening quotation from Michel Foucault. This study of spaces around the gate, analysed in terms of its symbolism and especially of power and its relations—including the very Foucauldian theme of surveillance—is traced through various biblical texts reflecting the different periods of late monarchic, Babylonian and Achaemenid, again following Foucault's method of careful scrutiny of literary texts. For all students of social-scientific history-writing, Wright offers a substantial vindication of the usefulness of an approach that reconstructs historical configurations through careful and critical analysis of the literature which looks not primarily for the narrated data but the symbolism and power relations conveyed by the discourse as clues to the social context of the literature.

For the Achaemenid period, here are Wright's conclusions:

> Power reconfigures the Achaemenid period. The city is an ethnic-national center. City walls and gates create a national-military boundary, a place for the nation to gather. Temple gates still maintain their control over the temple court; now, however, royal power presides over both the gates and the courts. The economic goods of the society shift within the fortified confines of the temple complex. Power, however, concentrates chiefly on the space outside the temple gates—the city square. The square defines national citizenship, a place where those of proper patrimony may gather. In gathering in the square, however, the citizenry is subjected to the gaze of the royal/governmental power. Surveillance is achieved over an otherwise diffuse population (p. 49).

In Wright's analysis the urban architecture of Jerusalem (the only major city of Judah in this period) reflects the structure of political and social power, and indeed the social identity of the inhabitants. At the same time, however, Wright's study underlines the problem raised by Hoglund's claim that the early Achaemenid period is essentially rural. Without necessarily contradicting that conclusion, this essay prompts us to ask how such an elaborate urban discourse presents itself in Second Temple literature, and, if Hoglund's conclusions are accepted, at what stage in the development of Achaemenid Yehud we can recognize *historically* the growth of such an urban centre. At any rate, not before the end of the fifth century at the very earliest, if the chronology of the book of Nehemiah is accepted.

The theme of 'Hellenism' dominates the other two sections of the volume. Part II opens, appropriately, with an assessment by Lester Grabbe of the major work of recent decades on the topic, Martin Hengel's *Judaism and Hellenism* (1974). Hengel's thesis of the thorough 'Hellenization' of

Palestine has figured prominently in recent decades and (building on the previous work of Tcherikover and Bickerman) has succeeded, by and large, in dismissing the value of a simple opposition between 'Judaism' and 'Hellenism', itself—again taken over from the ancient Jewish literature such as the books of Maccabees and the writings of Josephus.

Grabbe not only conveniently summarizes the major points and reactions but also, in his subsequent appraisal, makes it clear that Hellenization was not homogeneous and that Oriental or Greek elements might predominate in different loci:

> Hellenistic civilization was *sui generis* and must be considered from a variety of points of view, for it concerned many different areas of life: language, custom, religion, commerce, architecture, dress, government, literary and philosophical ideals (p. 62).

Any assessment of such a process, then, must begin by defining that process itself; and Grabbe makes it clear just how problematic interpretation of the data can be. He also makes the point that the process began well before the so-called 'Hellenistic' period. Indeed, as we know, Greek penetration in the Levant can be traced back not only into the Persian period, but also into the era of the Babylonian and even Assyrian empires. Greek presence in this area was, indeed, the logical outcome of the Assyrian policy of westward expansion, one goal of which was opening, politically, the way between the Mediterranean and the Tigris-Euphrates region.

Longer perspectives are essential for sociological studies of this kind, and Grabbe alludes to this in his comment that 'the day-to-day life of the bulk of the population in the Near East probably changed little between the third millennium BCE and the nineteenth century CE' [p. 63]! Certainly, Hellenization, whatever that means, needs also to be understood as part of the slower and longer cultural and economic trend that saw the centre of gravity of Eastern Mediterranean civilization move westward, not only in terms of politics and economics (becoming essentially maritime), but also with respect to religious and scientific lore. And such trends do not depend only on political configurations. Commerce is always a more powerful instrument of cultural exchange. As Grabbe views it, within the Greek-type *poleis* of the Levant, there was no interest in cultural imperialism as such by the Greek rulers. Rather, most of the influence came through the willing adoption by Orientals of Greek language and elements of Greek culture. Nevertheless, as the following paper by Hoglund documents, the Seleucids did engage in a deliberate urbanizing policy.

In his conclusion, Grabbe also notes, importantly, that the opposition

Hellenization/Judaism is a contrast of unequal phenomena. Many if not all local cultures negotiated with the Greek presence and in so doing created different forms of 'Hellenism'. To the vast majority of ancient Jews, those who lived outside Palestine especially, Greek-speaking and Greek-thinking Judaism was part of the 'Hellenized' world. Grabbe suggests, nevertheless, that 'however Hellenized they might be, observant Jews could never be fully at home in the Greek world' (p. 66).

Hoglund's second essay is a review of the material culture of the Seleucid period. Drawing attention again to the deplorable lack of archaeological resources for this period of Palestinian/Judaean history, and the lack of adequate classification within the 'Hellenistic' period of this region generally, he points above all to a process of urbanization that saw a transfer of a proportion of the population from countryside to city and the establishment of new cities, often together with the abandonment of older urban sites. He also notes evidence of a shift in wealth creation and economic activity away from agriculture (still typical of the Ptolemaic period, if the Zenon papyri are as typical as they are often taken to be) towards trade and related activities. These would include not only taxes on the passage of goods, but also the growth in number and size of markets, the provision of accommodation for traders and their goods and of course the surplus value created by exchange, stimulated by the increased use of coinage.

Hoglund suggests, against Grabbe, that promotion of 'Hellenization' was indeed a Seleucid policy. Such changes in the material culture invite exploration of the relationship of 'Judaism' and 'Hellenism'. And although Hoglund's remit does go beyond the material culture, he comments on the possible beneficiaries of such a policy; a core of citizens (in Jerusalem as elsewhere) committed to 'Hellenistic' values, but perhaps for economic reasons above all. We are thus prompted to ask: how far is the issue of 'Hellenism' in Judea implicated with the creation of a new kind of elite? The essays that follow Hoglund's re-engage this question, for education will certainly have been a key factor in the rise and establishment of such an elite.

The first of these essays, by Richard Horsley and Patrick Tiller, probes the social configurations reflected in the book of Ben Sira, engaging critically with the theory of G. Lenski (1966) on power and privilege. In particular, they challenge the notion of a distinct priestly *class*, and indeed prefer to concentrate rather on class *relations*:

> And it makes a considerable difference in what catches our attention if we focus less on the different social strata or 'classes' than on the basic political-economic-religious relations between those social strata, for

example, on the relations between (higher) ruler and subordinate governing class and the relations between the governing class and the peasant producers (p. 89).

The urban-rural dimension re-emerges here, as Horsley and Tiller revise Lenski:

> If we were then to place Lenski's various classes not as a scheme of social stratification (the predilection of much American social sociology) but in a scheme of fundamental political-economic relations, following precisely the information provided by Lenski, it is clear that the fundamental/basic or controlling relationship lies between the rulers and the agricultural producers, the peasantry who comprise the vast majority (90%) of the people of such an agrarian society (p. 90).

The reconstruction of Seleucid (and by implication Ptolemaic) Judean society adopted by Horsley and Tiller is one in which the priesthood ruled and had the allegiance of all, including the peasants. This allegiance was crucial to stability and if the priests compromised too much with alien culture the equilibrium would be lost.

Was there, then, no internal conflict in Ben Sira's society? There is a strong possibility that already in the third century, the Enochic *Book of the Watchers* reflects a priestly rivalry. But Horsley and Tiller believe that while the Enochian sages served a priestly party that (at least in the third and second centuries) unsuccessfully competed for influence and authority, they nevertheless fulfilled a sociological role identical to that of Ben Sira and his students. They did not disrupt the social structure itself. They conclude with the following question:

> Is Ben Sira's picture of a social structure that is stable and quiet despite its deep divisions a reliable picture of Judea, and its differences with other sources to be explained as representing the calm of the early second century just before the storm unleashed by the Hellenizing reform of 175? Or should Ben Sira be seen as an accurate observer of the basic social structure but himself a conservative supporter of the high priesthood (and one perhaps simply oblivious to the roots of the impending social conflicts)? Or should Ben Sira's picture of a relatively simple basic social structure in Judea be dismissed as inaccurate insofar as it must miss a more complex structure and division in the society? (p. 103).

This question is answered in one way by Horsley and Tiller, but in quite another by John Halligan, who takes the Jerusalem temple itself as a focus for analysis of Second Temple Judaism in the Seleucid period. As he puts it:

The Hellenistic period saw the growth of non-priestly power groups who needed to be accommodated to the increasingly dominant power of the ruling high-priestly dynasty. And of course this fault-line was connected to the other: political allegiance to Seleucids or Ptolemies implied a stake in the political and social power structure of Judea (p. 109).

With the ideology of Ben Sira, often thought to represent a 'Jerusalem consensus', as a springboard, Halligan exposes the faultlines that must have already existed in Ben Sira's time. By focusing on two specific strands, which lie at different ends of the spectrum of ideologies, Halligan demonstrates the complexity of Temple ideology in the Seleucid period: for Jason, the continued primacy and privilege of the Oniad dynasty could best be preserved by some accommodation with the new non-priestly groups, and, without wishing to diminish the status of the Temple, he offered these persons a status within the Seleucid empire, as citizens of one of its *poleis*. That his bid failed is evident, and the Jewish sources, despite their clear bias against him, reveal some of the real reasons.

Halligan's second probe, the case of the Qumran literature shows, by contrast, how strong allegiance to the Temple—allied with a commitment to one particular priestly tradition—led to an effective boycott of that temple, provoking other ideologies to replace it. Between the cases of Jason and of the Scrolls, linking them both and the entire spectrum, is the problem of accommodating competing views of the temple without creating factionalism. This challenge proved impossible and, as Halligan concludes, 'only the destruction of that temple, perhaps, would in the end resolve the problem of who should run the temple' (p. 115). If colliding with the analysis of Horsley and Tiller, Halligan is developing the thesis of a new rich, lay class hinted at by Hoglund.

One of the key aspects of such a class would have been its education, and their hegemonic challenge to the priestly establishment was not least in respect of literacy, something they would perhaps need professionally but might also have the leisure to acquire, to emulate their Greek counterparts (I have argued elsewhere [Davies 1998: 142-51] that this issue is closely tied to the process of canonization and that some biblical books were written by and for this class). Robert Doran offers a review of Jewish education in Ben Sira, in Alexandria and finally in the Jerusalem gymnasium built by Jason. Of Ben Sira, he concludes:

...the one teacher we know of in pre-Hasmonean Jerusalem is someone who maintains a strong interest in Jewish traditional literature but is not averse to including in his curriculum suitable literature from other traditions (39.4), nor would he discourage the study of foreign languages (p. 122).

Gleaning clues from the numerous fragments of Jewish writers from Alexandria, Doran can also demonstrate the existence of 'biblical education' being carried on in Greek.

Finally, on the matter of the gymnasium in Jerusalem, Doran argues that 'Hellenization' and 'assimilation' do not furnish sufficient grounds to explain its construction, since there is little evidence of such institutions in second-century Syria or Palestine, that is, within the Seleucid realm. What other motives are left for Jason's initiative? Partly in support of Halligan's analysis, Doran suggests that Jason needed political support to bolster his own position after ousting Onias III from the position of high-priest. Controlling access to the gymnasium would provide him with a means of bestowing favours and thus of building his own political base:

> ...it was a means of securing stability in a buffer state and making it into a center devoted to the Seleucid cause. Such an explanation of the building of the gymnasium says nothing about its curriculum in literature, and certainly does not require any change in ancestral religion, laws and constitution. It is the author of 2 Maccabees who has given it this spin. One does not therefore have to posit motives of Hellenization, that is, apostasy from Judaism or an enlightened reform of Judaism, to explain why a gymnasium was built in Jerusalem (p. 131).

Several contributors to this volume, then, are concerned to offer explanations for the developments in Jerusalem under Antiochus IV that do not simply rely upon a conflict between 'Judaism' and 'Hellenism' as two opposing cultures, nor upon a religious explanation for the crisis that this engendered. The reasons, and the processes, have also to do with class relations and with economics. Horsley's investigation of the Hasmonean expansions also looks for political rather than religious reasons for the 'conversion' (he rightly deems the term inappropriate) of neighboring territories. From his quite detailed investigation of the relations between the Hasmonean regime and subjected peoples, particularly the Idumeans and the Galileans, he concludes that

> Those relations, far from being susceptible of understanding in terms of religious conversion, must be dealt with in terms of the political-economic-religious structure of an ancient temple-state that expanded its territory and power during a period of imperial weakness. In the case of the Hasmoneans, the new incumbents of the high priesthood in Jerusalem were, to start with, illegitimate occupants of the office whose power depended on the military forces built up during the resistance against the declining Seleucid imperial regime. Beyond the confined ideology of 1 Maccabees there is no indication that Hasmonean expansion was a religious crusade (p. 163).

The Hasmoneans, indeed, employed non-Judaean mercenaries in their professional army and established an increasingly Hellenized administration. They exploited Seleucid decline to expand their own domains in Palestine. The Seleucid and Roman decrees do not represent 'the laws of the Judaeans' as pertaining to the polity or constitution of the state and its relations with its subjects.

> Thus when subject peoples were required to live according to those 'laws of the Judeans', it pertained to the relations of the people in their village communities to the Hasmonean state. There is no direct evidence of any attempt to press the subject peoples to apply 'the laws of the Judeans' in their conduct of local community and family affairs. Of course, insofar as observing the laws of the Judeans in relations with the central government impinged adversely on the conduct of local affairs, then structural conflict would have developed (p. 164).

Pasto's quite wide-ranging essay covers essentially three major, related topics. First, he argues that the history of modern scholarship has reflected a pro-Greek bias in its depiction of the conflict between 'Hellenizers' and 'Judaizers'. Thus, for example, he refers to 'discursive practices that already differentiated the referent of "Jew" in terms of limited and expansive, or national and religious, identities, and always in terms of Christian origins as the triumph of universalism over particularism' (p. 176).

Pasto documents his case well, but it strikes this reader of the scholarly literature that in most textbooks at any rate, the Hellenizers are, following the Jewish literature of the time, the villains. Receptions histories can have more than one stream! Nevertheless, he is very probably justified in suggesting that our modern attitudes to this question are informed by cultural preferences and prejudices that we bring to our interpretation; and a particularly crucial period is late nineteenth- early twentieth-century Germany, with the growth of *Wissenschaft des Judentums*, reformed Judaism and the issue of Jewish vs. German nationality. The tragic consequences (but also the brilliant scholarly outcome in so many cases) of this do cast a shadow over much of the debate about 'Hellenization'.

Pasto's second topic is the existence of 'Judaism', which he presents in terms of a 'big tradition'; this social-anthropological category enables him to re-describe the nature of Jewish 'parties' and 'sects' in terms of 'little traditions' which of course always imply a 'big tradition'. At any event, Pasto wants to reinstate the 'Judaism' of this period as something very real. As he puts it: '*Jewish normativity and Jewish diversity are complementary, not contradictory, features of the social reality of the time*' (p. 184). Lest one be tempted to think that this is merely a different way of describing the same phenomenon of related 'Judaisms', Pasto is also redefining what *kind* of an entity 'Judaism' is:

> In terms of Jewish history and Hasmonean origins, we might best be served by distancing ourselves from the concept of 'ethnicity' as a major category for social formation and self-reference, especially if this is configured in the destitute frame of inclusive versus exclusive forms of identity and set against the category of 'religion' (p. 177).

Finally, as a third topic, Pasto engages in a couple of models, using comparative data. The first is a fascinating description of the Hasmonaeans as 'local strongmen' using comparative data from nineteenth-century Ottoman Palestine; the second is a comparison of Hasmonaean and Ashanti expansion in West Africa in the early eighteenth century.

At the end of this very rich, detailed, suggestive and of course controversial essay, Pasto makes two important general points: first the Jews are not a special case in antiquity; and second, they were not undergoing some great cultural crisis in the mid-second century BCE. He pleads for an understanding of 'Judaism' that is 'outside Christian hegemonic categories' (but, I would query, also outside Jewish ones?). The 'post-Orientalist' and postcolonial perspectives that Pasto urges do indeed help to steer sociological analysis away from the categories of interpretation that the traditional theological and humanistic-historical approaches to such questions have employed and, like several of the contributions to this volume, demonstrate the power of social-scientific methods to deliver entirely new analyses and insights.

Although the volume ends, not inappropriately, with the case of the Samaritans, by definition, not 'Judean', Samaritanism is nevertheless often understood as a 'Jewish sect'. It also encountered cultural forces and underwent similar social developments similar to those in Judea. Thus, in Grabbe's own words:

> The history of the Samaritan community seems similar to that of Jews but in miniature, since the Gerizim community was apparently smaller than that of the Jews. They had much the same basic customs, with the main difference being the appropriate place for God's temple. They both had a Diaspora population. They both suffered religious suppression or persecution, the Samaritans suffering also at the hands of the Jews and possibly vice versa (pp. 216-17).

Unfortunately, as his excellent review of the data and the problems demonstrates, we know too little (as opposed to being told too little, which may also be true but a different matter) about these Samaritans, whether from their own sources or from those of others. Crucially disputed, of course, is when and why their rift with Judaism came about. Again, as Grabbe reminds us right at the end, we could be in danger of oversimplifying; perhaps dealings with Samaritans differed according to class (and possibly other social formations)?

I have benefitted enormously from the task of editing these contributions, yet I remain aware of the need to revisit and rethink a host of issues with which this volume grapples. I end this introduction with the hope that readers will feel the same, and perhaps 'go and do likewise'. For there does indeed remain much to be done.

Part I
THE ACHAEMENID PERIOD

THE MATERIAL CULTURE OF THE PERSIAN PERIOD
AND THE SOCIOLOGY OF THE SECOND TEMPLE PERIOD

Kenneth Hoglund

This essay reflects an attempt to place the study of the material culture of the Persian period on a more theoretically correct footing. As such, it may appear unnecessarily restrictive to some who are used to a more discursive style of approach to Syro-Palestinian archaeology, but the reasoning behind the analysis undertaken here is part of the ongoing effort to make the questions, and the assumptions behind those questions, explicit before arriving at possible answers.

Much of anthropologically informed archaeology is distinguished from older forms of approaches by its insistence on an explicit research design before undertaking an analysis. Behind this insistence is the understanding that empirical data says nothing in and of itself. It speaks only when we ask the right kinds of questions. To put it another way, the 'archaeological record' is silent until we approach it with a set of theoretical understandings and assumptions that allow it to be perceived as having something to say. The selection of what data to consider, the establishment of temporal and spatial boundaries, and the assumptions regarding the import of various lines of data must all be voiced and explained for the true measure of an archaeological analysis to be tested.

All this serves as a prologue to an effort to establish such a research design for the Persian period in the Levant that will serve to provide some insight into the sociology of the period. The SBL Sociology of the Second Temple Group, by which this paper was originally commissioned, as a whole posed two issues to those addressing the Persian period: What was the extent of postexilic society? What constituted membership of postexilic society?

From a material culture perspective, several related issues need to be addressed. What is meant by the term 'postexilic society'? Is this a spatio-temporal entity that can be relatively fixed? When we speak of the 'extent' of this entity, are we speaking in spatial terms of effective political control, of spheres of regular contact and influence, or of the furthest distribution of isolated trade items?

For the purposes of this study, I have understood the Group's use of 'postexilic society' to refer to those elements of the population located in the region surrounding Jerusalem, that is, the community that gave rise to the biblical materials of the early postexilic period (Haggai, Zechariah, Ezra–Nehemiah, 1 and 2 Chronicles). This regional definition immediately raises the question of a co-identification with a political entity: that is, is the region surrounding Jerusalem coextensive with the political boundaries of the 'district (Aramaic *medina*)' of Yehud? Further complicating this issue is the debate over the historical foundation of Yehud as a distinct political (and hence, social?) entity (see now Carter [1999] for a comprehensive discussion of the issues of boundaries, settlement and demography).

While there is no consensus on these points, some distinctions need to be made before an effective database can be arrived at for analysis. For my purposes, the region under consideration may also reflect the boundaries of Yehud as a political entity; certainly there will be considerable overlap. However, no presumption will be made that the region of inquiry was in its entirety 'Yehudian', nor that Yehud's boundaries were a subset of the region.

As far as the historical debate over the foundation of Yehud is concerned, I will assume that elements were in place from the dedication of the Second Temple (c. 515 BCE) onward to create administrative and social differentiation, without presupposing that the Temple cultus itself was the means of such differentiations (as argued by Weinberg [1973]; see also Weinberg [1992]). However, the existence of such a religious center in an area removed from Samaria would have necessitated some form of local administration to oversee the distribution of regional funds for support of the cultus. The impetus toward differentiation would have been accelerated in the mid-fifth century by the mission of Nehemiah (and Ezra, if he is assigned to the 458 date) whether one takes Nehemiah to be the first 'true' governor of the district (as does Alt [1953] and his followers) or a reform-minded governor in a long line of such political figures (Cross 1975; Avigad 1976). This would allow for the region to be perceived as possessing a certain identity apart from Samaria whether that identity was the result of administrative and political independence or not.

Having delineated the grounds for assuming some form of cultural distinction to the region, it remains to set some spatial boundaries to the area of analysis. Traditionally, the boundaries of 'Yehud' have been established on a perceived congruence between two distinct forms of data: the various toponomic lists of Ezra–Nehemiah, and the distribution of the 'Yehud' jar-stamps and/or coins (Avi-Yonah 1966; Stern 1982). Both lines of evidence are problematical, and the suggested congruence between them is hardly conclusive.

Regarding the toponomic lists, each has a series of literary problems within its setting that seriously undermines any effort to use it as an historical source. For example, the lists of returnees at Ezra 2 and Nehemiah 7 are derived from some source other than an authentic list of the late sixth century BCE, and are intimately related to the final redaction of the narratives (Eskenazi 1988). Stern has shown that the list in Nehemiah 11 giving the places that supplied population to Jerusalem is modeled on portions of the book of Joshua and represents an idealized portrait of the postexilic community (Stern 1977). The list of workers in Nehemiah 3 apparently does not represent districts of the region but the organization of corvée units (Demsky 1983). In sum, not a single list in Ezra–Nehemiah can be unequivocally utilized as a reflection of the boundaries of Yehud in the Persian period.

Regarding the Yehud jar-stamps and coins, a distinction should be made between the two kinds of artifact, both in terms of date and possible function. As for the jar-stamps, Stern is probably correct in assuming that the jar-stamps in Aramaic script are the most pertinent to the Persian period, since the Hebrew script forms are almost certainly of a second century BCE date (Stern 1982: 202-206). It should be noted that no published example of an Aramaic Yehud jar-stamp has yet come from a stratigraphically clear context, and thus the dating is derived from paleographic comparisons rather than association with closely dated strata. The dilemma with this procedure is that the scripts of these stamps are in a mixture of lapidary and cursive forms of Aramaic that is particularly difficult to date (Cross 1982: 132). While there are no conclusive reasons to question the consensus dating of the Aramaic jar-stamps, until stratigraphically certain contexts are established for such finds, their relative dating must remain tentative.

The assumption that such jar-stamps represent some form of governmental function is a common, though undemonstrated, assumption among those using the stamps as evidence for the boundaries of Yehud. First, as regards their governmental function, the assumption is based on a total of eight seals found only at Ramat Rahel in a stratigraphically mixed setting where *yhd* (Yehud) is linked with *hphw'* (the Governor). While most writers have taken the term *phw'* to relate to an official office ('governor' related to the Akkadian *bel piḥati*), this consensus has recently been seriously questioned (Lipiński 1989). Even if one follows the identification of this term as 'governor' and accepts the paleography as being consistent with the fifth–fourth centuries BCE, neither the context of the find nor the term 'governor' being connected with the official name of the district provides a clear sense of the function of the jar-stamps. If one is to assume that their distribution will in some manner conform to the political boundaries of Yehud, it is necessary to determine their function.

Secondly, even if one takes all the Aramaic Yehud jar-stamps of this type as indicative of some official function, their findspots range from Jerusalem, Ramat Rahel, Tell en-Nasbeh, Jericho, to En-gedi (Stern 1982: 203, types A, B and D). Those who use the Yehud jar-stamps for determining the boundaries of Yehud do not differentiate between those jar-stamps of genuine fifth–fourth centuries BCE (Stern's types A, B and D) and the paleo-Hebrew Yehud stamps of a certain second-century BCE date (Stern's type C). This mixing of types of differing dates and possible differing functions only confuses the issue of the boundaries of Yehud. If the distribution of the Aramaic jar-stamps is studied on its own terms, it is evident these can contribute little to defining the boundaries of the district.

If neither the biblical toponyms nor the Yehud jar-stamps provide unequivocal evidence for the boundaries of Yehud, then is it possible to define the district's boundaries on the basis of any 'objective' criteria? The answer to this question is a qualified 'yes'. A careful consideration of the environmental constraints within which any human occupation of the Judean hill country must function provides general parameters for a geopolitical entity centered in the hill country. To start with, to the east the terrain and available rainfall drop off rapidly east of Tekoa. Consequently, apart from isolated sites along the shores of the Dead Sea (such as En-gedi), most of the region under consideration will have been situated west of a line drawn from Tekoa to Kain (modern en-Nebi Yaqin). To the west, a natural boundary area is the rapid descent of terrain where a line of Senonian chalk has been eroded. In the past, this line has served as the boundary between the Judean hill country and the Shephelah (Baly 1974: 36, 81). This line also marks a major change in rainfall patterns, the gently rolling Shephelah receiving 400-500 mm/yr while the abrupt rise of the Judean hill country receives 500-700 mm/yr.

The border of this region to the south is problematical. A number of scholars, noting the absence of Yehud seals south of Beth-Zur and the notice in 1 Macc. 4.29 that Beth-Zur was in 'Idumean' hands, have assumed that the region south of Beth-Zur was occupied by Edomite groups in the Persian period, and thus that the southern border of Yehud is placed at Beth-Zur (Stern 1982: 246-47). The Yehud seal data are questionable, and it seems even more speculative to use literary notices of the mid-second century to reconstruct conditions of the fifth–fourth centuries. If the possibility of 'Yehudian' settlement south of Beth-Zur is granted, then it is most sensible to draw the line about 12km south of Hebron, where the rainfall drops off to 300-400 mm/yr. To the north, there is no secure point to place a boundary. Presumably it would have been in the vicinity of the traditional border between Israel and Judah, somewhere to the immediate south of Bethel.

Having delineated this region in spatial terms, it is possible to make some general statements about the contribution of material culture to the reconstruction of the social forces acting on the postexilic community. Unfortunately, excavations within this area are limited, and there are no real indicators of burial customs, cultic observances or linguistic traits that might provide clues as to the ethnic character of the region.

The actual settlements of the Persian period in this region do offer some very suggestive indications of the economic and social organization of the postexilic community. The primary source for settlement data in the region is the 1967 survey published under the general editorship of Moshe Kochavi (1972). The Kochavi survey was conducted under extreme conditions, and efforts to confirm the results of the survey have met with little success. A more recent survey has been undertaken by A. Ofer, but at the time of writing no data from this survey have yet emerged.

From the Kochavi material it is apparent that the Persian period was marked by an intensification of settlements. Some 63 per cent of the Persian period sites in this region had no prior Iron II occupation and represent new settlements (Hoglund 1990). In addition, these sites are largely unwalled farming communities, spaced in a pattern that maximizes agricultural production. This same pattern of settlement during the Persian period has been reported for the northern portion of the Ephraimite hill country where 58 per cent of located sites were without Iron II precedents (Zertal 1990).

The overall portrait that emerges in the postexilic community is of a decentralized, ruralized population spread across the central Judean hill country. Such a pattern calls into serious question any reconstruction of the social constitution of the postexilic community that requires an urban aristocracy or an extensive integration of population. It suggests that a more fruitful approach might be to bring a variety of social observations about rural agrarian society to the postexilic biblical materials in an effort to set them in an appropriate social context.

A TALE OF THREE CITIES:
URBAN GATES, SQUARES AND POWER IN IRON AGE II, NEO-BABYLONIAN AND ACHAEMENID JUDAH

John W. Wright

> A whole history remains to be written of *spaces*—which would at the same time be the history of *powers* (Foucault 1980: 49).

Analyses of Israelite cities have dealt largely with Iron Age II and Helle-nistic-Roman urban configurations. Evidence from the Achaemenid period has largely been subsumed into earlier and later periods to help 'fill out' otherwise incomplete models. As a result, the Israelite city has been largely viewed as static, unchanged until the 'importation' of the 'foreign' form of the *polis* in the Hellenistic age. While we have begun to under-stand Judean society as dynamic and changing in the Achaemenid period, we have yet to develop a keen sense of its urban setting, an oversight crucial in light of the probability that what later became the Hebrew Bible was either preserved or composed within an Achaemenid urban environment (i.e. Jerusalem). In this essay I will attempt to make a place for the configuration of the Judean city in the Achaemenid period through a social analysis of three urban spaces: the entrance of the gate; the gate; and the city square. Urban spaces change geographically and socially as the power that embodies them shifts location. A spatial analysis of the urban configuration can provide one perspective on the changing social dimensions in Iron Age II, neo-Babylonian, and Achaemenid Judah.

I will begin with a social analysis based on the literature of the Hebrew Bible. While certain dangers inhere in such an endeavor, the standard critical chronology of writings allows the formation of a coherent typol-ogy. This typology, then, can aid in the clarification of the dating for more controverted writings. Different urban configurations and their supporting ideologies emerge. I will seek to explicate the historical contingency and disjunction within the history of the Israelite/Judean city.

City Gates and Public Squares in Iron Age II Israel: The Literary Evidence

Within pre-exilic biblical texts, city gates constitute an important social boundary between the 'insiders' and 'outsiders' of the Israelite city. Forti-fied entryways into the city gates represent 'civic space' *par excellence* within the Israelite city, an architectural institution that regulated much of the city's civic life. In contrast, the square, urban open space, falls within an anonymous social realm between the domestic and the civic. Squares are dangerous places of transience between the ordered realms of the household and the *civitas*. As the household played an important role within the *civitas* of the city, the 'public' square represents a spatial dimension that escaped the social ordering of the Judean city. The square's social ambiguity reinforced the positive significance of the city gate.

I would like to analyze the social configuration of the Israelite city as indicated by the literary evidence by moving geographically from the out-skirts of the city to its interior: from the entrance of the gate (פתח־השער) to the gate complex itself and finally into 'empty' urban space, the square. Careful attention to the social dynamics in each location can help recon-struct the latent significance of each location.

Outside the City: The Entrance of the Gate

The 'entrance of the gate' seems to represent a technical label in pre-exilic Israel for the geographical and social boundary between the city and the neutral countryside. It is an area outside the jurisdiction of the city and its governance, a location nearby, but not part of the city. The entrance of the gate represents the boundary between inside and outside the city. The פתח, not the gate itself, was the threshold to the pre-exilic Israelite city.

As a threshold or boundary, the entrance of the gate formed a neutral zone for social interaction related to the city during non-military occa-sions. When Ahab and Jehoshaphat enter an alliance against Syria, the two kings, both in their royal regalia, meet 'at the threshing floor in the entrance of the gate of Samaria' (1 Kgs 22.10). This location is not accidental. City space permitted only the presence of one king. A foreign monarch may enter the city (i.e. the gates) only as visitor or vanquished. The entrance of the gate, therefore, provided an institutional setting that recognized the royal status of each king, enabling the royal conference without mixing social signals to the inhabitants of Samaria. The entrance of the gate functions similarly in the procedure by which a person might obtain sanctuary. The involuntary manslayer 'shall stand [in] the entrance of the gate of the city and speak his words in the ears of the elders of that city; then they will admit him into the city with them and they will give him a place and he will dwell with them' (Josh. 20.4). Outside the city, the entrance of the gate allows communication to take place with the 'elders' of the city without endangering the city space itself. A person enters city space only after the elders have decided favorably in his or her favor.

The entrance of the gate was related closely to the city without strictly being part of the city space itself. During the Assyrian siege of Jerusalem, lepers stayed at the entrance of the gate (2 Kgs 7.3)—protected by the city walls from the Assyrians, their physical condition did not permit entrance within the city proper. Along with the street, the top of the walls and the squares, the entrance of the gates provides the setting in which Wisdom chastises the 'fools' for not heeding her call (Prov. 1.21).

The entrance of the gate was truly liminal—the last stop before one entered or exited the city.[1] It therefore possessed great military significance. It provided an early defensive front for the city, with retreat into the city always a possibility (cf. 2 Sam. 10.8).[2] In a military conflict, the entrance was a dangerous space, both for the attackers and the defenders. In David's wars against the Ammonites, Uriah the Hittite dies when the Israelites force the Ammonites back 'into the entrance of the city gate' (2 Sam. 23.18).[3] Yet if the entrance of the gate could be gained, the fall of the city could soon ensue (cf. Judg. 9.44-45). Jeremiah 1.14-19 plays upon this spatial imagery. God will bring forth enemies from the north to besiege Jerusalem: 'They will come and each will place his throne [in] the entrance of the gates of Jerusalem...then I will speak judgment against them for all their wickedness with which they forsook me' (Jer. 1.15). In contrast, God will make Jeremiah a 'fortified city and bronze walls against all the earth' (Jer. 1.18).[4] Jeremiah himself will stand inviolate as a city able to defend the entrance of its gates.

Finally, symbolic activities display the entrance of the gate's character as related to, but not of, the city. Even though Joshua has thoroughly

---

1.   Cf. also Prov. 8.31 for a similar setting, although the term פתח־שער is not used.
2.   Cf. also Judg. 18.16-17.
3   To approach the 'entrance of the gate' so early in a siege seems to have been commonly recognized as military folly. Joab expects David's anger at taking the troops so close to the wall (2 Sam. 11.20-21). See also the initial days of Abimelech's war against Shechem for casualties 'to the entrance of the gate' (Judg. 9.40).
4.   Following LXX.

destroyed Ai and its inhabitants, he buries the king of Ai under a pile of rocks 'in the entrance of the gate of the city' (Josh. 8.29). He thus symbolically denies the king's membership in the city in death[5] and constructs a political message for those who might enter the ruins of the city with hopes of reconstruction. In Jehu's purge of the house of Ahab, Jehu orders that the heads of the 70 sons of Ahab spend the night 'in two piles in the entrance of the gate' (2 Kgs 10.8). The next morning, then, Jehu 'went out and stood and addressed all the people' (v. 9). The location in the 'entrance of the gate' is symbolically significant. The heads never enter the city— such would signal their legitimacy, their affiliation with the city, and call Jehu's usurpation into question. The entrance of the gate provides a 'neutral' space, easily accessible to the city, for Jehu's speech. Decomposing royal heads stacked outside the city communicated the illegitimacy of the house of Ahab, and thus Jehu's legitimacy.

To sum up this section: the entrance of the gate composed an important social space in the Iron Age II Israelite city. A neutral territory, it played an important social function in providing a distinct space from the city, yet one monitored and controlled by the civic authorities. The entrance of the gate constituted the boundary of the city, close by, but not of. To be of the city, one had to enter into the city gate.

The City Defined: Inside the Gate

The city gate represents the civic space *par excellence* within the Iron Age II Israelite city. The gate provides a spatial definition of membership within the city: one's presence 'in the gates' qualifies one as a member of the society. The gate is not liminal space. Though at the city's periphery geographically, it lies at the city's center socially. As the spatial marker of social membership, the gate is laden with key social functions, the means by which the city 'elders' exercise their control over the city. Though ostensibly fortifications against 'outside threats', the city gate more commonly functions as a means of control and surveillance of the city inhabitants themselves.

Though geographically close, the social gulf between the gate and the entrance of the gate is immense. The gate is *civitas*, the space where the inhabitants of the city, or at least its adult males, may gather. Men (there is no evidence that women participated in this activity) often sit in the gate, awaiting either the close of the day (Gen. 19.1) or the reception of news

---

5.   Cf. Jer. 22.19 concerning Jehoiakim: 'With the burial of an ass he shall be buried, dragged and cast forth beyond the gates of Jerusalem'.

(1 Sam. 4.18; 2 Sam. 18.24). The gate provides a place for civic interaction: it is the fool who must keep quite within its confines (Prov. 24.7). In the gate 'old men' congregate (Lam. 5.14), a prophet meets the appointed king (1 Sam. 9.18), the men of a city confer (Gen. 34.20-24), and a prince unwittingly steps into the place of his own assassination (2 Sam. 3.27). The gate is thoroughly civic—feigned madness within its walls results in explusion from the city (2 Sam. 21.13-14).

To be in the gate is to be in the city; once within the gate, no other place exists that defines city space more completely. The gate marks both the extent and the center of the city's jurisdiction. Within the gate, the men of a city await in ambush in order to capture an enemy who has entered their space (Judg. 16.2) and the king of Jericho concentrates his surveillance upon the gate in order to keep enemy intruders within his grasp (Josh. 2.3-7). The gate represents the city and its authority. For an enemy to enter the gate is to conquer the city (e.g. Isa. 22.7; Obad. 11; 13) or to undertake a heroic risk for one's leader (2 Sam. 23.15-16). Gates therefore spatially mark membership within a city. Abraham negotiates a property transaction with Hittites, 'all who went in the gate of his city' (Gen. 23.10-18).[6] In Isa. 38.10 Hezekiah fears that he will soon join the citizenry of Sheol: 'I am consigned to the gates of Sheol for the rest of my years.'

As one's presence within the gates signals membership within the city, the gate becomes the focus of power within the city. The 'elders', the male ruling aristocracy of the city, meet in the gate (Prov. 31.23). Following the death of Absalom and on the verge of complete political upheaval, order is restored when David 'took his seat in the gate...and all the people came before the king' (2 Sam. 19.9). As the center of the city's power, political dissent, even sarcastic remarks made to the governing power, results in the immediate 'execution of justice' (2 Kgs 9.30).[7] The gate therefore receives military surveillance and significance. The king of Syria appointed a special 'captain on whose hand he leaned to have charge of the gate' (2 Kgs 8.17) and a 'gate of the guards' plays a key role in Jehoida's usurpation of the throne from Athaliah (2 Kgs 11.6, 19). Finally, it is in the side of the gate that David acknowledges his army as they march out to quell Absalom's rebellion (2 Sam. 18.4). David's presence within the gate, the civic

6. Note especially v. 10a: 'sitting among the Hittites'.
7. The episode of Jezebel's confrontation with Jehu highlights the civic significance of communication within the gate. The gate is the select place for political dissent to mount a serious challenge. Jehu's question seeking the support of clients, 'who is on my side?', shows the strength of Jezebel's challenge.

space and the center of governmental power, legitimates the mission of the army to intervene within a dynastic dispute.

The gate unified the exercise of power within the Iron Age II Israelite city. The societal powers administered legal questions and the economic redistribution of goods, that is justice (מִשְׁפָּט), from their meetings in the gate. The gate provides the legal setting for 'reproof' and the legal plea (Isa. 29.21). Absalom intercepts persons 'beside the way of the gate' who 'had a suit to come before the king for judgment' (2 Sam. 15.2). He points out the problem to the individual: 'Your claims are good and right; but there is no man deputed by the king to hear you... Oh that I were judge in the land! Then every man with a suit or cause might come to me, and I would give him justice' (vv. 4-5). The gate spatially reinforces Absalom's tactics. Court is not in session—the king is incompetent. A new king, namely Absalom, would establish justice. Absalom then receives obeisance within the gate (v. 5), the civic space, thereby broadening his political patronage.

Closely related to legal workings within a patronage system is the economic distribution of goods. The gate represents the point of economic interchange, both in trade and in care for the disenfranchised. 'In the gate of Samaria' Elisha predicts 'a measure of fine meal shall be sold for a shekel, and two measures of barley for a shekel' (2 Kgs 7.1), even though the city was currently under siege. As the place of economic transactions, the gate also served as the institution for patronage/welfare system. Job recounts his righteousness in the 'gate of the city' (Job 29.7-25). His status within the city's aristocracy exceeded even that of princes and nobles (vv. 9-10) for he 'delivered the poor who cried' and 'caused the widow's heart to sing for joy' (vv. 12-13). Amos rails against the Israelite aristocracy for hating 'him who reproves in the gate' (Amos 5.10) and refusing aid to 'the needy in the gate' while still accepting a bribe (v. 12). Amos's solution? 'Hate evil, and love good, and establish justice in the gate' (v. 15); in other words, uphold the patronage-client system that spatially centers on the gate and its inhabitants—the elders. Amos does not have a radical social ethic, a redistribution of wealth and the elimination of the causes of social inequity. He merely calls for the proper maintenance of the power structure of the city as formed by the social definitions generated by the gate. All who enter the gate are members of the city; therefore the city proper (i.e. the male elite who control the civic space, the gate) must care for the basic needs of the poor.

The Israelite city, therefore, functioned according to a patronage system much like that of later Greco-Roman times. Yet a striking difference exists generated by the spatial location of civic space governing the patron-client relationship in the gate rather than the household or estate. By focusing societal power within the confines of the geographical space of the gate, city membership is conceived as a unity. The aristocracy bears a responsibility for the poor as a whole; failure to care for the poor is not the failure of one patron, but of the entire aristocracy. Thus the prophetic condemnation of aristocratic abuses of the system, the call for 'justice' in the care of the underclass, and the certainty of destruction of the entire society. Further, social 'benevolence' is encouraged, as competition for status through the accumulation of patrons takes place in one civic space before one's peers (Job 29). With social definition and control emanating from one space, the poor are more liable to receive at least some meager portion of the society's goods. By contrast, the elite maintain tight control and surveillance of the poor through the spatial limitation of the distributions of goods and 'justice'. The system seeks equilibrium. The poor receive food, yet remain powerless 'beneficiaries' of the 'benevolence' of elite. The elite must share a small portion of their wealth for the disenfranchised, a small price to pay for firm control of the society's goods and power. An ideology of 'justice in the gate' emerges, divinely sanctioned, that legitimates the economic and social location of power in the hands of the male elite: Yahweh calls for the elders to act as patrons for the poor. As the equilibrium depends entirely on the power of the elite, it may become upset only if the patrons fail to 'provide' for the poor. Failure to provide benevolence, therefore, ultimately risks the well-being, not of the poor, but of the elite. In other words, the prophetic criticism of aristocratic economic abuses actually justified the continued oppression of the poor. The gate as the locus of civic space mediates and sustains the power of the society efficiently and effectively.

In sum, to be in the gate was to be a member of the Israelite city and society. The city bears a responsibility to all its inhabitants. Those who controlled the gate, however, controlled the majority of the members of the city. The city was stratified into two main groups: the aristocracy and the rest of the population. By their position 'sitting in the gate', the power of the city remained in the hands of the male elite. Political power, military surveillance, legal and economic patronage all focused on the gate and reinforced the social position of the male elite. The city, by defining its membership spatially in terms of the gate, provided a means of control to insure that any shifts in power within the city would be shifts within the male aristocracy of the city.

The Deuteronomistic law code exhibits these social dynamics of the gate. 'Your gates' (שעריך) is used throughout the legal sanctions as synonymous for the city. Therefore, the centralization of the Passover in Jerusalem demands that 'you shall not offer the Passover sacrifice within any of your gates which the Lord your God gives you; but at the place which the Lord your God will choose' (Deut. 16.5-6a). The gates can also assume military significance when representing the city: if the laws are not heeded, enemies will come and 'besiege you in all your gates throughout your land' (28.52). As a result of the siege, 'your enemy shall distress you in [all] your gates' (28.55, 57), although the gates are essentially civic space and not fortifications; it is the 'high and fortified walls' which represent the defences 'in which you trusted' (28.52).

Gates thereby mark membership within the city, open to those who may partake in the goods and ceremonies of the city. If one is within the gates, one maintains at least some civic privileges and responsibilities. The 'sojourner' (גר) who is 'in your gates' must rest on the Sabbath (5.14), be paid for his labor (24.14) and listen to the public reading of the law (31.12). The Levite 'who is within your gates since he has no portion or inheritance with you' (12.12) must participate in the city's offering and festivals in Jerusalem (12.12, 18; 16.11). If a Levite 'from your gates' decides to join the Jerusalem clerical corps, then he must receive equal portions to eat (18.6). Whether one is poor (15.7) or a widow (16.14), once 'in your gates' they should receive benevolence from the other members of the city. Indeed the phrase 'in any of your gates' marks all members of society, male or female who are under the society's regulations (17.2). Yet Deuteronomy also exhibits the same two-tiered social stratification discussed above. While one's presence 'in your gates' qualifies one as a member of the society, it also places one subject to the society's elite— those addressed in the masculine, second person plural, who mediate the laws to the rest of the society. The disenfranchised, whether Levites, sojourners, poor, widows or women in general, do not own the gates. They are consistently distinguished from the patriarchal authority to whom the commandments are addressed. Their presence in the gates qualifies them as members of the society, but only at the price of surveillance and control by the male elite of the city.

Legal proceedings and economic functions in the gate display this social control. The gate represents the normal setting for legal decisions, and only difficult cases are to be referred to the central Levitical court in Jerusalem (17.8). 'Judges and officers' are to be appointed 'in all your gates' to 'judge the people with righteous judgment' (16.18). The gate is where the widow may claim her right of levirate marriage to the elders (25.7), where the elders summon the brother-in-law to pursue the matter further (25.8a), and where the widow may publicly humiliate her irresponsible in-law in case he refuses to marry her. Deuteronomy 22.13-22 seemingly typifies the legal proceedings in the gate. The issue in question is the virginity of a woman at the time of her marriage. The city's elders meet in the gates for the dispute between the groom and the bride's father; a woman herself has no legal voice in the gate except to admit her economic helplessness. Charges are heard (vv. 14-16; the defense is a counter-charge, rather than a mere statement of innocence), evidence presented (v. 17), decision made (vv. 18a, 20a) and sentence carried out (vv. 18b-19, 21). By such a process, the male elders exercise control over the sexual activities of women—a matter of the most concern for the 'honor' of Israel (vv. 19, 21). The woman's sexuality is a public, not private matter, and therefore subject to the surveillance of the civic powers in the gate.

The economic function of the gate helps regulate those who are otherwise not under the direct control of the elders. The Levite, sojourner, orphan and widows, those who have escaped the direct lines of patriarchal control in domestic space, are brought back within the elder's sphere through the economic storage and distribution of surplus goods in the gates (14.28-29). Economically disenfranchised according to society's proper laws, subsistence is gained through submission to the social elite within the gate.

The Deuteronomistic law code therefore consistently portrays the civic role of the gate found elsewhere in pre-exilic biblical writings and traditions. Deuteronomy, however, highlights the gate as the focus of power in the city in an additional manner: the gate functions as a space for the spectacle, for public punishment and execution. As discussed above, in the gate, the brother-in-law who fails to marry his late brother's wife receives public humiliation, verbal and symoblic abuse by one who has no voice in the gate. The man who falsely accuses his wife of a pre-marital sexual encounter is beaten and fined within the gate. The place of humiliation in both cases is significant. The male offenders have not committed crimes against the women, but against the city, especially, in the second case, the woman's father. The civic order—that is, the elders—has been challenged, and must be restored within the civic space, the gate. As Foucault states,

...public execution has a juridico-political function. It is a ceremonial by which a momentarily injured sovereignty is reconstituted. It restores that sovereignty by manifesting it at its most spectacular... Its aim is not so

much to re-establish a balance as to bring into play, as its extreme point, the
dissymmetry between the subject who has dared to violate the law and the
all-powerful sovereign who displays his strength (Foucault 1977: 48-49).[8]

The juridico-political function of the gate, the 'ordered space' of the
city, appears in its most concentrated embodiment in its site of public
executions. The gate is designated as the place of execution in two occa-
sions: a 'stubborn and rebellious son' (Deut. 22.18-21) and 'idolaters'
(17.2-5). In both cases, the offender disregards the civic structure and
power, the parents and the city's god Yahweh. Punishment, therefore,
must be extracted within the civic space by the elders, the representatives
of the parents and the deity. At issue is not vengeance, retaliation or
justice, but the integrity of the society which has been violated: 'so shall
you purge the evil from the midst of you' (Deut. 17.7b). Stoning within
the gate, a ritualized atrocity, seeks to re-establish and reinforce the city's
sovereignty, the elders, in its proper place. While Foucault directly describes public executions in sixteenth and seventeenth-century France, his
words accurately pertain to stonings within the gate:

> It was the effect...of a certain mechanism of power: of a power that not
> only did not hesitate to exert itself directly on bodies, but was exalted and
> strengthened by its visible manifestations; ...of a power that presented rules
> and obligations as personal bonds, a breach of which constituted an offence
> and called for vengeance; of a power for which disobedience was an act of
> hostility, the first sign of rebellion, which is not in principle different from
> civil war; of a power which, in the absence of continual supervision, sought
> a renewal of its effect in the spectacle of its individual manifestations; of a
> power that was recharged in the ritual display of its reality as 'super-power'
> (Foucault 1977: 57).

Anonymous Space within the City: The City Square

As societal power focused on the periphery of the city within the city gate,
inner city open space, the square (רחוב), seems to have constituted a
public realm outside the regulating control of the societal forces. The
square is a 'no-man's land' in the midst of the city, an area where the lion

---

8.   It is interesting to note that in Deuteronomy a woman, if deemed guilty of
sexual indiscretion, is executed in the door of her father's house. The difference of
punishments reveals different relationships of power. The male lies within the power
structure of the city, and only needs to be publicly shamed to reactivate the society's
power. The woman is outside the city's direct power, under the control of the patriarchal family. She has transgressed, not primarily the power of the city, but the power of
her father.

slays the lazy person (Prov. 22.13; 26.13) and the Philistines bury the bones of Saul, an enemy king (2 Sam. 21.12). The square is public space, a place in which wisdom calls (cf. Prov. 1.20); yet it is space where normal identity seems lost in a social vacuum, a vacuum filled with eroticism and illicit sexuality. Here a woman seeks for her lover (Song 3.2) and a prostitute practices her seductive trade that threatens the patriarchal control exercised in the city gates (Prov. 7.12, 24-27). Squares seem especially dangerous to strangers, wayfarers with no pre-existent social relationships within the city. Strangers open themselves to sexual violence by staying in the square in the evening, violence that does not stop even when someone opens up their own domestic space (cf. Gen. 19.1-14; Judg. 19.15-30). Judges 19 is especially explicit. The anonymity provided by the square and the night combine to produce sexual terror. An unnamed Levite and his concubine enter the city of Gibeah 'and sit down in the square of the city; for no man took them into his house' (19.15).

Filled with ambiguity and latent sexuality in times of peace, the square becomes an area for destruction and mourning in times of war. Chariots rush through the squares, wreaking havoc among the city's inhabitants (Nah. 2.3). Following a losing battle, the square becomes a place of public mourning (Amos 5.13) and the location for the incineration of the goods of the city (Deut. 13.17). Outside domestic and civil space, the square becomes an area in the social shadows void of a positive role in the social definition and control of the Iron Age II Israelite city.

Conclusion
The entrance of the gate, the gate, and the city square form three distinct geographical and social spaces. Yet together they form a system that focuses societal power and control in the gate. One is not in the city in the entrance of the gate. This may be achieved only by passing *into* the gate. Societal power flows from outside the city into the gate. Though technically within the city, the anonymity of the square bears no real definitional quality of membership within the city—it only distinguishes members from strangers. Social definition may be obtained, not within the square, but within the gate. The center of the city in Iron Age II city was on its periphery—the city gate. All who were in the gate were members of Israel; however, this membership, defined by the gate, was also controlled by it. Power was embodied spatially within the confines of the gates and those who sat within it—the elders. Through the gate's social functions, the elders were able to maintain strict coercion and surveillance of the city, while generating an ideology that legitimated their control as benevolent and just

according to the will of the society's deity. The city represents a social system enclosed by its walls, isolated against 'outsiders' in order to maintain the delicate equilibrium within the city itself. Urban space is neither commercial nor sacred space. It is political space that defines its inhabitants by their presence 'in the gate'.

Literary remains from Iron Age II Israel preserved in the Hebrew Bible are largely the product of the ruling elite who sat within the gate—we do not possess the perspective of those who were excluded from the sphere of the gate's power. Interestingly, while present, the role of the gate as the city's fortification does not play a major role within the literary evidence. Rather than control versus outside aggression, the literary evidence suggests that gates functioned primarily as control of the city itself. It therefore provides new questions to examine the architecture of the gate and the gate's relation within 'city planning'.

The City Gate and Public Square in Neo-Babylonian Judah

The Judean city did not merely evolve in the early sixth century BCE; it underwent a complete social reconfiguration. With the neo-Babylonian conquest of Jerusalem, new power embodied city space and created a new place. In the process, the definition of membership within the city was altered. The city ceases to be an enclosed space, with membership defined by those who dwell within its gates on the periphery of the city walls. It becomes an ethnic space within a larger imperial reality. Power shifts to the temple complex itself. Admission to the society is now limited to those who may gain access to its temple. The elders, uprooted from their place in the city gate, now attempt to maintain power by creating a new space in the temple area, joining with the priests to maintain the new order and thus avoid conflict with imperial forces.

Problems abound in the reconstruction of the Israelite city in the first two-thirds of the sixth century BCE. The prose sections of Jeremiah and the book of Ezekiel provide our information on gates and squares in this time-frame. Yet each presents its own share of critical problems in constructing sixth-century social realia. Compositional history, dating, and geographical province of the works alone necessitate caution in a historical reconstruction. Further, whether the works reflect any actual social configuration is at best questionable. Nevertheless, Ezekiel and the prose sections of Jeremiah present a coherent and consistent conception of urban spatial dynamics, a conception that at least represents the imaginative reconceptualization of Judean urban society. With the Judean monarchy disem-powered (and later replaced), new forces demanded a new space as a new means of control over a new population.

It is therefore not surprising to find the spatial configuration of the Judean city radically changed. The entrance of the gate no longer forms an important social boundary. The city gates themselves, even if remaining part of the city's defense system, seem to have been bereft of their earlier social significance. More importantly, gates penetrated the inner space of the city, especially the temple complex. The inner city itself became forti-fied. City squares, however, according to the sparse information that we possess, still maintain their anonymous character. Access to the fortified temple complex, rather than mere residence within the city, defined full membership within the society.

Within the neo-Babylonian Judean city, the lines of social control are less geographically defined than in the Iron Age II. It is no longer possible to reveal lines of social control by a simple movement from outside to inside city walls. By tracing the different locations and functions of the entrance of the gates, the gates themselves, and the square in the neo-Babylonian period, it becomes possible to see the social reconfiguration of the Judean city in the years of Persian rule.

The Entrance of the Gate in the Neo-Babylonian Period
The entrance of the gate disappears as an institution connected to the exterior fortifications of the city; it relocates to the inner city as part of the temple complex. No longer a 'no-man's land', the entrance of the temple gate becomes a civic-temple institution, inheriting in the process some of the spatial authority of the Iron Age II gates.

The entrance of the gate as an institution associated with the city occurs only once in a postexilic biblical text, Jer. 19.2, where Yahweh instructs Jeremiah to preach his sermon in the 'entrance of the Potsherd Gate'. A close reading of the passage, however, indicates that the author artificially constructs the setting to fit his conception of Jerusalem before the exile. Jeremiah is sent *outside* the city's jurisdiction in order to speak to the 'kings of Judah and the inhabitants of Jerusalem' (v. 3).[9] The entrance of the gate no longer possesses symbolic social significance as marking the boundary of the city. It merely serves as a passage for commerce in and out of the city

9.　This contrast suggests that a significant social-chronological gap exists between the prose and poetry sections of Jeremiah, poetry from the neo-Babylonian period and prose from the late neo-Babylonian or Achaemenid periods.

walls, a place where 'kings'[10] and others might travel. Indeed, the author
cannot consistently maintain the literary fiction throughout the scene.
Jeremiah never explicitly delivers the prophecy in the entrance of the gate.
Instead, he gives a shortened version of the same sermon to the citizenship
of Jerusalem in the temple court, the new space that defines Judean citizenship (Jer. 19.14-15).

The 'entrance of the gate' remains an important social boundary, a
transitional social space; however, it is now within the city, located outside
the fortified temple complex. The entrance of the gate represents the space
just outside the sacred precincts. It is where Ezekiel begins his visionary
tour of the temple (Ezek. 8.3) and the 'people of the land' gather 'before
the Lord' to worship 'on the sabbaths and the new moons' (Ezek. 46.3).
Only on special festival days may the people of the land enter the temple
court and here in a carefully ordered procession with the prince (נשיא) at
their head (Ezek. 46.9-10). The entrance of the gate represents the closest
geographical space to the sacred area that defines membership within the
society.

This proximity to the temple complex seems to have filled the entrance
to the temple gate with significant political authority within the city. The
entrance of the 'New Gate' of the temple provides a location for
Jeremiah's trial for sedition (Jer. 26.10). The geographical movements
within the text reveal the entrance of the gate as a meeting place between
the sacred and profane powers. The 'priests and the prophets and all the
people' arrest Jeremiah within the temple courts; they must move outside
the temple for the trial. They do not have authority within their sphere to
declare Jeremiah guilty of a capital crime. The 'princes of Judah', later
called the 'elders of the land' (Jer. 26.17), must travel from the 'house of
the king' to their seats in the entrance of the gate to decide Jeremiah's
fate (Jer. 26.10). Unable to enter the temple area proper, the entrance of
the gate provides an institutional setting for the civic authorities to partake of the sacred legitimation of the temple complex. It provides a space
for legislating the city. No longer a space for the marginal, the social
reconfiguration of the city imparts governing authority upon the inner
city 'entrance of the gates'. It is in the entrance of the eastern gate of the
temple that Ezekiel envisions 25 men, including two 'princes of the
people' (Ezek. 11.1). These are the city's ruling council, the 'men who
plan evil and who counsel evil wicked strategies in that city' (Ezek. 11.2).

---

10. Note the plural. The author inadvertently reveals the symbolic intent of the
passage, rather than a precise historical description in which only one king would rule.

These figures seem engaged in city planning and conceive of themselves as the civic authority (Ezek. 11.3). The death of one in the entrance of the gate while Ezekiel prophesied contained extreme symbolic significance to Ezekiel—the utter destruction of Israel (Ezek. 11.13). As the power of the city, the elders meeting in the entrance of the gate represented the total society. It thus provided an ideal setting for the depiction of Baruch's reading of Jeremiah's scroll to all the people (Jer. 36.10).

The Gate in the Neo-Babylonian City

Gates undergo several transformations in the neo-Babylonian period, changing place and function. Gates are transfered from their exclusive, or at least predominant, place along the city walls to inner city structures, especially the temple complex. In essence, the temple becomes the fortified center of society. With this transference, the social function of the gate changes. It is no longer the locus of civic power, the boundary between 'inside' and 'outside' the city. Rather, it creates new space, the temple courts.

The book of Jeremiah again illustrates the crucial point of transformation. In poetic sections, gates remain at the city walls, a place that summarizes the economic plight of Judah during drought (Jer. 14.2), where winnowing takes place (15.7), and the exterior of a city's fortifications (51.58). In the prose sections, however, the locus includes inner city gates—the Benjamin Gate of the temple, the gate of the palace, and the gate of the temple complex. Certain ambiguities that exist suggest a conscious attempt to archaize the setting of the narratives, an attempt that is not altogether successful.

Benjamin's gate plays a significant role in the prose section of Jeremiah. Though a city gate, a temple gate is also associated with it. As a city gate, it can function similarly to its Iron Age II predecessor. The Benjamin Gate is a seat of political power; the king rules within its space (38.7).[11] Yet the socially defining role of the gate has changed. The Benjamin Gate does not serve as an urban boundary to identify those within as members of the society. It is a commercial institution, conveniently located for social surveillance. Yahweh assigns Jeremiah to the Benjamin Gate, 'in which the kings of Judah enter and leave', to deliver a message reminiscent of Nehemiah: to limit economic activity on the sabbath. A sentry apprehends Jeremiah in the Benjamin Gate as Jeremiah attempts to leave the city,

11. Note, however, that later on in the narrative, the king meets Jeremiah *within* the temple complex.

accusing him of deserting to the enemy (37.13). Despite the redactor's efforts to maintain a literary fiction, the city gate no longer serves as a civic boundary, defining civic membership. The city gate remains coercive space, yet without representing civic space. Its central concern is to regulate passage in and out of the city (39.4). The city gate diffuses and applies power embodied elsewhere. With the 'exterior' boundary weakened, it comes as no surprise to discover that suddenly within the city itself, fortifications arise. Gates appear as space within the center of the city (note, e.g., the 'middle gate' during the neo-Babylonian conquest, 39.3).

Inner city gates appear in the prose sections of Jeremiah related to two spaces: the palace and the temple. As power shifts away from the city's edge, it bifurcates, creating royal and sacred spheres. In Jeremiah 22, Yahweh assigns Jeremiah to the king's palace to address the king, his servants, and 'your people who enter these gates' (the royal court, v. 2). The oracle offers as incentive to 'do justice and righteousness' a promise that a royal retinue 'will come in the gates of this house' (v. 4). This retinue, the king, chariots, horses, servants, and people represents a significant military force, located within the city. The palace gates mark a boundary within the city between the royal and civil realms. Fortifications exist to control access to the monarch and to concentrate military control of the environs within royal space. Power has shifted from the periphery of the city to its center within the royal palace itself. The king need not be in the gate to rule as king, since the palace now defines his power.

Royal space, once created, must define itself against other aristocratic forms of power in a society. Temple gates thereby accompany the creation of palace gates, forming a new means of control and definition of citizenship within the city. In Jer. 7.2, Yahweh instructs Jeremiah to 'stand in the gate of the Lord's house' to deliver his message to 'all you men of Judah who enter these gates to worship the Lord' (26.2; the parallel takes place in the temple courtyard). Temple gates are liminal, the portal by which the citizens, the men of Judah, enter a civic space, the temple courtyard. Yet the nature of civic space has been altered. Under the control of a sacred elite, civic space is also the realm of the society's deity. Temple space defines membership in the society. Cultic requirements may now control the city's population. Power embodies the temple complex; public worship of Yahweh unifies the society, generating (and excluding) a newly defined citizenry.

Jeremiah 20 exemplifies new power embodied within the Temple gate and personnel. The priest Passhur, 'the chief officer of the house of the

Lord' (Jer. 20.1), arrests and punishes Jeremiah without consulting any other authority. The narrative of ch. 20 depends upon the events of ch. 19. Jeremiah delivers an oracle against Judah in the 'Potsherd Gate', a setting meant to highlight the symbolism of the smashing of a flask, not the destruction of *civitas*. To emphasize this, Jeremiah moves to the temple court (חצר), the new space created by the temple gates. Now located within the religio-civic center of the city, Jeremiah declares Yahweh's judgment 'upon this city and upon all its towns' (19.15). Jeremiah's 'crime' is not merely his words; rather, such words in the temple court constitute treason against the city-nation. Passhur therefore acts in accordance with the power granted him as custodian of the temple space, beating and incarcerating Jeremiah.

The prose sections of Jeremiah witness to a different Israelite city than its Iron Age II predecessor. City space no longer equals membership within the society; civic space itself has been relocated within the temple court, a new space created by the temple gates. Although terminology changes, the book of Ezekiel seems to portray a similar urban structure as the prose sections of Jeremiah. Now fortified, the temple complex embodies the power of society.

City gates as exterior fortifications appear in Ezekiel, though devoid of their significance as the civic place. In a series of oracles of judgment in response to an inquiry by the 'elders of Israel' (Ezek. 20.1), Ezekiel states that 'many' will 'fall in all their gates' (21.20) and that the king of Babylon will 'set battering rams against the gates' (21.27). The place of battle, the city gate, remains at the center of the city's fortifications. Yet even within these oracles, the definition of city space has changed. Ezekiel is commanded to 'set your face toward Jerusalem and preach against their sanctuary; prophesy against the land of Israel' (20.7) The city, Jerusalem, is used parallel to the 'their sanctuary' and the land of Israel. Urban life is defined by the sanctuary, the temple, which also represents the land of Israel.

This shift in definition explains Ezekiel's preoccupation with the temple complex, a description that signifies the change of place of power in Israelite society. Here civic and sacred power converge. The gates, both to the outer and inner court, are liminal, openings into the outer temple court, which defines societal membership with its royal head, and the inner court, which defines the priestly aristocracy. As liminal, gates demand surveillance to control those who may enter and the behavior of those within. Levites are the temple gatekeepers, 'having oversight in the gates of the temple and serving in the temple' (Ezek. 44.11). While Levites are excluded from sacrificial service, they are the temple administrators, appointed 'to keep charge of the temple, to do all its service and all that is to be done in it' (44.14). They thereby receive rooms within the inner court of the temple in the side of the north gate that faces south (40.44-45a).

Ezekiel identifies temple gates by their directional orientation and place relative the temple's sacred center. All exterior gates possess the same dimensions, as do the interior gates. The northern and southern gates to the temple courtyard mark the normal boundaries of entry, not just into the temple itself, but also into sacred-civic space. Following Ezekiel's visionary tour through the temple complex, six 'executioners of the city' enter the temple courtyard through the north gate (9.1-2). Judgment against the city proceeds from the court, the civic space created by the gate (vv. 3-10). The north and south gates control movement into the temple precincts. Only the citizens, the 'people of the land', may enter the temple court through the north and south gates of the temple 'at the appointed feasts', marking their membership within the society (46.9). Their movements, however, are very controlled: 'whoever enters by the north gate to worship shall go out by the south gate; and he who enters by the south gate shall go out by the north gate: no one shall return by the way of the gate by which he entered, but each shall go out straight ahead. When they go in, the prince shall go in with them; and when they go out, he shall go out' (46.9b-10). A processional, the citizens (all male) may not wander or change directions within the sacred-civic space. Order provides a means of control; behavioral deviance is not permitted within space which embodies so much power. The prince provides additional surveillance within the temple court. Civic and sacred space are merged. Sacred space identifies civic power, which in turn reinforces the 'sacredness' of the space. The north-south gates and axis mark a significant social boundary. They control who may enter, and thereby membership within society, and also control the members of society under the royal and temple personnel.

The transference of liminality from the entrance of the city gate to the temple gates renders the old definition of civic membership irrelevant. The inner city becomes subject to increased regulation and surveillance. Ezekiel 'enters' the temple via the north gate to the front of the temple and receives important instructions:

> Son of man, mark well, see with your eyes, and hear with your ears all that I shall tell you concerning all the ordinances of the temple of the Lord and all its laws; and mark well those who may be admitted to the temple and all those who are to be excluded from the sanctuary. And say to the rebellious

house, to the house of Israel, Thus says the Lord God, O house of Israel, let
there be an end to all your abominations, in admitting foreigners, uncir-
cumcised in heart and flesh, to be in my sanctuary, profaning it, when you
offer to me my food, the fat and the blood... You have not kept charge of
my holy things; but you have set foreigners to keep my charge in my
sanctuary (Ezek. 44.5-8).

Ethnic-cultic affiliation, rather than geographical location, defines membership within the city. Ethnic-cultic regulations serve to distinguish and
control persons who inhabit the city, but are not members of the society.
The temple gate serves to monitor and define the population for the royal
and cultic powers that embody the temple complex.

The east gate possesses unique significance. The divine representative
meets Ezekiel in the gate, most likely the east gate (40.2; cf. 40.6), for
Ezekiel's tour through the temple, 'a structure like a city' (40.2). The
temple's east gate defines the sacred-royal power. It is the divine gate. As
the 'glory of the Lord' exits the temple, the cherubim 'stood in the door of
the east gate of the house of the Lord; and the glory of the God of Israel
was over them' (10.19). In 43.4 (with Ezekiel watching in the east gate, v.
2) the divine glory re-enters the temple through the east gate. The direct
association of royal power within this gate, therefore, bears special import.
The east gate is reserved only for Yahweh and the prince:

> Then he brought me back to the outer gate of the sanctuary, which faces
> east, and it was shut; it shall not be opened, and no one shall enter by it; for
> the Lord, the God of Israel, has entered by it; therefore it shall remain shut.
> Only the prince may sit in it to eat bread before the Lord; he shall enter by
> the way of the vestibule of the gate, and shall go out by the same way
> (Ezek. 44.1-3).

In the east gate, the prince offers sabbath and new moon sacrifices, with
the citizenry required to observe his special power from the entrance of the
same gate (46.1-8); indeed, all the prince's offerings, freewill, burnt or
peace, seem to be offered from the east gate (46.12).[12] Within the gate, the
prince 'owns' a section of the sacred sphere. He is unique among all persons within the society in the association of divine entrance and exit with
his entrance and exit. The east gate legitimates the prince's power,
equating him with the divine presence within the society.

Another series of temple gates, those to the inner court of the temple,

---

12. It is interesting to note the presence of the Benjamin Gate in the middle of the
east side of the city, showing a possible correlation to the political role of the gate in
the prose sections of Jeremiah.

delineate the realm of priests, embodying their power within the society. The inner court must be open to visual surveillance from the outer court to insure the cultic activities proceed as necessary; however, entry into this space must be carefully controlled to protect the power of the cultic personnel. The inner gates therefore receive special ritual attention. The ritual of the sin offering carefully marks boundaries between various spheres within human-divine interaction. The blood of the sacrificial lamb is smeared on the doorposts of the temple, the gateway into the deity's dwelling, the corners of the altar, the gateway to communication with the divine, and 'the posts of the gate of the inner court', the gateway into the sacred and powerful realm of the priests (45.19). The priests must change their apparel as they enter and exit the inner gate 'lest they communicate holiness to the people with their garments' (44.17-20). Such ritual activity distinctly marks the power of the priests so that 'they shall teach my people the difference between the holy and the common, and show them how to distinguish betweeen the unclean and the clean. In a controversy they shall act as judges, and they shall judge it according to my judgments' (44.23-24).

Gates within the temple complex thus spatially configure urban power differently from the Iron Age II Israelite city. Temple gates create a new space—the sacred-civic temple courts. The courts form a social hierarchy which diffuses societal power within their space. The outer court defines and regulates the elders, the patriarchal aristocracy of the city (cf. Ezek. 8.7). Kitchens exist in each of the four corners of the temple court in order to feed the elders in isolation from the rest of society during the cultic festivals (46.21-24). The elders, though in a new place, still represent the 'city' in the broad sense of the term. Therefore, Yahweh instructs the 'executioner of the city' to begin the slaughter of Israel 'in my sanctuary. So they began with the elders who were before the house' (9.6b). The spectacle ends with order restored, the divine honor upheld by the placement of the bodies within the sphere of their influence and power: 'Defile the temple and fill the courts with the slain' (9.7).

In their displacement from the city gates, however, the elders lose their hegemony of power. Priests now embody a space closer to the deity, the inner court, the place where one might see the 'glory of Yahweh fill the temple' (Ezek. 43.5). Priests dwell in this place, offer sacrifices and receive their food (cf. 42.13; 46.20). Surveillance of this privileged elite increases within this realm. Alcohol consumption is prohibited (44.21), the defiled priest now made clean must report into the inner court to offer a sin offering (44.27), and attire is controlled. The center of the city resides with

Yahweh, who dwells within the temple. Yahweh's place generates and legitimates the priest's surveillance of power over the elders.

The third place within the temple complex, the east gate, spatially defines the royal sphere. Neither elder nor priest, but the prince mediates between the elders and the priests. The head of the citizens, the elders may enter the outer court only with the prince within their midst. While excluded from the priestly space, the priests stand ready to offer his sacrifices under the gaze of the prince (46.1-2). Further, the east gate, the exclusive place for the prince, embodies his power as the representative of the divinity. With the opening of the east gate of the inner court, the presence of the divine is mediated to the 'people of the land' standing in the entrance of the gate (46.2-3). Without his presence, priestly and divine power remain isolated within the inner courts. In tandem with priests, the prince exercises power over the city.

The gate system in neo-Babylonian Judean understanding creates a new city. A four-tiered society emerges, in contrast to the two-tiered society of the Iron Age II city. The prince, the priests and the elders compose the membership of the society. Excluded from the sacred-civic space of the temple, women, children and foreigners constitute those subject to, but not partakers of, power. Even elders, once the embodiment of power, are brought under surveillance through the temple space and the civic cult. Priest and prince reign in a symbolic relationship which controls the rest of the society through the coercion and privileges the temple confers upon the elders. In a sense, the city has ceased to exist; the sanctuary has taken its place.

The Square in the Neo-Babylonian City

The sixth-century shifts apparent in the entrance of the gate and the gate itself are not apparent in the literary evidence concerning the square. The square remained much as it had before the sixth century. Prostitutes are still victimized there (Ezek. 16.24, 31); people are still sought but not found (Jer. 5.1). Mourning and destruction become especially connected to the square, a fact not surprising due to the grim realities of the neo-Babylonian conquests of Jerusalem (see Jer. 9.20; 48.38; 49.26//50.30; Lam. 2.11, 12; 4.18). While the evidence does not sufficiently indicate whether the square still cast its chaotic aura upon persons in its space during this period, the social significance of the square still does not seem to have been altered from its Iron Age II predecessor. The gate, now part of the temple complex, still embodied the power of the Judean city.

Conclusion

By removing the city walls and the city gate, the center of the city shifts from the city gate to the temple complex. In a sense, the city becomes the temple complex. Membership within the city is defined by new space created by the temple courts. Even legal proceedings gain authority by moving into the entrance of the temple gate. As the locus of power, the temple complex functions as a vacuum. The city gate cannot maintain its social significance and the square remains void of any defining power. Cultic surveillance provided by the temple and its personnel replace the geographical surveillance provided by the city gate within an enclosed city space. Civic membership is cultic, rather than nationalistic.

The neo-Babylonian conquest of Jerusalem destroyed not merely Jerusalem, but the Iron Age II configuration of an Israelite city. A new city emerged in, at least, Israelite understanding, if not social realia. The imperial power formed new spaces within the city. The Israelite city did not evolve; it was eclipsed and grew anew in a radically different configuration. Within the historical rupture, the temple-state replaces the city. The new space of the temple constructed a more stratified society. Membership in society becomes membership within a ethnic-cultic community founded within a central shrine. An elite of the elite, the prince and the priest, controlling the elite, the elders. In turn, the elders controlled each other and the non-citizens of the urban environment. Such a system possessed benefits for the imperial power, which remains hidden from the gaze of the interpreter, present only in the replacement of the 'king' (מלך) by the prince (נשיא). With power concentrated within the temple complex, the imperial control may be maintained through a relatively small number of native citizens. As this elite benefits from the temple system, they provide the surveillance for other sources of social disruption within the society.

City Gates and Public Squares in Achaemenid Judah

'The survivors there in the province who escaped exile are in great trouble and shame; the wall of Jerusalem is broken down, and its gates are destroyed by fire' (Neh. 1.3). The conditions of Jerusalem that inspire the return of Nehemiah do not necessarily indicate social unrest or rebellion, but the eclipse of the city in the neo-Babylonian period. Nehemiah requests that Artaxerxes 'send me to Judah, to the city of my fathers' sepulchres, that I may rebuild it' (2.6). Nehemiah requisitions timber to reconstruct the city, 'to make beams for the gates of the fortress of the temple, and for the walls of the city, and for the house which I shall occupy' (2.8). The city has again been reconfigured. A fortress now guards the temple, walls surround the city, and an imperial palace rises in the city's midst. The city is back, though its form has scarce continuities with its Iron Age II predecessor.

The eclipse of the city in the neo-Babylonian period evolved into the 'de-urbanization' of Judean society in the Achaemenid period (see Hoglund 1992). Persian imperial power relied largely upon a series of fortresses for control of society (Hoglund 1991: 62-64; 1992; Briant 1982). Hellenistic economic force, however, entered Palestine by the late sixth century and pervaded the society by the end of the fifth century (Stern 1982). This Hellenistic power ultimately embodied itself within a widespread re-birth of the city in Palestine (Arav 1989), a renaissance that continued into the Roman era. Within Achaemenid Yehud itself, first steps towards this urban reconfiguration were on their way. Persian, Hellenistic and local power coalesce to eliminate and revise old urban space; a new city, akin to, yet different from the *polis* emerges.

In biblical texts generally dated to the Achaemenid period, the social configuration of the Judean city (at this time primarily Jerusalem) has again changed. The entrance of the gate disappears. The city gates re-emerge, but constitute a military-national border void of civic significance. The temple complex still exists, embodying its sacred-civic power. City squares, however, ruled by a clerical or lay ruler of society, constitute *the* civic space. Participation in civic meetings here, rather than residence within the city, define full membership within the society. Temple and square stand together; the square, however, rules the temple, utilizing the sacred for surveillance of its citizenry. The city becomes a national place, centered upon the square outside the temple. Not necessarily residential, the city exists for the national/provincial cult, government and protection.

The Entrance of the Gates
Present in the first three quarters of the sixth century BCE, the entrance of the gate seemingly disappears by the fifth century. It is not found in later biblical literature. While an argument from silence is always dangerous, opportunities for the term do occur in later texts. A comparison of 2 Chron. 23.15 with its source, 1 Kgs 11.16, highlights this. In 2 Kings 11, Jehoiada has Athaliah killed in 'the horses' entryway of the palace' (דרך מבוא הסוסים, v. 16). Unfortunately for Athaliah, the palace was not fortified. The Chronicler, however, changes the location of the assassination to 'entry of the gate of the horses of the palace' (אל שער הסוסים,

v. 15) The execution takes place outside the palace, its boundaries now marked by gates (i.e. fortifications). In response to the Persian king's decree against the Jews, Mordecai goes 'in the midst of the city' and 'before the king's gate' to mourn because ritual mourning, a political protest, is not allowed within the king's gate (Est. 4.1-2). An inner city space immediately outside the gates seems indicated in both instances; yet the term 'court' no longer characterizes this space. By the middle of the Achaemenid period, the square replaces the entrance of the gate.

Urban Gates in Achaemenid Jerusalem
In Achaemenid biblical texts, gates generate multiple places. Gates as entryways within the exterior urban fortifications re-emerge. These gates, however, do not regain their former significance as civic space. The city gates represent a military border that enclose the national space. One enters the gates, not so much to enter the city per se, but to proceed to the power that defines the nation. The liminality of temple gates, however, loses its significance as a locus of power. Rather than generating civic space, temple gates emerge as economic institutions, controlling the economic resources of the society. One temple gate from the neo-Babylonian city does maintain, and possibly increase, its power. The east gate of the temple becomes the gate of the king, an institution that embodies the royal power over the society.

City walls in the Persian period create military space; exterior gates provide entry into a fortified space in case of an emergency. Nehemiah must inspect the ruined fortifications at night; his plan to rebuild the city walls is interpreted as a sign of rebellion against his Persian overlords (Neh. 2.19). As the work proceeds, the surrounding nations see the rebuilding as an act of war (4.7-9). The rebuilding itself becomes a military operation: 'Half of my servants worked on construction, and half held the spears, shields, bows, and coats of mail; and the leaders stood behind all the house of Judah, who were building on the walls... And each of the builders had his sword girded at his side while he built' (4.16-18).

In constructing the walls, Nehemiah does not merely rebuild a city; he estabishes a national center which upsets the balance of power within the region. Sanballat perceived Nehemiah's building program as a nationalistic agenda in an open letter, a piece of literary propaganda for the benefit of the Persian court (6.6-7). While Nehemiah accuses his opponents of fantasy (vv. 8-9), he revels in the political power gained as a result of the walls' completion: 'And when all our enemies heard of it, all the nations round about us were afraid and fell greatly in their own esteem; for they perceived that this work had been accomplished with the help of our God' (6.16-17). Jerusalem's walls restore Yehud to national status. Jerusalem becomes a city-state. Nehemiah's 'Memoirs' attempt to preserve the delicate balance between his nationalistic agenda and his status as a Persian vassal.

Gates within the exterior fortifications of the city mark the entrance into a new national-civic space, regaining symbolic significance. The symbolism has shifted, however. The gate is no longer the embodiment of the city but a means to enter the city as the center of a city-state. Gates emerge in key roles in the Second Temple prophetic visions concerning the restoration of Israel. Through the gates, 'the righteous nation which keeps faith may enter in' (Isa. 26.2). Gates provide the symbolic repertoire to indicate the establishment of Jerusalem as an national-imperial center, receiving tribute from the other nations: 'Your gates shall be open continually; day and night they shall not be shut; that men may bring to you the wealth of the nations, with kings led in procession' (Isa. 60.11). Open space within the city now bears positive social significance—gates are the openings that allow entry into the new space.

As a military-national boundary, descriptions of gates change, reflecting an architectural shift. Gates demand gatekeepers; military surveillance focuses upon these liminal spaces. In 2 Chron. 33.14, Manasseh purportedly builds an outer wall in Jerusalem 'for the entrance into the Fish Gate, and carried it round Ophel, and raised it to a very great height' as part of his militarization of Judah. Strength must be given 'to those who turn back the battle in the gate' (Isa. 28.6). Upon completion of the city walls, Nehemiah assigns his Levitical militia to control the newly established military border simultaneously with his establishment of his brother of the fortress in Jerusalem (Neh. 7.1-3). The gates provide the military post for Nehemiah's control of trade on the Sabbath (13.19); however, as gates define a military, rather than civic boundary, trade continues outside the confines of the wall (13.20) until Nehemiah threatens military action against them, staged, most likely, from the city gates (13.21). Levites (Nehemiah's servants?) receive their permanent commission to 'come and guard the gates, to keep the sabbath day holy' (13.22).

As the relocation of power into city space shifts the functions of gates, descriptions of exterior gates and their architecture seemingly change. Bars and doors, present but rarely mentioned in the Iron Age II city gate, dominate the description of gates. Gates are not massive monumental works that provide a meeting ground for the elite. To build a gate is to 'set its doors, its bolts, and its bars' (Neh. 3.3, 6, 13, 14, 15) and 'bars of your gates' signify 'peace in your borders' (Ps. 147.13-14). Towers are not considered part of the gate complex, but independent structural units built to reinforce the military border (Neh. 3.11b, 25, 26). In 2 Chron. 26.9, Uzziah 'built towers in Jerusalem at the Corner Gate and at the Valley Gate and at the Angle, and fortified them'. As within Hellenistic fortifications, towers are separate architectural features (Arav 1989). Gates protect the national space inside the city; they control military surveillance of the city. The social power seeks to control the citizenry in its new space, the city square.

As gates re-emerge in their new form on the city's exterior, interior fortifications around the temple remain. A subtle shift, however, seems to have taken place in the role of the temple gates in the Achaemenid period as royal power dominates temple power. Spatially, the temple court, while still present, loses some of its definitional power as the civic place to the city square, now placed outside the temple gates under the clear domain of the civic authorities. Temple gates do not become insignificant; their function seemingly shifts to economic control of the society's goods.

Temple gates remain a focus of interest in Achaemenid period literature. The Chronicler depicts David as especially concerned that the temple gates have their necessary materials. After providing the forced labor to dress stones for the temple, 'David also provided great store of iron for nails for the doors of the gates and for clamps, as well as bronze in quantities beyond weighing, and cedar timbers without number' (1 Chron. 22.3-4a). Gates clearly constitute an important architectural feature within David's plans for the temple. The space created by the gates, the temple courts, still possesses cultic-civic significance. Temple courts embody the space where national-cultic convocations occur. Responding to the military threat of Moabites and Ammonites,

> Jehoshaphat feared, and set himself to seek the Lord, and proclaimed a fast throughout all Judah. And Judah assembled to seek help from the Lord, from all the cities of Judah they came to seek the Lord. And Jehoshaphat stood in the assembly of Judah and Jerusalem, in the house of the Lord, before the new court, and said, 'O Lord, God of our fathers, art thou not God in heaven?'... Meanwhile all the men of Judah stood before the Lord, with their little ones, their wives, and their children. And the Spirit of the Lord came upon Jahaziel...a Levite of the sons of Asaph, in the midst of the assembly. And he said, 'Hearken, all Judah and inhabitants of Jerusalem, and King Jehoshaphat: Thus says the Lord to you, "Fear not, and be not dismayed at this great multitude; for the battle is not yours but God's"'... Then Jehoshaphat bowed his head with his face to the ground, and all Judah and the inhabitants of Jerusalem fell down before the Lord,

worshiping the Lord. And the Levites...stood up to praise the Lord
(2 Chron. 20.3-6a, 13-15, 18-19).

The temple courts accommodate the members of the nation who are gathered for a sacred purpose by governmental power (see Neh. 8.16 for the
Feast of Tabernacles). The assembly's composition, however, has changed.
Now women and children are allowed within the temple courts. It is a
national assembly, marked not so much by gender but by kinship. Within
this 'assembly', the king dominates, addressing the people and God. God
responds through a Levitical prophet.[13] The convocation concludes with a
national act of worship. The temple court space embodies the cultic-national identity; the royal authority therefore stands at its head in surveillance and control to insure the continued existence of the society.

Given this function of the temple courts, temple gates possess a significant role as liminal space into the national-cultic place. Therefore, David
assigns gatekeepers as an integral part of his temple bureaucracy (1 Chron.
26.1-19; and even to guard entrance to the tabernacle, 1 Chron. 16.42).
Jehoiada the priest, depicted by the Chronicler in royal terms,[14] 'stationed
gatekeepers at the gates of the house of the Lord so that no one should
enter who was in any way unclean' (2 Chron. 23.19). Following his successful coup, Jehoida secures the national-cultic space through control of
the entryways to it—the temple gates. Temple gates permit royal surveillance of the citizenry through the cultic personnel under his power.

Royal domination of the national-sacred place seems also to have
created a new space associated with the gates, temple-gate storehouses.
Temple gates, under royal-Levitical control, incorporate the economic
power within the society. 1 Chronicles 9.23-26 anachronistically depicts
gatekeepers, assigned by David and Samuel, to 'the gates of the house of
the Lord, that is, the house of the tent, as guards. The gatekeepers were on
the four sides, east, west, north, and south;...for the four chief gatekeepers, who were Levites, were in charge of the chambers and the treasures of

13. See also 2 Chron. 24.20-23. Zecharaiah, a priest-prophet, 'stood above the
people' to deliver a divine oracle, arousing royal indignation. As a result, 'by command
of the king they stoned him with stones in the court of the house of the Lord', the place
of his indiscretion. The socio-spatial dynamics are very similar to 2 Chron. 20. The
temple court defines 'the people'; in their assembly, a prophet speaks—but royalty
controls this space. As Zecharaiah offends this royal power, the stoning occurs within
the confines of the temple court, the sacred-royal embodiment of power.

14. See 2 Chron. 24.15-16, where Jehoida's death is recorded in a royal formula,
including a notice of his burial 'among the kings'.

the house of God.' The gatekeepers assigned to the temple by David must watch these storehouses (1 Chron. 26.14, 17), as did Mattaniah, Bakbukiah, Obadiah, Meshullam, Talmon and Akkud in Nehemiah (Neh. 12.26; cf. 2 Chron. 8.14-15). In the collection of the temple tax in the reigns of Joash and Jehoiada, the king commands that a chest be made which is placed 'outside the gate of the house of the Lord' (2 Chron. 24.8). The temple gates thereby control economically the landowners, and centralize the economic activities of the nation (see also Neh. 10.32-39). Nehemiah's purge of Tobiah from 'a chamber in the courts of the house of God' most likely represents his attempt to monopolize control over the economic productivity of the province (Neh. 13.4-9). In such a spatial embodiment of economic power, gatekeepers could possess significant administrative authority within the society (see Wright 1990).

With the hegemony of royal authority over temple gates and space, the east gate of the temple formally receives the designation 'the king's gate' (cf. 1 Chron. 9.18). Though evidence is sketchy for the province of Yehud, gatekeepers assigned to the east gate seemingly possessed significant administrative authority (see 1 Chron. 9.18; Wright 1990: 74-76) and socio-economic status.[15] In the book of Esther, however, 'the gate of the king', separate from a temple complex, embodies the administrative operations of the king. The king's gate marks the passage from the royal sphere to society; it mediates the royal power over society. Those who can control the gate, control the diffusion of the royal power. The king's gate, therefore, is a politically loaded space. Much of the political struggle that frames Esther takes place in or around the gate of the king. It is where Mordecai sits, uncovers a coup attempt against the Persian monarch, and conveys the message to Esther (Est. 2.19-23). It is where Mordecai refuses to do obeisance to Haman, the second power in the kingdom to the king himself (3.2-5). In this governmental setting, such a denial of power leads to the conspiracy against the Jews. Incorporating royal power over society, no one is allowed to enter the king's gate in mourning attire, a fact that causes Mordecai to express his public dissent just outside the king's gate (4.1-3). Mordecai's presence in the king's gate with significant contact to the king through Esther identifies him as a political threat to Haman,

15. Shemaiah, the son of Shecaniah 'the keeper of the East Gate', had sufficient social standing and economic resources to repair a segment of the wall during Nehemiah's governorship (Neh. 3.29). Shemaiah may have been part of an aristocratic group that returned with Ezra (cf. Ezra 8.5). Shecanaiah is also the familial name of a group who returned with Zerubbabel (Neh. 12.3).

someone who can get away with not honoring his presence (5.9-13). As the story unwinds, it is clear that Haman's concerns were not fanciful!

Whether it is possible to transfer the imperial space of the king's gate in Esther to the cultic-national space of the east gate in Achaemenid Yehud is questionable. Yet given the domination of royal or governmental authority over temple gates and space in Achaemenid literature from Yehud, it seems reasonable to understand the king's gate as the embodiment of royal power that mediates the sacred-national space of the temple to the society. As the king's gate, it creates a new space: the square outside the temple gate where governmental authority may apply its power to the society.

Gates in Achaemenid literature thereby reveal a new configuration of the Israelite city. The city is now a national space, a fortress in need, an imperial center in hope. As the city becomes a city-state, royal power reconvenes, co-opting the space and the power of the priestly aristocracy. The balance between temple and governmental power in the neo-Babylonian period tips strongly in favor of royal power. Membership within the community, therefore, is not strictly determined through the cult alone (and thus excluding minors and women) nor by residence within the city; membership is determined by kinship. Ethnicity, the family's lineage, becomes the chief means of societal regulation. Control and surveillance of the society shifts to genealogical (and thereby marital) concerns. A new space is created—the city square, a concentrated space that also includes women and children where the royal power may survey the genealogical purity of the national citizenry who otherwise live far outside its gaze.

From Chaos to Civic Space: The City Square
As the entrance of the gate disappeared, the city square becomes connected to inner city gates. In the process, its earlier negative connotations dissolve. The square becomes the civic space. Zecharaiah sees the squares of future Jerusalem as a place for old women and men to sit and girls and boys to play (Zech. 8.4-5); Mordecai, dressed in regal attire, receives a royal accommodation on horseback in the midst of the square (Est. 6.9-11). Earlier in the story, Hathach seeks and even finds Mordecai in the midst of the square (Est. 4.6). The square has lost its darkness and anonymity; those who enter the square now enter public space, the space of nobility and citizens.

In fifth-century Jerusalem, the city squares, located outside the Temple, become the space for civic assemblies. Whereas in Iron Age II the troops meet outside the city walls before a military campaign, the Chronicler depicts Hezekiah appointing military leaders over the people: 'and he gathered them to him to the square of the gate and he spoke to their hearts' (2 Chron. 32.6). The king addresses his citizenry within their place, the square. Similarly, when Hezekiah gathers the priests and Levites to commission them to begin his temple reforms, he addresses them within the eastern square, before the gate of the king (29.6). In the square, the royal power gazes at its citizenry, both lay and clerical. In the square, no other power exists in competition with the king. The temple in the background confers authority to him; he mediates the sacred authority even to the temple personnel.

The city square spatially defines citizenship within the fifth-century Jerusalem city-state. The narrative of Ezra 10 displays the social power embodied within the square. In the attempt to strip social standing from members who had married non-Judean wives, 'a proclamation was made throughout Judah and Jerusalem to all the returned exiles that they should assemble at Jerusalem, and that if any one did not come within three days, by order of the officials and the elders all his property should be forfeited, and he himself banned from the congregation of the exiles' (10.7-8). The assembly takes place in a specific location in Jerusalem, in the square before the temple (10.9), despite heavy rain. The composition of the assembly, however, has changed from the neo-Babylonian period. While the elders dominate the proceedings of the square, societal power, now creating the city as a ethnic-national center, includes women and children in order to observe ethnic 'purity'. By making presence in the square mandatory, the means for surveillance lost by the geographic diffusion of the population is re-embodied within the space of the square. Absence from this space means absence from citizenship. This concentration of power within the space, however, receives a democratic legitimation. Within this space, all citizens may debate civic policy; its is the council of the citizens that decide policy. Ezra's word does not go unchallenged; dissent exists (10.15). Once the decision in the square is completed, however, the square creates a genealogical record that enables the ethnic-national city to exercise control over its dispersed citizenry: 'On the first day of the tenth month they sat down to examine the matter; and by the first day of the first month they had come to the end of all the men who had married foreign women' (Ezra 10.16b-17). Power embodied within the city square casts its gaze throughout the whole society.

This concentration of power within the square before the gate emerges in Nehemiah as well. The narrator assigns the events of Nehemiah 9 to the 'square before the Water Gate' (Neh. 8.1-2). Here 'all the people gathered as one' to hear the governmental authority (Ezra is here 'scribe', not 'priest') read the national law to the people, 'both men and women and all who could hear with understanding'. It is a civic meeting in the civic place. Membership in the society is defined by a person's presence within the square where he or she may be put under direct supervision by the authorities. Those who take their place in the front of the square, exercise power over the society, defined genealogically, through the public square. The square embodies the legal authority of the society, becomes the locus of justice (or injustice, depending upon one's social position): 'Justice is turned back, and righteousness stands afar off; for truth has fallen in the public squares, and uprightness cannot enter' (Isa. 59.14).

In the Achaemenid period, power creates the city square; it incorporates the application of the power over the society. The square creates the assembly and excludes all others from power. Yet while creating the privileged caste, the square also creates a means for their control and surveillance. In a society defined by ethnicity and nationality, the square concentrates a potentially diffuse, and therefore, difficult-to-control population into a small geographical space. From this place, the royal/governmental power may keep its hegemony over the elite, while creating an ideology of participation and equality.

Conclusion

Power reconfigures the Achaemenid period. The city is an ethnic-national center. City walls and gates create a national-military boundary, a place for the nation to gather. Temple gates still maintain their control over the temple court; now, however, royal power presides over both the gates and the courts. The economic goods of the society shift within the fortified confines of the temple complex. Power, however, concentrates chiefly on the space outside the temple gates—the city square. The square defines national citizenship, a place where those of proper patrimony may gather. In gathering in the square, the citizenry is subjected to the gaze of the royal/governmental power. Surveillance is achieved over an otherwise diffuse population.

Urban space therefore re-emerges in the Achaemenid period, but in a vastly different form. Membership in the society is determined by access to the square, not the city itself. One may be within the city, but not a member of society (cf. Neh. 13.1). The square creates an ethnic, rather than geographical, definition of members. Control is exercised through economic and social rather than physical coercion; or rather physical control is dispersed through economic and social institutions within the temple and the square. Such an urban configuration is also 'democratic', possibly even egalitarian—for those within. Women and children re-emerge as members within the society. While clerics maintain economic control, Levites and laity exist equally in the same space outside temple; governmental/royal power reigns over the square and thus over both equally.

The Achaemenid city is made for commerce. As an ethnic-national center, it encourages the movement of persons and goods conducive to trade. With roots in the ethnic-cultic organization of the neo-Babylonian period, the Achaemenid city opens itself to the Hellenistic model. With the rise of the square, we might detect birth of the *polis* within Judea.

Conclusion

No geographical entity 'city' existed in ancient Israel. The tale of the Isra-elite city in antiquity is a tale of at least three cities. The city is a civic place, where membership is defined by residence within its gates. The city no longer exists; it is an ethnic-cultic place, where membership is defined by access to the temple courts. The city is an ethnic-national center, where membership is defined by one's presence in the square. As power inhabits the urban landscape, it creates its own geography for the control and surveillance of society and its own ideology to legitimate this control. Urban gates and city squares provide us a means of access into these embodiments of power.

Part II
THE 'HELLENISTIC' PERIOD(S)

THE JEWS AND HELLENIZATION:
HENGEL AND HIS CRITICS

Lester L. Grabbe

The question of the Jews and Hellenization seems to be one of perennial interest. Because of the influence of Martin Hengel's various books on the subject, he serves as a useful focus to address the question. Most of the issues have been discussed by him, and those who have taken a different position in recent years have usually done so with explicit reference to him. The purpose of this paper is to give a 'once over lightly' to the subject but to introduce the main issues and questions, as well as giving my own conclusions (for fuller information, see Grabbe 1992: 147-70). The focus of this paper is on the Ptolemaic period, though no discussion can be confined exclusively to that time.

Hengel's Basic Thesis

Summary
Martin Hengel's *opus magnum* which appeared in English in 1974 is probably the most significant work to deal with the question of Judaism in its relationship to Hellenism, though certainly building on and influenced by earlier authors, especially Bickerman. While limiting himself formally to the period from Alexander to the Maccabean revolt, he discussed the later period in passing at many points. Further, his later monographs (Hengel 1980, 1989) filled in certain aspects of the post-Maccabean period. Hengel's major work is a highly concentrated book which cannot be easily summarized. His main thesis relates to the cause of the suppression of Judaism as a religion under Antiochus IV, and in this he comes out forcefully on the side of the proposal already advanced by E.J. Bickerman (1979). But in reaching that conclusion he takes a thorough look at the whole process of Hellenization and concludes, among other things, that Judaism and Hellenism were not mutually exclusive entities (Hengel 1974: I, 2-3) and that from 'about the middle of the third century

BC *all Judaism* must really be designated "Hellenistic Judaism" in the strict sense', so that one cannot separate Palestinian Judaism from Hellenistic Judaism (Hengel 1974: I, 103-106).

In order to demonstrate this thesis, Hengel does not just advance a series of arguments or proofs. Rather, by a thorough description of Judaism during this period and by setting out its context in the Hellenistic world of the time, the conclusion forces itself forward that the Jews of Palestine were not successful in—indeed, did not particularly attempt—holding themselves aloof from the dominant culture. Judea under the Ptolemies and Seleucids was a part of the wider Hellenistic world, and the Jews of Palestine were as much a part of this world as the other peoples of the ancient Near East. Thus, in order to disprove Hengel, one would have to give positive evidence that the Jews wanted to resist all aspects of the Hellenistic culture, that they were able to distinguish between 'Hellenistic' and 'native' elements, and that they prevailed in their resistance. Hengel has successfully put the onus of proof on any who would challenge the view that Palestinian Judaism was a part of Hellenistic Judaism of the time. Although a summary cannot do justice to the detailed study, Hengel's major points and arguments are essentially the following:

1. The Jews of Palestine, far from being isolated, were thoroughly caught up in the events of their time, particularly the rivalry between the Ptolemaic and Seleucid kingdoms. Palestine itself was a disputed territory, claimed by the Seleucids with a certain legality on their side but nevertheless under Ptolemaic rule for the century before 200 BCE.

2. Ptolemaic (and later Seleucid) administration reached to the lowest levels of Jewish society. Every village was supervised by the Greek administration and had its officials seeing that the various sorts of taxes were paid. Although natives were often delegated as supervisors at the lower levels, Greeks and Greek-speaking natives were very much in evidence, especially at the higher levels.

3. International trade was a feature of the Hellenistic world; indeed, trade with the Aegean had already brought many Greek influences to the Phoenician and Palestinian coasts long before the time of Alexander. Palestine itself was an important crossroads in the trade between north and south and between Egypt and Arabia.

4. The language of trade and administration was Greek. The use of Greek for official purposes is well illustrated already by the mid-third century and its direct influence on the Jews can be deduced from a variety of sources.
5. Greek education also had its influence on Jews and Jewish education.
6. Greek influence on Jewish literature is already documented as early as Alexander's conquest and can be illustrated from literature in Hebrew and Aramaic as well as those works composed directly in Greek. Evidence of the influence of Greek philosophy occurs in such quintessentially Jewish circles as Qumran and writings such as *1 Enoch*.
7. The 'anti-Greek' forces which followed on the Maccabean crisis did not succeed in erasing the pervasive Greek influence of the previous century and a half, and Jewish Palestine even as it gained basic independence under the Hasmoneans still remained a part of the Hellenistic world.

In his later writings, Hengel's position overall has seemed to remain the same. However, he has nuanced it somewhat to meet some of the criticisms made (see next section): he recognizes that in the period before 175 BCE, 'we only have very fragmentary and sporadic information about the Jews in Palestine and in the Diaspora' (Hengel 1980: 51). He also accepts that Hellenization was perhaps a lengthier process than originally allowed for: 'A more thorough "Hellenization", which also included the lower classes, only became a complete reality in Syria and Palestine under the protection of Rome... It was Rome which first helped "Hellenism" to its real victory in the East...' (Hengel 1980: 53).

Criticisms of Hengel
Of the many reviews which have appeared—including those by such well-known specialists in the Hellenistic period as Fergus Millar (1978), Arnaldo Momigliano (1970) and Louis H. Feldman (1977, 1986)[1]—the

---

1. In the 1977 review Feldman summarized Hengel's work in 22 points and then proceeded to attack each of them as invalid or not supporting Hengel's thesis in a significant way. His 1986 article covers some of the same ground but in a more diffuse way. There is no doubt that Feldman has some important criticisms and has drawn attention to areas where Hengel is weak or where the data do not give strong support to his argument. Unfortunately, he vitiates the impact of his arguments with two major flaws: first, there seems to be a strong, underlying assumption that being Hellenized

majority have been impressed by Hengel's breadth of learning and by his basic arguments about the Hellenizing of Judaism. Feldman has been the main one to reject Hengel's thesis completely. The major areas where Hengel is weakest or most controversial (aside from his main thesis about the cause of the suppression of Judaism as a religion under Antiochus IV) are the following:

1. While Greek influence on Jewish literature in Greek is easy to demonstrate, such is much more difficult with literature in the Semitic languages. For example, Hengel takes the view that Qohelet shows knowledge and terminology of Greek popular philosophy, a thesis by no means universally accepted, as Feldman among others has noted.[2] In other examples, one can show Greek parallels and make a cogent case for Greek influence, yet without demonstrating that other potential sources are not equally possible. Thus, Hengel's arguments, which are generally quite strong with regard to Jewish literature in Greek, become much less certain and more likely to be disputed in the area of Hebrew and Aramaic literature.

2. Many of the examples that Hengel uses actually belong to the post-Maccabean period, partly because our knowledge of the Ptolemaic period is so problematic (see Momigliano 1970). Of course, in many cases it seems legitimate to extrapolate to the earlier period (e.g. the evidence of the Qumran scrolls), thereby suggesting that the crisis that arose in Jerusalem was not primarily one of Hellenizing but of religious suppression. Yet Hengel was not always careful in his original study to make clear that some developments in Hellenization may have come about only in post-Maccabean times, while the exact path of Helleni-

means ceasing to be a proper Jew (e.g. 1986: 85); secondly, his arguments often depend on interpretations which would not be accepted by the majority of specialists. For example, in his 1977 review he dates *1 Enoch* 12–36 much later than is generally done (his point no. 21) and doubts the identity of the Qumranites as Essenes (point no. 22). In the 1986 article, he assumes, for instance, that only Gentiles attended the various amphitheaters and sports stadia erected by Herod and others (104) and that the ossuary inscriptions in Greek were only to prevent non-Jews from molesting the graves (88). Overall, his complete rejection of Hengel's thesis therefore seems unjustified.

2. Contrast Braun (1973), who develops the thesis at length, with O. Loretz (1964), who argues strongly that there is nothing in Qohelet which cannot be explained from pre-Hellenistic Near Eastern tradition.

zation in Judea during the Ptolemaic period may not be so clear as he first implied. One of the most valuable of Feldman's criticisms is to cast doubt on the speed with which Judaism was Hellenized. Other contributors have also noted this (cf. also Hengel's response noted above [p. 54]).

3.   In the way that examples are selected and presented, Hengel appears to exaggerate the place of Greek education and language in Palestine. The examples used go only so far; that is, they demonstrate that some Jews had a reasonable knowledge of Greek and many more had a smattering, but the actual number of Jews who could be considered monolingual or bilingual in Greek in Palestine was probably rather less than Hengel seems to conclude. In any case, the evidence is certainly not conclusive for a pervasive use of Greek throughout Jewish society in Palestine. As for the question of education, we simply have almost no information about education at all in Judea at this time, much less education in Greek.

Analysis

Terminology

One of the major problems in the debate is that of terminology. Not all scholars necessarily mean the same thing when they use the terms 'Hellenize/Hellenization', a fact that has resulted in confusion and much dispute over simple misunderstandings. In discussing the question of terminology, it is unavoidable that I anticipate some of the points made below. Nevertheless, it seems best to take up the question here rather than later.

There seem to be several legitimate ways in which the 'Hellenization' can be used. First is in reference to the general situation in the Orient after Alexander. Much remained the same, at least for the time being, but there was a qualitative change overall. Greece, Asia Minor, Egypt and Mesopotamia now all fell under the rubric 'Hellenistic' in that they made up the Hellenistic world. All Eastern peoples, the Jews included, were a part of this world.

Second is the cultural phenomenon, with its complex set of cultural elements derived from both Greek and Near Eastern sources. It was neither 'Greek nor Oriental', but neither was it homogenized. There were some loci (regions, social and economic classes, institutions) which were almost purely Greek and others which remained unadulteratedly native, and there were mixtures of various sorts (though this element—that of *Verschmel-zung* [or 'blending together']—should not be exaggerated, as will become clear). However, the balance of the different elements and their relation-ships were not static but constantly changing and developing. Thus, Hellenistic culture can be adequately described only as a process. The Jews were fully a part of this process. There is no indication that they differed from the other peoples within this world in both adopting certain Greek elements and practices and yet also preserving their own cultural heritage.

Third, there is the question of the individual, the extent to which specific Greek practices were adopted or conformed to. The Hellenistic world included far more than just the culture of classical Greece. But one could be said to be 'Hellenized' if an effort was made to adhere to Greek ideals and customs. From this point of view, individual Orientals—including individual Jews—might be more Hellenized than others. This last point seems to be the one often in mind (perhaps even unconsciously) when Hellenization of the Jews is discussed. A further complication concerns the extent to which the adoption of some Greek cultural elements implies a religious apostasy.

The Question of Language

In the post-Alexandrian centuries 'Greek' came less and less to be an ethnic designation and more and more one of education, especially in good Greek style. There is clear evidence that many educated and upper-class Orientals were knowledgeable in the Greek language. The question is how far this knowledge penetrated. Although it is often asserted that Greek became the official language of the conquered territories, this seems mistaken (Kuhrt and Sherwin-White 1987: 5-6, 23-25): the Seleucid empire was multilin-gual, with local languages continuing to be used in official documents (with perhaps a few exceptions[3]).

A similar situation pertained in Egypt (see Samuel, 1983: esp. 105-17, on the linguistic situation). Although Egypt is famous for its finds of papyri in Greek, the accumulating evidence suggests that at least as much material was produced in Demotic during the same period of time. There was clearly a flourishing native literary tradition in all sorts of genres, not just temple literature, during this time. More significant, though, is the amount of Demotic papyri relating to the administration. The native Egyptian legal

3.   For instance, slave-sale documents after 275 BCE were issued only in Greek, according to Doty (1980: esp. 85) and Rostovtzeff (1932: esp. 65-69).

system was still administered alongside the Greek, but the Demotic documents cover far more than the legal sphere, encompassing bureaucratic
activity up to a fairly high level. Contrary to a frequent assumption,
Egyptians could and did rise to high positions in the administration, and
much of the work of the bureaucracy was done in bilingual mode. In short, a
great deal of business and everyday life was still carried on in the Egyptian
language by Egyptians at all levels of society.

A major question is one of interpretation. One can point to such
examples as the Armenian king Artavasdes who cultivated Greek learning
and even wrote Greek literature; at a birthday celebration, the Bacchides
of Euripides was performed for his court (Plutarch, *Crassus* 33). Or the
Buddhist king Asoka who erected inscriptions in good Greek (as well as
Aramaic) in the remote area of Kandahar (Pugliese Carratelli and Garbini
1964). But what conclusion should be drawn from this? How far can such
examples be taken as typical? For instance, Hengel states that 'Galilee,
completely encircled by the territories of the Hellenized cities...will
similarly have been largely bilingual' (Hengel 1989: 14-15). Martin Goodman gives a more nuanced and somewhat less categorical view. While
recognizing that Greek had its place in Galilee, he notes that it was not
dominant, with Aramaic—not Greek—being the lingua franca: 'In Upper
Galilee there is almost no evidence of Greek at all... But in Upper Galilee
and probably in the area around Lake Tiberias, Greek was only a thin
strand in the linguistic cloth...' (Goodman 1983: 67-68). Was Galilee
bilingual? Evidently not, if one means that Greek was widely used
everywhere. The mere presence of some Greek usage does not necessarily
deserve the term 'largely bilingual'.

Greek certainly did function as a *lingua franca* in many parts of the
Hellenistic East, as Aramaic had done under the Assyrian, neo-Babylonian
and Achaemenid empires. Royal inscriptions and many other sorts of
documents were issued in Greek, yet there was no attempt to impose it as
the sole language of administration. Traders no doubt found some
acquaintance with Greek useful, not only in dealing with officialdom but
also for getting around in areas with a multitude of local languages. If the
buyer or seller one was dealing with knew a second language, however, in
many parts of the Seleucid empire it was more likely to be Aramaic than
Greek.

The complexity of the penetration of the language is illustrated by two
examples. An ostracon in Aramaic from about the middle of the third
century BCE already contains two Greek words (Cross 1981). Another
ostracon from Khirbet el-Kom in the Idumean area, dated about 275 BCE,

is bilingual in both Greek and Aramaic (Geraty 1975). By contrast, there is only one formal bilingual inscription so far known in the entirety of Syria, that from Tel Dan about 200 BCE (Biran 1977; cf. Millar 1987a: 132). Thus, Hengel's demonstration of the widespread use of Greek in his various writings cannot be doubted, yet the significance of this fact is not so easily assessed. For one thing, this use of Greek seems to have been confined to a certain segment of the population, especially the educated upper class. To what extent it penetrated into the lives of the bulk of the population is more difficult to determine; however, the number of Jews outside the Greek cities who were fluent in Greek seems small.

Hellenization Elsewhere in the Ancient Near East

An older view emphasized the Greek influence on the original civilizations of the ancient Near East and the dominance of Greek institutions. Such an attitude can be found in the classic work of Tarn and Griffith (1952) and is also the prevalent view in the first edition of volume 7 of the *Cambridge Ancient History* (though Rostovtzeff gives a more nuanced approach in his articles in that volume). The most recent work has recognized not only the Greco-centric view of so much older scholarship but has found evidence in new discoveries as well as old that the earlier cultures were far from obliterated under Greek rule (Kuhrt and Sherwin-White 1987; Sherwin-White and Kuhrt 1993).

The spread of Greek institutions and culture to the remotest parts of the Greek empire can be seen in the Greek remains in such unlikely places as Ai Khanum (Bernard 1967), and the island of Failaka (ancient Icarus) in the Persian gulf (Roueché and Sherwin-White 1985). The presence of Greek communities, as indicated by inscriptions, architecture and literary remains, show that no region could escape some influence. The question is to what extent the Greek presence produced merging, adoption or change in the indigenous cultures. A 'mixed culture' was slow in coming in most cases, if it ever occurred as such.

The cities of Babylon and Uruk provide useful evidence about Hellenization in Mesopotamia. Alexander originally made Babylon the capital of his empire. It has often been assumed that, with the founding of Seleucia-on-the-Tigris, Babylon declined to the point of desolation. The foundation of Seleucia was probably done deliberately to provide a new Hellenistic center, but Babylon itself continued not only to survive but also to thrive (Sherwin-White 1987; van der Spek 1987). The native tradition of kingship, in which the Seleucid ruler acted in the same capacity as the old native Babylonian kings, is attested as continuing and seriously supported by at least some of the Seleucids (Sherwin-White 1983; 1987: 8-9, 28-29; Kuhrt 1987: 51-52, 55-56).

Neither Babylon nor Uruk is certainly known to have been a *polis* in the early Greek period, though evidently some Greeks were there (Sherwin-White 1982, 1987; van der Spek 1987: 66-70, 72-74). The Greek names found in cuneiform sources fall into four periods which seem to correspond well with the history of the city under Greek rule (Sarkisian 1974; van der Spek 1987: 60-74): First stage: Greek residents but no involvement with the native inhabitants (Greek names practically absent); second stage (223–187 BCE): Greeks begin to take part in civic life, with some intermarriage (limited Greek names among the Babylonians); third stage (middle of second century): influx of more Greeks, probably because of the policy of Antiochus IV (Greek names more frequent); fourth stage (after 140): the Arsacid conquest halts the Hellenization process (Greek names continue sporadically for a time but gradually die out).

Syria and Phoenicia

The question of Hellenization in Syria generally is very important since ths area formed Judea's immediate environment. Hengel has also emphasized the part played by Phoenicia and Philistia as the intermediaries of Greek culture to Judea (Hengel 1974: I, 32-35; 1980: 28). Millar has also produced two seminal essays on this topic (1983, 1987a). One of his major points is that, perhaps apart from Phoenicia, it is difficult to draw general conclusions about Hellenization for the Syrian area simply because of the paucity of evidence (Millar 1987a: 111-13, 129-31). After extensive discussion, he concludes on a rather negative note, 'The enigma of hellenistic Syria—of the wider Syrian region in the hellenistic period—remains' (Millar 1987a: 129). It is not just a question of the paucity of data for the Hellenistic period but also for the Achaemenid period: you cannot talk about changes after Alexander if you do not know what it was like before him.

This lack of remains can lead to widely differing interpretations of what little there is. To take one example: Hengel places a good deal of emphasis on the writers and philosophers who came from the Syrian region, including such individuals as Meleager of Gadara (Hengel 1974: I, 84-86; 1980: 118). Millar, on the other hand, comments with regard to Meleager, 'But there is nothing in the quite extensive corpus of his poetry to show that he had deeply absorbed any non-Greek culture in his native city...' (Millar 1987a: 130).

But it is not the case that only a negative conclusion can be drawn from Millar's study. As the editors note in their introduction, 'his careful examination of a scattered body of material is susceptible to a more positive interpretation than he himself allows...' (Kuhrt and Sherwin-White 1987: x). One of the points that does emerge is the strong continuation of the native culture in that area, which was clearly not generally submerged by the Greek or absorbed into it. Millar has also produced evidence of changes under Hellenism which included the spread of Greek culture in certain ways.

Phoenicia is a useful example of how Hellenization could penetrate the culture yet not displace the native traditions. The influence of Greek culture actually began well before Alexander (Millar 1983: 67; Hengel 1974: I, 32-35). Although the precise course of Hellenization is difficult to document (Millar 1983: 60), the cities of the region gradually evolved into Greek *poleis* (Millar 1987a: 123-24). Nevertheless, it is also clear that Phoenician culture continued at all levels, both in Phoenicia itself and in its colonies overseas. We find Phoenician names alongside Greek, some individuals having both sorts. Coins have both Greek and Phoenician writing. Philo of Byblos wrote a work (supposedly based on the work of the ancient author Sanchuniathon) which preserves many details of Canaanite religion from antiquity, yet Philo's work is itself thoroughly Greek in form (Barr 1974–75). One would have to say that the major Phoenician cities were Hellenized in some sense, yet they also remain Phoenician with a strong continuation from their past.

Resistance to Hellenization

The reactions against Hellenization were complex and diverse, but the Jews were by no means the only people to fight it. Although much of the evidence has no doubt disappeared, enough survives to show that there were anti-Hellenistic moves of various sorts among a wide range of the Near Eastern peoples. The most obvious form of resistance was armed rebellion against Greek political domination and the attempt to restore native rule. The Jewish state stands out in this because it successfully gained independence whereas most other rebels met with failure; yet the Jews of Palestine were certainly not the only ones to aspire to independence or to attempt to gain it by force of arms. Among the Egyptians in particular, there were a number of uprisings, though none successful (cf. Peremans 1978; Lloyd 1982).

Even gaining independence from Greek rule did not necessarily mean the overthrow of Hellenistic culture or the rooting out of all Greek elements or influences, as is made clear by the example of the Hasmonean state which threw off the Seleucid yoke but made no attempt to eliminate the overt Greek elements in Jewish culture. On the contrary, Judea under Hasmonean rule was typical of Hellenistic kingdoms of that general period. In this one may compare modern 'nativistic movements'. They often react against some cultural elements of colonial powers simply because they are symbolic of oppression (La Barre 1971: esp. 20-22), yet many elements taken over from the colonizers will be accepted, either because they have become so well integrated that they are no longer recognized as foreign (Worsley 1957: 23) or because they are useful or symbolically neutral to the movement.

Another sort of reaction was the production of anti-Greek propaganda, generally of a literary type. We find a whole genre of such writing from the Hellenistic period produced by a variety of peoples, often taking the form of oracles or *ex eventu* prophecies. In Egypt there were prophecies predicting the overthrow of Greek rule, including the *Oracle of Bocchoris* (or *the Lamb*), the *Potter's Oracle*, and the *Demotic Chronicle* (Eddy 1961; Collins 1979: 168-70). From Persia came the *Oracle of Hystaspes* (Eddy 1961; Collins 1979: 46-47). The Jews produced fake *Sibylline Oracles* (Collins 1979: 46-47). This literature itself was a way of kindling hope and venting frustration. What effect it had from a practical point of view is uncertain; probably little in most cases, though there may have been times when it served to inspire the native peoples to active resistance and revolt.

Conclusions

Hellenization was a long and complex phenomenon. It cannot be summarized in a word or a sentence. It was not just the adoption of Greek ways by the inhabitants of the ancient Near East or of Oriental ways by Greeks who settled in the East. Hellenistic civilization was *sui generis* and must be considered from a variety of points of view, for it concerned many different areas of life: language, custom, religion, commerce, architecture, dress, government, literary and philosophical ideals.

Hellenization represented a process as well as a description of a type of culture. Whatever Alexander's ideals may have been, his successors were highly Greco-chauvinist. Pride of place in society was to go to Greeks alone, with the natives usually at the bottom of the pyramid. Greek ideals were preserved in the Greek foundations, with citizenship and membership of the gymnasium jealously guarded for the exclusive privilege of the Greek settlers. Orientals might live in the Greek cities but they were not citizens and were mostly barred from becoming so. There was no interest in cultural imperialism as such by the Greek rulers.

However, over a period of a century or so after Alexander's death, things gradually began to change. Local nobles and chieftains were often of use in the Ptolemaic and Seleucid administrations, and they employed Greek secretaries. A good example of this is the Jewish noble Tobias for whom we have a number of letters in Greek from the Zenon archive (see Tcherikover, Fuks and Stern 1957–64: I, 115-30). These individuals were also likely to see the need to have their sons given a Greek education. Thus, it is that already early in the Greek period, we find educated Orientals who have some knowledge of Greek. Individuals such as Manetho in Egypt and Berossus in Babylon were already writing treatises in Greek in the early part of the third century. In the Tobiad romance, Joseph and later his son Hyrcanus (second half of the third century) deal with the Ptolemaic court on an equal footing (Josephus, *Ant.* 12.4.2-11[160-236]); there is no indication that they have to communicate by translator or that their educational background is considered inferior.

The life of the average person was not strikingly affected. The poor peasant continued to work the land, only noting that he had a new landlord or had to pay taxes to a new regime. Yet in stating this, one must not forget that the day-to-day life of the bulk of the population in the Near East probably changed little between the third millennium BCE and the nineteenth century CE. The coming of the Greeks did not radically change their lives—but neither did the coming of the Assyrians, the Persians, the Romans, the Arabs, the Turks or the British. However, there were constant reminders of the new culture, most obviously in the language of administration and commerce. Certainly, anyone who wished to engage in trade would probably find it advantageous to gain some acquaintance with Greek, and those who could afford it would be under pressure to provide some sort of Greek education for their offspring. Yet the native languages continued to be used in administration, and most people could get by quite well without any knowledge of Greek. As an analogy, one might consider the Anglicization of India in the nineteenth century or the Westernization of Japan in the post-World War II era.

This state of affairs means that, on the one hand, Hellenization was a centuries-long process in which all were engaged and from which no one escaped; therefore, all peoples of the Near East, the Jews included, were part of the Hellenistic world, were included in this process, and were from this point of view Hellenized. On the other hand, one could also speak of degrees of Hellenization in the sense of how far individuals went in consciously imitating and adopting Greek ways. From such a perspective it would be legitimate to talk of a particular individual as being 'more Hellenized' or 'less Hellenized' than another and Hellenization in this sense represents a spectrum encompassing many shades of Greek influence from the limited to the intense. This means that it is important to make clear what is being referred to in each context, though many writers on the subject fail to make such distinctions and talk as if it were all or nothing, as if someone were Hellenized or not.

Although there are many points to be debated in current study, Hengel's dictum is becoming more and more accepted: one can no longer talk of Judaism *versus* Hellenism nor of Palestinian *versus* Hellenistic Judaism. To do so is to create an artificial binary opposition and to reduce an enormously complex picture to stark, unshaded black and white. It is also to treat a lengthy process as if it were a single undifferentiated event—as if conception, pregnancy, birth, childhood and adulthood could be simultaneous. At the risk of repeating points made in the previous section, the following aspects relate to the Jews specifically.

1. Hellenism was a culture whereas Judaism was a religion. Some aspects of Hellenistic culture were irrelevant to Jewish religious views. Other aspects were viewed as irrelevant by some Jews but highly subversive by others. And from any point of view, certain aspects of Hellenistic culture, especially those in the religious sphere, had the potential to bring about major transformations of Judaism. The stark dichotomy of 'Hellenizers' and 'Judaizers' of 1 Maccabees has been used too simplistically and thus has caused gross distortion (see Grabbe 1992: 221-311). It assumes a narrow, prejudicial definition of what it means to be a loyal Jew with no allowance made for those of a different opinion. It is as if, to take a modern analogy, the only form of Judaism allowed to be 'Jewish' were Orthodox Judaism. This may indeed be the view of some Orthodox Jews, but it is hardly the perspective of Conservative, Reform, Liberal, Karaite, Falasha, and other forms of Judaism. It is not the job of the historian to take sides or adopt the denominational prejudice of the sources.

2. Those called 'Judaizers' (or, misleadingly, 'orthodox' in some modern works) were not totally opposed to all aspects of Helle-

nistic culture. What they opposed were certain things affecting their religion, though this opposition sometimes used—or reacted to—cultural symbols as a means of expressing their loyalty to a particular form of Judaism. (One might compare a common reaction among 'nativistic movements' in which overt elements of the colonial culture are attacked even though much has been absorbed without even recognizing it.)

3. The attitudes of those called 'Judaizers' seem to have covered a wide spectrum, including the *Hasidim*, the Maccabees, those who refused to defend themselves against their enemies, the partisans of Onias, and those who wrote Daniel 7–12; the same is true of the so-called 'Hellenizers'. As far as we know, none of them rejected the label 'Jew', even Menelaus and his followers whom many would regard as the most extreme of the Hellenizers. Nevertheless, to be 'Hellenized' did not mean to cease to be a Jew. Take for example Philo of Alexandria: here was a man with a good Greek education, who wrote and thought in the Greek language (probably knowing no Hebrew), and lived a life which in many daily habits did not differ from the Greek citizens of Alexandria, yet who considered himself nothing less than a loyal and pious Jew (see especially Mendelson 1988; Cohen 1999). Or we might consider the message of the *Letter of Aristeas* which is that Jews can be a part of the Hellenistic world without necessarily compromising their Judaism. A final example is the Jason who became high priest (2 Macc. 4.7-22); he evidently considered himself a full and faithful Jew, yet he was the one who obtained permission for Jerusalem to become a Greek foundation. The fact that some Jews may have judged him an apostate is irrelevant to the question of his own self-designation or Jewish identity (see the discussion in Grabbe [1992: 221-311]).

4. The native cultures continued to thrive to a greater or lesser extent all over the Near East, not just in Judea. Greek remained a minority language and did not displace the many local languages nor the old *lingua franca* of Aramaic. Hellenization as a process —not just a static culture—continued with the coming of the Romans and the growth of their empire.

5. It is indeed true that Jews were unique and did not lose their identity—a fact with which some writers on the subject seem obsessed—but one could also make the same statement about

many of the native peoples. Each ethnic group was unique in its own way and was just as attached to its own identity, culture, native language and traditions as the Jews. This also in many cases included particular religious cults which were as important to them as Yahwism was to the Jews. One can readily accept the Hellenization of the Jews without denying their uniqueness, loyalty to religion, careful maintenance of tradition and custom, or continual contribution to Hebrew and Aramaic literature.

6.   In accommodating to Hellenistic culture the Jews always maintained one area which could not be compromised without affecting their Judaism, that of religion. The Jews alone in the Greco-Roman world refused honor to gods, shrines and cults other than their own. Thus, even those Jews who were most at home in the Hellenistic world, such as Philo or the author of Pseudo-Aristeas, still found themselves marked out—and marked off—by this fact. For the vast majority, this was the final barrier which could not be crossed; we know of only a handful of examples from antiquity in which Jews abandoned their Judaism as such. Thus, however Hellenized they might be, observant Jews could never be fully at home in the Greek world.

THE MATERIAL CULTURE OF THE SELEUCID PERIOD IN PALESTINE: SOCIAL AND ECONOMIC OBSERVATIONS

Kenneth Hoglund

Broadly speaking, the Seleucid period of Palestine dates from the final victory of Antiochus III at Paneion in 200 BCE to the overwhelming victories of Judas Maccabeus in 165 BCE (Noth 1960: 350, 368-69). The seemingly precise nature of these historical events conceals a certain indefiniteness about both the beginning and end of the period, since protracted times of turmoil marked both transitions. For example, Ptolemaic coinage was issued in the Levant after 200 BCE, and Seleucid coinage is found well within the Hasmonean period at Judean hill country sites (Mørkholm 1983; Rappaport 1984: 31; Schäfer 1977: 576-77). However, for the generation or so that Seleucid power ruled unchallenged in Palestine, the Seleucid rulers were able to reshape the relatively relaxed Ptolemaic rule of the region into a more dynamic process of governance.

Archaeologically speaking, there are clear indicators allowing the dating of remains with considerable precision. Thus, the ceramics of the period show no clear breaks from 200 BCE until well into the first century CE (Lapp 1961: 225), but refinements within the period are clear enough to frequently differentiate 'Seleucid' from 'Hasmonean'. Of greater significance is the increasing circulation of coinage, and the importance of datable Seleucid issues to administrative life (Rappaport 1984: 31; Rostovtzeff 1939: 290-91).

Despite the potential for such chronological refinement, few researchers attempt to differentiate subphases within the broader Hellenistic period (333–37 BCE). Indeed, the most recent synthetic studies of the material culture of the period do not attempt to isolate and describe a Seleucid period, within the larger Hellenistic framework (Arav 1989; Halpern-Silberstein 1989; Rappaport 1991). When such sub-phasing is encountered, it is usually characterized as Hellenistic 1 (333–152; Ptolemaic and Seleucid) and Hellenistic 2 (152–37 BCE; Hasmonean). This scheme has been adopted by the Archaeological Survey of Israel and the *Encyclopedia of*

Archaeological Excavation in the Holy Land (see Kuhnen 1990: 38 n. 6). Dividing the period into Ptolemaic-Seleucid and Hasmonean phases makes it difficult to interpret the results of surveys as they apply to the foundation of new settlements or the abandonment of older sites in the Seleucid period. As a result, in the presentation that follows little can be said on the basis of survey data alone without further efforts to pinpoint the ceramic dating of sites designated 'Hellenistic'.

While it is not possible in such a brief format to offer a comprehensive portrait of the material culture of the Seleucid period in Palestine, it is possible to isolate various components of the archaeological data and suggest several observations that may be drawn from such sources of information. Each component bears on certain aspects of the religious and social organization of Seleucid Palestine. Settlement patterns and types of settlements, largely derived from intensive regional surveys, may provide an indication of the kinds of resources being utilized to sustain the local economy, or may point to the prevailing economic factors in the choice of population concentrations. The spatial organization of urban centers dating from the period may also disclose the relative importance of market-place activity or the presence of an urban elite. Evidence of administrative activity in the form of garrisons or public buildings may point to the degree of penetration achieved by the Seleucid central administration. Tombs and the evidence of customary burial practices may assist in tracing the existence of elites in the society and the degree to which 'Hellenization' may have impacted different social groups. While this list does not exhaust the possibilities, it will provide a workable set of data with which to consider the period.

Settlement Patterns

The settlement data from various regions around the Levant show that nearly 15 per cent of the Hellenistic settlements were founded at previously unoccupied locations (Zori 1977). While the survey evidence as published will not allow the foundation of all these new establishments to be assigned to the Seleucid period, it seems probable that a majority may date to that period.

Excavations at various sites seem to further reinforce this conclusion. For example, at Tel Anafa in the Upper Galilee, the dating of the first Hellenistic phase of the site is somewhat ambiguous but appears to be early second century BCE, or Seleucid (Herbert 1979).

Samarian and Judean Hill Country

For the Samarian hill country, the same pattern seems to be in evidence. Survey data point to a dramatically different occupational pattern from the Persian period to the later Hellenistic period. For example, in the 1967 survey of the Occupied Territories, in the territory of Ephraim and Manasseh, some 81 sites were designated Persian, while only 47 were located from the Hellenistic period. Of these, 39 represented continuous settlement from the Persian through the Hellenistic period (Kochavi 1972: 237-38). In the survey of the land of Benjamin, a similar picture emerged. There, some 14 sites were considered Persian, while only 12 were located from the Hellenistic period, with only three of these representing continuous Persian-Hellenistic occupation (Kochavi 1972: 189-90).

More intensive surveys in the same region have amplified these trends. Zertal has reported that out of 235 Persian period sites in the region of Manasseh, 64 per cent were abandoned in the succeeding Hellenistic period. Further, the character of occupation dramatically shifted, from small-scale farming communities in the Persian period to more urban sites in the succeeding Hellenistic phase. Zertal summarized his data by stating, 'in the Hellenistic period the importance of the old [urban] centres declined, while new ones were developed' (Zertal 1990: 15). In particular, Zertal saw a focus on the centers of Mt Gerizim and Arubboth-Narbatta during the Hellenistic period. Zertal could well have mentioned the urban center of Dothan itself, where excavation revealed an extensive Hellenistic occupation dating to the Seleucid period (Free 1954: 15).

To the south, preliminary reports on the excavations of an extensive Hellenistic city surrounding Mt Gerizim have noted the extraordinary planning that went into the city. Ceramic and numismatic evidence clearly place the foundation of the city within the reign of Antiochus III (Magen 1986).

In Judea, at Tel Goren the Hellenistic phase was restricted to a fortified enclosure at the summit of the tell. The founding of this phase was dated to the late third/early second centuries BCE by the excavators, though all of the published pottery came from the early second century (Mazar, Dothan and Dunayesky 1966: 39-44). It is probable that this stratum also marks Seleucid efforts to fortify the region south of Jerusalem. The citadel at Beth-Zur is another classic example of this process (Sellers 1933; Lapp 1961). At Lachish, the so-called 'Solar Shrine' was founded in the first half of the second century and possibly destroyed c. 150 BCE (Aharoni 1975: 3-5).

Coastal Plain

Along the Coastal Plain, a number of sites also show the increasing urbanization and formation of new settlements under Seleucid governance. Along the Plain of Sharon, the initiation of Seleucid rule is also marked by newly founded cities (Roller 1982). The earliest city at Caesarea Maritima appears to have been founded in the first decades of the second century BCE (Roller 1980). At Tel Mevorakh, after a gap in activity of the site from the end of the fourth century, the city is refounded in the early second century (Stern 1978: 25, 84). The continuing excavations at Tel Dor have demonstrated that while initially fortified under the Ptolemies, Dor was extensively rebuilt in the Seleucid period (Stern 1985). Survey data also points to a diminished number of rural Persian period sites in favor of more urban settlements. For example, in the southeastern corner of the Plain of Sharon, there is a 50 per cent reduction in the number of sites from the Persian into the Hellenistic (Ne'eman 1990).

Farther to the south, Ashdod revealed a significant Hellenistic phase, the initiation of which appears to have been in the early second century BCE (Dothan 1971: 44-45).

Transjordan

The survey work that has been done in this area has not provided adequate chronological precision to say if a site was founded in the earlier or later part of the Hellenistic period. The survey of Ibrahim *et al.* indicated the Hellenistic period was marked by the emergence of several large cities, though no specification was made as to where in the Hellenistic period these should be placed (Ibrahim, Sauer and Yassine 1976: 58). The Wadi el-Hasa survey revealed a number of sites from the 'Late Hellenistic' period, though no characterization was made as whether these were villages or urban centers (MacDonald 1988: 190). In the survey of the Heshbon region, most Hellenistic materials were evidenced at larger urban centers, and these tended to be more of the 'Late Hellenistic' period (Ibach 1987: 169-70).

Based on what little excavation has been conducted in the area, we may be able to say that these cities were established in the Seleucid period. For example, though the evidence is scant, it would appear that Gerasa was formed into a fully Hellenistic city during the period of Seleucid domination (Kraeling 1938: 30-31). At Tell es-Sa'idiyeh, stratum 2 was dated to the 'Hellenistic' period, possibly the beginning of the second century BCE. The tell was largely abandoned, the only remains encountered being a presumed fortress (Pritchard 1985: 69-73). At Pella, there is a substantial enlargement of the city in the early second century that the excavators attribute directly to renewed Seleucid interest in the Transjordan (Smith 1987: 55).

Urban Forms

It is regrettable that after so many decades of archaeological research in Palestine, we still lack clear examples of a Seleucid urban form. The best known is that of Marissa, excavated in the first part of this century. The final phase of the site's occupation, and the phase from which the most complete city plan may be recovered, dates to the Seleucid period (Avi-Yonah 1977: 786).

The long-established custom of defining an urban form as 'Hellenistic' based on a Hippodamic grid pattern has been effectively refuted by Horowitz's study of the Seleucid city of Marissa (Horowitz 1980). The excavations at the seaport of Dor have also shown a grid pattern to have existed in the Persian period (Stern 1985). Where any semblance of a full city-plan has been revealed, the interior organization seems to be along a central street with blocks of shops and housing occupying the areas behind the street (Halpern-Silberstein 1989: 14). The main city gateway led into an open courtyard where presumably temporary stalls might be erected by vendors.

Administrative Structures

The only directly administrative structures recovered to date are a series of fortresses and urban fortifications (Halpern-Silberstein 1989: 3-13). These structures are almost identical to similar installations in the larger Hellenistic world, suggesting that the sciences of welfare and defense had achieved the same degree of sophistication throughout the region.

Burial Practices

Out of the diversity of tomb types in the Persian period, the early Hellenistic period shows a tendency toward the adoption of the *kokim* form of tombs as normative. The earliest and most elaborate examples come from Marisa where richly decorated *kokim* tombs of the Ptolemaic period have been excavated (Peters and Thiersch 1905; Halpern-Silberstein 1989: 18-20). By the Seleucid period it appears that family *kokim*, where the body was placed into a coffin and then deposited in one of the loculi of the tomb, was the dominant practice. Certainly by the time of the Hasmonean dynasty, there is little variation in funerary customs (Hachlili and Kille-brew 1983).

It should be noted how difficult it is to date these tombs in the absence of burial goods either through violation of the tomb or the preferences of funerary customs. An example of the problems this raises may be seen in Kuhnen's study of tombs from the Carmel region where many of the structures were identified by their excavators as 'Hellenistic-Roman' (Kuhnen 1987). Thus throughout the Ptolemaic to Seleucid periods, the use of *kokim* tombs was being adopted, and it is currently impossible to offer any further chronological refinement on this process. The earliest evidence for the Jewish use of ossuaries appears to be after the close of the Seleucid period, probably in the Hasmonean period (Figueras 1983: 1, 7-9).

Summary and Conclusions

The evidence from settlement patterns and what limited excavation has been conducted points to a Seleucid emphasis on urbanization. This process took two forms: the expansion of existing indigenous cities and the founding of urban colonies with non-indigenous populations. While there has been no systematic study of the placement of these new urban centers, it appears that they are frequently situated along major roadways and secondary trade routes (Arav 1989: 144-45).

Though not limited to the Seleucid phase of the Hellenistic period, the general diminishment of rural agricultural villages from the Persian period continued throughout the Hellenistic period. Given the number of new cities founded under Seleucid impetus, one might assume that the depopulation of small settlements was increased during this time. The unanswered question is what became of the former residents of these villages. Perhaps this is the origination of an urbanized underclass that provided day labor and occasionally an unsettled mob.

There is the additional possibility that it is in this urbanization process that we see the emergence of a new urban elite that had not been part of the Levantine world prior to this. This group, which many have identified as the carriers of a Hellenization impetus within the Jewish community, would represent a new and distinct social development.

The founding of new cities along overland trade routes would suggest that commerce played a more critical role for the Seleucid economy than it did under the Ptolemies. Several studies have noted the importance of tolls for revenue generation under the Seleucids, a practice attested to in Syria-Palestine (Taylor 1979).

All of this suggests that some group was the beneficiary of an increased pace of commerce. It was the allure of new wealth through trade that fueled the attraction of Greek ways. Consequently, creating a core of citizens committed to Hellenism was a Seleucid goal in most urban areas. For example, the Akra in Jerusalem was a demonstration of the allure of Hellenistic culture attracting to its precincts a well-off clientele (Dequeker 1985: 196-97).

Outside of these macrosocial observations, the level of research into the dynamics of the Seleucid period as revealed in the material culture is dreadfully lacking. The one thing that can be said, that the Seleucid period was marked by an intensive urbanizing process, was noted many generations previously when orators, reflecting on the greatness of Antiochus III remarked, 'there was no suitable place to receive a city that he left bare' (Libanius, *Orat.* 11.101). Clearly the way is left wide open for additional assessments of the archaeological remains of the period and their interpretation.

BEN SIRA AND THE SOCIOLOGY OF THE SECOND TEMPLE

Richard A. Horsley and Patrick Tiller

On Sociological Models

The most influential recent literature portrays Second Temple Judea as suddenly abuzz with commercial activity in the Hellenistic period. Hengel relies heavily on the Zeno correspondence which, he claims, gives the picture of a very active, almost hectic commercial life, originated by that host of Greek officials, agents and merchants who flooded the land in the truest sense of the word and 'penetrated into the last village of the country' (Hengel 1974: I, 43). He finds this picture confirmed by other evidence of key indicators of commercial activity: the monetarization of the economy, expanded foreign trade, and tirades against such commercial activity in traditional Jewish literature such as the book of Sirach. 'Finds of coins are a further indicator of the commercial boom in Palestine at this time... By and large, one might say that minted money was finally established in Palestine only through Ptolemy II, and largely superseded barter' (Hengel 1974: I, 43-44). Hengel finds 'the increase of foreign trade in the course of the third century BCE is attested by the many stamped—and partly datable —jars from Rhodes and other parts of the Aegean which are to be found throughout Palestine west of the Jordan' (1974: I, 44). He further claims that 'it may be assumed that in Palestine, as in Egypt, agricultural and commercial production was considerably increased, leading not only to a substantial increase in revenue from taxes but also to an increase in the population itself' (1974: I, 47). Finally, Hengel states, opposition to 'economic and cultural contacts with the non-Jewish environment is most clearly expressed by Ben Sira in his polemic against the hectic concern with earning money and against the...deceptive merchant' (52).

There are some serious problems with this picture in several interrelated respects, problems which are not peculiar to Hengel's unusually thorough scholarship, but pervade the present state of inquiry into Second Temple history generally. First, Hengel and others have not asked very precise questions in their evaluation and use of numismatic, archaeological and other evidence. In order to evaluate finds of coins, we would have to ask not only about the location of the sites at which they were found, but also about their use or function at those sites. The vast majority of coins cited as evidence for the monetarization of the economy in Palestine generally, including Judea, were found at Samaria, Shechem and Scythopolis, that is, outside of Judea, or at Beth Zur, which means they were probably left there by a military garrison. This is hardly evidence for the monetarization of the economy, let alone that it may have penetrated the villages! Moreover, if the economy was monetarized, why were both crown and sanctuary both collecting taxes in kind in those 'great vessels' marked with the pottery stamps *yhd* and *yrslm* studied by Lapp and cited by Hengel (Lapp 1963; Hengel 1974: I, 25)? If we look more closely at the sites where the wine jars from Rhodes were found, most of the evidence comes from cities on the coastal plain, such as Ptolemais, Strato's Tower, and Ashdod, while inland the sites are again the military fortress of Beth Zur and the Acra garrison in Jerusalem (see the literature cited in Hengel 1974: II, 35 n. 342). Again, there is no evidence to suggest that foreign trade had penetrated very far into Judean society. Hengel admits the lack of evidence for an increase in 'agricultural and commercial production', yet extrapolates from the production of balsam around the Dead Sea, an utterly unique case which says nothing about the rest of the agrarian economy. We might also doubt whether the occurrence of literary metaphors in Qoh. 2.6 and Sir. 24.30-31 are solid evidence that 'artificial irrigation was probably also introduced into Palestine at that [second century BCE] time' (Hengel 1974: I, 46). Finally, except for the sharp polemics against the trader and retailer in 26.29–27.3, the passages from Ben Sira that Hengel cites as proof texts for his claim about hostility to foreigners and the busy money-making they represent require considerable imagination to be read in this way (1974: I, 127-28; II, 40 n. 404, 96 n. 284).

Much of the difficulty stems from the absence of any clear sense of what the actual concrete political-economic structure of Judea or other districts of Palestine would have been like in the Second Temple period. In the absence of any critically developed model of this or any other ancient society, Tcherikover, Hengel and others continue to project back the kinds of social relations and structure they are familiar with, namely, that of modern Western capitalist society, with its 'middle class' as well as commercialized market economy. Much of the standard picture of the social and economic world in Hellenistic times generally, moreover, is based on the monumental work of Michael Rostovtzeff, who himself projected back into ancient times the evolving capitalism of his native Russia in the early twentieth century (Rostovtzeff 1941). It seems obvious that we should be evaluating the limited evidence available, whether coins, wine jars or sapiental sayings, with a much more precise and complex set of questions and concepts and some overall picture of how an ancient society was put together. The obvious move would appear to be to borrow a model of how a whole society works from sociology.

We find problems, however, in the ways some biblical scholars have used sociology and with the kind of sociology they have used. Some efforts appear to do little more than illustrate from biblical texts a sociological scheme or model developed on the basis of modern societies, and pay little attention to the original literary and/or historical social context of the textual attested 'data' (as for example in Theissen 1978 and some essays in Neyrey 1991). The sociological method most prominently adopted to date in biblical studies has been structural-functionalism, which dominated sociology generally in the United States in the mid-twentieth century. But that method tends to slight the importance of historical change and to obscure social conflict (see the criticism in Elliott 1986 and Horsley 1989 [esp. the introduction, Chapter 2 and Appendices]). The frequently borrowed ancient model constructed by Carney (1975) does not project modern patterns back into the ancient world, but it is based primarily on evidence from Rome, and may not be readily applicable to the ancient Near East, at least until well after strong Roman influence in the East.

Given both the confusing and distorting situation in the scholarly treatment of Second Temple times and the problems with borrowing sociological methods and models, we must perhaps ask some rather simple and fundamental questions and take virtually nothing for granted. It is difficult to know where to start once we recognize that even the generation of data depends on the questions we ask of our sources. It seems best to proceed dialectically back and forth between textual, archaeological and other evidence, on the one hand, and a critical appropriation of concepts and models of traditional agrarian societies developed on the basis of comparative historical sociological studies, on the other. Thus, at the risk of repetition in this essay, we will start with what we believe is the pertinent textual information from Ben Sira, then critically adapt a widely used model of agrarian societies, and finally venture a historical sociological analysis of the Judean temple-state and temple-community based on Ben Sira's 'wisdom' along with related texts. Not surprisingly, texts all tell us the most about the people who produced them, in this case the scribes and sages of Second Temple Judea. In an attempt to make the most of the evidence available about this crucial social stratum, which mediated structurally between the rulers and the peasantry, we will attend also to the Enoch literature apparently produced just prior to Ben Sira.

Finally, we are engaged in what is primarily a historical inquiry in which sociological models should be used to elucidate textual and historical particularity, and not to dissolve or obscure it. We are drawing primarily on evidence provided by Ben Sira and adding sociological inquiry to the usual philological, archaeological, literary and historical investigations in an attempt to further our understanding of the social conflicts and events of Second Temple Judea.

Indications of Social Structure and Roles in Ben Sira

Because we want to work from the textual and other evidence and not simply impose a sociological model that may not 'fit', we begin with a search for indicators of social positions, roles and structures in Ben Sira's 'wisdom'. We took this first step in our investigation, based on close reading and philological examinations of the Hebrew and Greek texts and on key secondary literature, before one of us had read for the first time and before the other had read again for the first time in 12 years the principal sociological model we will criticize and adapt below. We hope, therefore, that the results of our investigation in this first section have not been determined by the adapted model to be utilized below.

We believe that Burton Mack (1985) has made an important breakthrough both in understanding what Ben Sira was about and in approaching the fundamental social structure of Second Temple Judea. Looking for a larger frame of reference in which to read Ben Sira's 'Praise of the Fathers', Mack found help in the suggestion of structural linguistics that a text emerges from and is rooted in a larger cultural system of signs (symbol system). Like other humanities fields and social sciences, so also biblical studies can develop a discourse that treats religion and culture, literature and society, as complex interrelated systems of signs. 'Regarding them as "texts", the scholarly endeavor is to "read" them together, "translating" from system to system, and so come to understand their "meaning"' (Mack 1985: 5). Breaking with the standard individualistic reading (exegesis) focused closely on particular terms and verses, Mack dramatically broadens the focus to take in the broader patterns that structure Ben Sira's paean of patriarchal praise. This enables him to notice the general pattern of characterization of 'the pious men' in Sirach 44–50.

The great ancestors of Israel are praised not for their individual achievements but for the offices they held. It is the offices and not the individual persons which are glorious. Their virtue lies in their fulfillment of their office. Their rewards are simply the bestowal of office. In the overall pattern, there are five principal offices, besides the distinctive functions of Moses, those of 'father' (Noah, Abraham, Isaac, Jacob), 'priest' (Aaron, Phinehas, Simon), 'judge' (Joshua, Caleb), 'prophet' (Samuel, Nathan, Elijah, Elisha, Isaiah, Jeremiah, Ezekiel), and 'king' (David, Solomon, Hezekiah, Josiah).

The focus and emphasis, however, is clearly on the priesthood, indeed the high priesthood. Several factors make this clear. Far greater attention is lavished on Aaron than on any other historical figure including Moses and David. In fact, the role of Moses appears almost instrumental to the establishment of Aaron in the priesthood and the Aaronite priesthood takes over the only continuing function of Moses, teaching Israel the commandments (45.5, 17). The everlasting covenant (promise) of the priesthood is established for Aaron and his descendants and this is done structurally in connection with and as the sequel to the everlasting covenants (promises) made with the founding fathers, Noah, Abraham and Jacob. By comparison, the later established covenant of kings is not characterized as everlasting and is used as a mere analogy in the assertion that 'the heritage of Aaron is for his descendants' (cf. 42.25; 47.11). According to Ben Sira's characterization, even the kings appear instrumental to the temple cult. Besides their respective fame for warfare and wisdom, David and Solomon function principally to establish the cult in Jerusalem (47.8-10, 13). The epic poem as a whole clearly climaxes in the elaborate praise of Simon, who receives more attention even than Aaron. And it is clear from the characterization of Simon that the high priesthood had taken over the functions of kingship (fortifications and water supply, cf. 48.17 and 50.2-4), while remaining focused symbolically in the temple-cult.

The overall and particular pattern of characterization thus indicates that the high priesthood is the outgrowth and continuance of all the glorious offices and their incumbents. Not only is it firmly established by the eternal covenant with Aaron and his anointing by Moses, but also it is further grounded in all the glorious offices of Israel's heritage, starting with the eternal covenant/promise to the fathers. Characterization of individual office-holders, the principal themes and motifs, and the overall structure of the poem all come to a focus on the high priesthood exalted in the temple. But just as the pious men thus praised are not merely paradigms of individual salvation, so the poem as a whole is about far more than a cult or religion called 'Judaism'. Ben Sira's praise of the fathers is a grand poetic and ceremonial charter of the Judean temple-state that he served in early second century BCE Jerusalem.[1]

We think that, building on what Mack has discerned, it is possible to be more precise with regard to the relationship between systems of signs, in particular, between the system of signs displayed in Ben Sira's book and that of Second Temple Judea. Mack works on the assumption that the 'complete system' of the hymn to the fathers 'is the structure of the covenant community with its arrangements of institutions and offices organized around the temple cult and the role of the high priest' (Mack 1985: 57). But perhaps Mack's reading has not yet brought the social structure Ben Sira portrays sufficiently and precisely into focus. The 'complete system' of the hymn corresponds not to the wider 'arrangement of institutions and offices organized around the temple cult and the role of the high priest', but focuses more precisely on the office of the high priest itself. Moreover, the characterization of the office of high priest suggests that the 'arrangement of institutions and offices' organized around the temple and high priest was unusually simple and virtually monolithic or 'monarchic'. The office of (high) priesthood had subsumed the functions of the other offices, particularly the teaching function of Moses and the political-economic functions of king. As evidenced in the hymn of praise, there was no 'structural differentiation' of separable political, economic and religious institutions such as that found in modern Western societies. We know from outside Ben Sira's hymn, of course, that the high priesthood in Jerusalem was politically and economically subject to the Seleucid imperial regime, as it had been previously to the Ptolemies and the Persians. But in Ben Sira's view, Simon is the 'head of state' in a more awesome way than David and Solomon had been. On the basis of Ben Sira's characterization, one suspects that, insofar as there may have been other offices or institutions in Judean society, they were subordinated to or delegated as part of the functions ostensibly of the high priesthood. In order to obtain access to the system of signs that corresponds to the structure of the covenant community as a whole and the wider arrangement of institutions and offices organized around the temple and high priest, we must go to the

---

1. Thus, according to Mack (1985: 144-45, 154-55), Ben Sira's answer to the 'wisdom crisis' was to accept 'the dislocation of wisdom from the social fabric' that was accomplished by the 'personification of wisdom as a mythic figure' and then to relocate wisdom in the social order by identifying it with the temple-state in Jerusalem.

book of Ben Sira as a whole (and whatever other texts may provide access to that wider system of signs).

Ben Sira's 'Readers'

It must be noted at the outset that the meaning discerned in a particular sapiental saying or instruction depends heavily on our assumption or determination about who is being addressed. Because readings of Sirach proceed without a sense of the particular social structure it presupposed, interpreters have rather a vague sense of Ben Sira's audience: for example, usually 'the broad sections of the population, sometimes...the wealthy' (Tcherikover 1979: 149). Any attempt to discern more precisely who Ben Sira's addressees may have been will be dependent on our hypotheses about the basic social structure he presupposed. But some preliminary observations seem warranted by certain passages in the text. The reflection on the function of the sage in relation to those in other stations in the society indicates that the speaker's position is somewhere between, that is, above the plowmen and artisans on whose labor a city depends but below and in service to those who rule (38.24–39.11). Other passages indicate that the addressees, like the speaker, stand beneath and somewhat vulnerable to the wealthy and powerful (8.1-2) and are learning 'to stand in the presence of chiefs' (μεγιστᾶσιν, שׂרים) (8.8). Yet the addressees apparently may themselves function in positions of relative power, able to rescue the oppressed when they render judgments (4.9). Much of the book, moreover, focuses on the substance and transmission of wisdom itself. It thus seems likely that Ben Sira and his book addressed primarily other sages (students of wisdom) and the prospective occupants of important scribal or judicial positions in the society. The book contains enough cautionary and critical remarks about the wealthy and powerful to suggest that they or their children were not the audience.

Some of the exhortations as well as some of the 'wisdom' appears to have been addressed more generally to the society at large, including the insistence on payment of tithes and offerings to the priests. As suggested in 38.24–39.11, however, the vast majority of the people, engaged in agricultural labor or making things with their hands, would not have had the 'leisure' to learn wisdom. It therefore seems likely that these exhortations have been included because they form a part of the standard content of wisdom teaching and not because the general population was expected to read or even listen to the reading of this book.

References to Rulers and/or the Priestly Aristocracy

It is at least conceivable that 'the king' from which one should not seek 'a seat of honor' (καθέδραν δόξης, מושב כבוד) or before whom one should not display one's wisdom (7.4-5) is the (Seleucid or Ptolemaic) emperor. However, this could simply be an archaic, traditional term from the origins of wisdom teaching under the Solomonic monarchy for the immediate societal ruler. Other references to a king (10.3, 10; 38.2; 45.3; 50.2) are not entirely consistent. According to 38.2 the physician is paid by the king, probably referring to any local ruler with the means to support the services of a physician. However, 50.2 clearly refers to the royal temple (מלך היכל). It is to be doubted that Ben Sira's readers were in a position to petition the emperor for any position of honor.

Although it is clear from the long sections on Aaron and Simon in the Praise of the Fathers, chs. 44–50, that the high priesthood ruled Judea, Ben Sira does not elsewhere refer to the rulers as (high) priests (unless this is implied in the exhortation to 'honor the priest' with first fruits, etc.). He uses a variety of terms, some of which appear to be interchangeable, to refer to the rulers, often in ways that indicate the relationship in which scribes/sages stand to these their apparent superiors.

In 10.24 those of highest standing in the society are the chief (μεγιστάν, שׂר), the ruler (δυνάστης, מושל), and the judge (κριτής, שׁופט). Chief (שׂר) is used for chiefs and rulers, often of subordinate status. In the Greek text of Sirach, it is translated by μεγιστάν, δυνάστης and ἡγούμενος. It does not seem to refer to a specific class of rulers; Ben Sira is a bit ambivalent about the status of his hearers (and of himself) relative to the שׂרים. According to 7.14 and 32.9 (cf. 35.13), one (especially if young) should not speak too much in the presence of these chiefs. On the other hand, by training one can hope to be able to stand in their presence (8.8),[2] and Ben Sira advises the שׂרים to listen to his instruction (33[30].19[27]).

מושל ('ruler', qal participle of משל) is translated by ἡγούμενος, κριτής, δυνάστης and κύριος, and seems to refer simply to anyone who rules, whether politically or otherwise (for non-political examples see 15.10; 37.18; and 44.4cd). While Ben Sira exhorts his readers not to show favoritism to a ruler (4.27), he implies that they may aspire to positions of rulership (7.6, especially if they are strong enough to oppose crime), and he identifies the skilled sage as the ruler of his people (9.17). In 33(30).19(27)

---

2. According to the Greek text of this verse, by training one can learn to serve (λειτουργῆσαι) chiefs. According to Di Lella (Skehan and Di Lella 1987: 212), to stand in the presence of chiefs means to be servant or courtier.

Ben Sira also advises the מושל to listen to his instruction. In the same vein, according to 38.33, the scribe (unlike the artisan) is found among the rulers, where presumably he expounds law, justice and wisdom.[3] Thus Ben Sira's readers (if we can assume that they were aspiring young scribes) could be at least informally identified as rulers, and they could formally become rulers at some level.

The word שופט is consistently rendered in Greek as κριτής. According to 10.1-2 a 'judge' is responsible for the training of his people and has ministers (λειτουργοί, מליצים) who are subordinate to him. One of the duties of a 'judge' was to settle lawsuits (see 8.14), but as in the Hebrew Bible, 'judges' seem to have been responsible for administering justice in other ways as well, including promoting stability (10.1) and general administration (4.15).[4]

Perhaps even higher in political rank is the noble (δυνάστης, נדיב) who according to 7.6 is in a position to dominate a judge. In 13.9 it is the נדיב from whom one is to maintain a proper distance. In the Hebrew Bible נדיב is used in poetry often as a rather neutral term for one who rules or is of high social standing. More frequently it is used in the context of the contrast between commoner and noble. For example, 1 Sam. 2.8 speaks of God causing the poor to 'sit with princes'. Likewise Ben Sira seems to use the term to imply a contrast between the social status of the ruler and those under his authority (e.g. 11.1).

Other terms for rulers are the 'master of the city' (שלטון עיר, μεγιστάν, 4.7)[5] before whom one should bow one's head, the 'chief' (נשיא, ἡγούμενος, 41.17) before whom one should be ashamed of falsehood, the officer (מחוקק, γραμματεύς, 10.5) to whom God grants majesty, and the leader (ראש) of a city, whose inhabitants emulate him (10.2).

The ways in which Ben Sira uses the various terms for rulers indicates that they all refer to local rulers of the Jewish temple-state. Most of the terms are used in construct (or other indications of relationship) with words such as city (עיר, 4.7 [emended text]; 10.2), people (עם, 9.17; 10.1, 33[30].19[27]), and assembly (קהל, 33[30].19[27]). Assuming that Judea was a temple-state with the high priest as political ruler, then these chiefs,

---

3. Although this verse is not extant in Hebrew, the original must have read במושלים, which was misread by the Greek translator as במשלים (παραβολαῖς), as Patrick Skehan has shown (Skehan and Di Lella 1987: 448).

4. Note also that in 10.1 the wise judge is parallel to the understanding one who possesses authority (ממשלה, ἡγεμονία).

5. Reading עיר with Syr. for עוד of ms. A.

rulers, judges and nobles must have been members of the priestly aristocracy of Jerusalem. In both 33(30).19(27) and 39.4 (Greek only) μεγιστᾶνες
λαοῦ (שׂרי עם) is paralleled by οἱ ἡγούμενοι ἐκκλησίας (משׁלי קהל),
suggesting that the priestly aristocracy were the rulers. One then has the
sense that there is some overlap or relationship between the μεγιστᾶνες
and ἡγούμενοι among whom the scribes/sages serve in 39.4 and the
πλῆθος πρεσβυτέρων among whom the sages stand and speak in 6.34
and 7.14.[6] In 10.1-2 the κριτής (שׁופט) of a people or city is parallel to the
sagacious one who possesses authority (ממשׁלת, ἡγεμονία) and to 'he
who rules a city' (ראשׁ עיר, ἡγούμενον τῆς πόλεως) and in 10.3 מלך
(βασιλεύς) is parallel to שׂרים (δυναστῶν) Although the words are
clearly not technical terms for specific offices, this suggests that the judge
of a people was not much different from the ruler of a city and that the
princes of a city were not very different from the king, the local head of
state.

On the other hand, there are indications of differences in status among
the ruling class. The fact that one who held authority (ממשׁלת, ἡγεμονία)
as a מושׁל (κριτής) might be partial to a נדיב (δυνάστης) (7.4-6) implies
that the former would have been somewhat lower in rank than, or subordinate to, the latter, though even a מושׁל might expect a little favoritism from
Ben Sira's readers (4.27). That Ben Sira exhorts his hearers not to seek
authority or to become a ruler (7.4-6) suggests that not all members of the
high-priestly families held offices and implies that such high offices were
theoretically open to scribes and/or that Ben Sira's audience included
members of priestly aristocracy families. The advice not to go to law
against a 'judge' (κριτής, שׁופט, 8.14), however, suggests that ordinarily
Ben Sira's audience, presumably largely nascent sages and scribes, did not
rise to such positions. His audience of scribes in the making would
ordinarily be in the position of bowing their heads low to the שׁלטון
(μεγιστᾶνες) (4.7).

Finally, it may be significant that the *gerousia* (which is often thought to
have played an important role in the politics of this period) is never, or
almost never mentioned by Ben Sira.[7] Sirach 38.32 mentions the people's

6. The Hebrew text of 39.4 is not extant and that of 6.34 is probably corrupt. Sir.
7.14 is either corrupt in Hebrew or πρεσβυτέρων is a rough translation of שׂרים.

7. Cf. ἡ γερουσία καὶ οἱ ἱερεῖς καὶ οἱ γραμματεῖς τοῦ ἱεροῦ καὶ οἱ
ἱεροψάλται (Josephus, *Ant.* 12.142). Hengel mentions the possibility that the עדתשׂרים
(πλήθει πρεσβυτέρων) refers to the *gerousia* (Hengel 1974: II, 21). The similarity
between the terms, however, is close only in the Greek version of Sirach, and עדה
seems to refer only to informal groups of people.

council (βουλὴν λαοῦ, omitted by all witnesses except for S^c L and Syr) in parallelism with assembly (ἐκκλησία). This, however, probably does not refer to any legally constituted senate, which in any case would not be referred to as a people's council. Where the Hebrew text is extant, עדה (translated by λαός, συναγωγή or πλῆθος) seems never to refer to anything but a band or multitude of people.

קהל is consistently translated ἐκκλησία and, as the parallelism and context shows, usually means the assembled people. Thus there is no clear evidence of an officially constituted senatorial body in Jerusalem. These were undoubtedly various assemblies where one could speak (15.5) or refrain from speaking (7.14), where the blameless could receive praise (31[34].11; 44.15), and, and before which Simon officiated at the altar (50.13, 20), but these are not legal governing bodies.

The Wealthy

As already noted on the basis of 7.4-6, apparently not all members of the priestly aristocracy would have occupied particular offices. Yet supposedly all members of the hierocratic families would have received (and controlled) the tithes and offerings, thus having somewhat the same basis of wealth as the high-priestly office-holders. Although all would have shared in the proceeds from the tithes, Ben Sira's polemics against bribery (8.2; 20.29; 40.12-13) show that those who actually held a particular office could substantially augment their income.[8] The potentially suggestive two successive warnings against 'contending with the ruler' and 'quarreling with the rich' (8.1-2) come in a longer series and are probably not intended as synonymous parallelism.[9] Hence although it seems likely on the face of it that the wealthy are basically the same as rulers, the textual references do not supply unambiguous evidence.

Also unclear and requiring further analysis is the relation between the wealthy, whom one should be cautious dealing with, and the sharp criticism of wealth generally, particularly ill-gotten riches (see 5.1, 8; 11.10; 13.24-25; 14.3; 31.3-9; 40.13,18).

8.   One of the indications of inequality of wealth among the ruling classes is that some of Ben Sira's readers were expected to have only one slave, while most had several (33[30].31[39]).

9.   According to Di Lella, 'V 2ab is in synonymous parallelism with v 1; as is usually the case, the rich are also the great' (Skehan and Di Lella 1987: 211). Yet the passage implies at least a technical distinction between the great and the rich. The powerful are dangerous because they possess power; the rich are dangerous because they can use their wealth to influence those who have power.

Tithes and Offerings

That Sirach includes four pointed passages on tithes and offerings indicates how important such revenues were to the temple-state. In the most elaborate of these passages, 35.1-12, the exhortation is framed by references to offerings as part of 'keeping the law/commandments' and to giving 'to the Most High as he has given to you', in the traditional understanding of tithes and offerings as something one owed to God. Two other passages, however, are more direct with regard to the actual function of such dues. The first-fruits, guilt offerings, the choice shoulder cuts from animal sacrifices, and so on, were tax revenues to 'honor the priest' because, in the eternal cove-nant bestowed on Aaron, these had been allotted to Aaron and his descen-dants as their 'heritage' (7.29-31; 45.20-21).

Scribes, their Position and Function

The principal role or function of the scribes or sages was 'to serve the chiefs' (μεγιστᾶσιν, שׂרים) (8.8). Ben Sira provides a number of indica-tions of what particular functions the scribes served for their superiors in the ruling priestly aristocracy of Jerusalem. In the course of the prolonged reflection on the scribes' position and activities in 38.24–39.11 he mentions that scribes were sought as advisers, if not members, of the collective leadership of Jerusalem and that they attained eminence among the populace as a whole (38.32-33). They were members of courts that heard cases, for they understood the decisions of courts and could expound judgments (38.33). They devoted themselves to the study of the law and to the wisdom of the ancients precisely for their service among the rulers, presumably the priestly aristocracy (39.1-4). Apparently this service of the high-priestly government also involved travel in foreign lands, possibly as ambassadors. Many other passages in Sirach confirm one or another of these functions of the scribe, whether it be a prominent role in 'the com-pany of elders/chiefs' (6.34; 7.14), wise counsel in the 'assembly' (15.5; 21.17), or serving on courts and the rendering of verdicts of judgment (4.9; 11.7-9; 42.2). Ben Sira also mentions that the sage 'instructs his own people', although it is difficult to discern whether this means the people generally, the Jerusalemites generally, or his own circle of disciples. If the former, then this special teaching function would also be part of the sage's service of the ruling aristocracy by instructing the Jerusalemites and/or peasants in the ideological basis for the priestly oligarchy.

Although these functions are explicitly understood as service of the ruling aristocracy, Ben Sira's instruction (for other sages) displays both a clear sense of the sages' sense of superiority to the peasantry and urban artisans and a special concern for the sages' role in protecting the poor and exploited. It is clear from the unflattering comparisons of the plowman, smith and potter with the scribe's σχολή for learning wisdom that the sages understood themselves as politically more important as well as culturally superior to the 'working class' below them on the social scale. Yet Ben Sira sees the scribe as responsible for protecting those vulnerable to exploitation. One of the two references to 'giving a verdict' is precisely for the purpose of 'rescuing the oppressed from the oppressor' (4.9). It may not be by accident of editorial arrangement that immediately follow-ing his exhortations to 'honor the priest' with the lawful payment of tithes and offerings—which may well have been the basis of the scribes' own remuneration for their services by the priestly aristocracy—come corre-sponding admonitions concerning special attention to the poor and suffer-ing (see 7.29-31, 32-36; 35.1-15, 16-26; and cf. 34.21-27). Moreover, one should not show partiality to a ruler (מושל, δυνάστης, 4.27). Clearly Ben Sira's view of the sage's function in society included more than simply an obligation to his aristocratic employers. It also included a perceived obligation to God to act on his behalf to limit the abuses of the powerful against the poor.

Ben Sira displays a similar ambivalence toward, as well as social-politi-cal distance from, the ruling aristocracy that he and others served with their wisdom. The sage must defer and bow low to the ruler (4.7). Not surprisingly the sages would be invited to dine at the table by their superi-ors and patrons. At two points Ben Sira thus offers extensive instruction for the proper deferential behavior on such occasions (13.8-11; 31.12-24). Yet despite this emphasis on subservience and deference to their superiors and patrons, Ben Sira also cautions his disciples about the potential dangers involved in dealing with the powerful (13.9).

Artisan, Smith, Potter; Physicians; Merchants

As a foil or counterpoise to the importance of the sage, Ben Sira mentions the artisan who cuts seals or paints images, the smith working with iron, and the potter making numerous vessels on his wheel (38.27-30). By comparison, physicians seem to enjoy higher social rank, like the sages themselves working among and being honored by the great ones.

Ben Sira also mentions merchants and traders (and buying and selling). Besides the brief references at 37.11 and 42.5, there is the sharp criticism in 26.29–27.2. Such a negative attitude of traders and merchants was common in ancient literature and the societies they come from.

Agricultural Workers

In contrast to trade and merchants, farm work is honorable, 'created by the Most High' (7.15), and the plowman is described positively, even if of lower rank than the sage himself (38.24-25). Clearly, if the priesthood depends for its income on tithes and offerings, then there must be many more 'plowmen' than priests by a factor of at least the inverse of the proportion of the crops received from the plowmen.

Slaves and Hired Workers

Interestingly, Ben Sira refers far more frequently and extensively to slaves (עֶבֶד, οἰκέτης) than to plowmen/farm workers. In these passages it seems that he is addressing people who have one or more slaves (see 6.11; 30[33].33[25]-40[33]; 42.5), although he also gives advice to those who have only one slave (30[33].39[31]). It would appear that these were household slaves, and not large gangs of slaves used in farming or mining. What is unclear is whether the hired laborer (שׂוֹכֵר, μίσθιος), parallel to the slave in 7.20, is also a household worker (cf. 31[34].27).

The Poor

The poor, whom Ben Sira mentions at several points, and with whom the scribes clearly have contact in the courts, are clearly not the same as beggars, whom he mentions differently (40.28). The poor have their own roofs over their heads, have some agricultural base, have holdings that can be (wrongfully) appropriated, and make appeals to the courts regarding their oppression by oppressors (see 4.1-6, 7-10; 7.32; 13.17-24; 29.1-8, 22; 34.24-27; 35.16-26).

Sociology of Agrarian Societies: A Critical Adaptation

In recent years even biblical scholars have recognized that, consciously or not, when we (re)construct history we make use of particular models of social structure and social relations. It is not a question of whether we utilize a particular model of society, but rather of whether we do so with some critical awareness. In this study we are purposely looking for help from the comparative historical sociology of Gerhard Lenski. This is partly because his study of power and privilege (Lenski 1966) has already been utilized extensively in analyses of the ancient Israelite monarchy and more recently in analysis of late Second Temple Palestine (e.g. in Saldarini 1988). Thus Lenski's model has already been injected into sociological discourse among students/scholars of Hebrew Bible. But Lenski's comparative historical model has certain advantages over other sociological methods and models as well. By contrast with the structural-functionalism through which Theissen and others have read Synoptic Gospel materials, Lenski's approach is fully aware, indeed is structured in terms of, the historical development of societies across long periods of time through different stages or types of social structures. Thus there is far less blatant projection of modern assumptions, for example, about the divisibility of certain social functions, back into historical circumstances in which they do not apply. Moreover, although he still uses certain conceptual terms appropriate only to the emergence of capitalism in early modern Western Europe, he recognizes that agrarian societies of the past involved a pre-market economy (for a summary of Lenski's thesis, see Lenski 1966: chs. 8–9; Saldarini 1988: 21-25, 35-45).

We cannot simply apply Lenski's model of *agrarian societies* to Second Temple Judea, however, because it has certain problems or limitations as historical sociology. Lenski himself was aware of some of them. In his overall evolutionary scheme keyed on factors such as complexity and technological developments, he sets up a limited number of stages or types, with *agrarian* societies standing between *horticultural* and *industrial*. He then lumps together all societies which appear to stand somewhere in between horticultural and industrial. In a moment of self-criticism, refreshing among scholars, he mentions in a footnote that Robert Bellah, in response to his discussion of agrarian societies, had argued for division of agrarian societies into three sub-types: city-states, bureaucratic empires, and feudal regimes (see Lenski 1966: 191 n. 5a). It then becomes evident as one reads through Lenski's discussion that the differences in precisely those three different kinds of societies keep cropping up when Lenski discusses variations within his broad agrarian type. For example, in European feudalism (or in the Classical Greek and Roman city-states for that matter), the 'state' is strikingly diffuse when compared with the far more centralized 'state' of ancient Near Eastern, Indian, Aztec, Inca and African societies. Or, in feudal Europe a good deal of mercantile or artisan specialization developed independently of feudal lords, whereas trade and artisans do not appear to have been independent of the 'state' in the ancient Near East and other bureaucratic empires. Or again, in feudalism, higher lords granted 'fiefs' to lower lords which included both relatively independent political jurisdiction together with a hereditary claim to the produce of the peasantry and even to the land, whereas in the ancient Near East rulers granted their high officials incomes from large landed estates without hereditary rights and without independent political jurisdiction.[10]

These differences, however, constitute a decisive systemic variation in the fundamental political-economic relations between ruler, governing class and peasantry! And it makes a considerable difference in what catches our attention if we focus less on the different social strata or 'classes' than on the basic political-economic-religious relations between those social strata, for example, on the relations between (higher) ruler and subordinate governing class and the relations between the governing class and the peasant producers. In some of the societies among Lenski's comparative materials, the ruler is the sole as well as central political authority figure who then economically supports the governing class with goods appropriated by the state from the peasants. In others, members of the governing class enjoy a combination of political authority over the peasantry and hereditary rights to the land or the produce of the land. Most of Lenski's materials illustrate the former system. For study of Second Temple Judea and other ancient near Eastern societies and ancient empires, which have such decisive differences from both feudal Europe and the city-states of Greco-Roman antiquity, a far more precise comparative model of agrarian societies could be constructed by focusing on the majority of Lenski's materials. The excluded feudal European materials and city-states of Greco-Roman antiquity could then be used as illustrations of different systems for comparison and contrast. Some of the remaining problems with Lenski's model are rooted in the basic systemic difference just outlined.

In his delineation of the 'priestly class' as separate and different from 'the ruler', the 'governing class' and the 'retainer class', Lenski was apparently making the Western differentiation between church and state, spiritual power and temporal power, religious and political institutions and roles normative for his model. In much if not most of his materials, however, these dimensions of life have not been differentiated, or have been unevenly differentiated at different levels. The very use of terms such

---

10. To cite just one 'important variable' mentioned by Lenski himself, the governing class 'in most of early medieval Europe...was made up of a feudal nobility whose power and privilege rested on their membership in a hereditary legal class. In other societies, such as the Roman, Byzantine, Ottoman, and Chinese Empires...the governing class consisted...of bureaucratic officials whose power rested on their occupancy of offices which were not usually inheritable and who did not constitute a legally defined class' (1966: 229-30).

as 'king' and/or 'priest' or 'manager' may be a projection based on a different social system. Since the category of 'the priestly class' is not central or determinative in the majority of Lenski's materials, it should not be included in our model of agrarian societies. We will thus be better able to discern cases in which priests and non-priests both occupy certain social positions or carry out certain social functions.

If we were then to place Lenski's various classes not as a scheme of social stratification (the predilection of much American social sociology) but in a scheme of fundamental political-economic relations, following precisely the information provided by Lenski, it is clear that the funda-mental/basic or controlling relationship lies between the rulers and the agricultural producers, the peasantry who comprise the vast majority (90 per cent) of the people of such an agrarian society. By virtue of their power, military and other, the rulers are able to demand rent/tithes/tribute from the peasant producers whom they rule (but who are otherwise virtu-ally self-sufficient). Then, as Lenski himself explains variously, the rulers (official ruler and governing class) use part of what they appropriate from the peasantry; (1) to support a staff of military and legal-clerical 'retainers' through whom the society is governed, (2) to organize or support traders who obtain the luxury and other goods the rulers desire, (3) to pay or sup-port artisans who make the various products needed by the rulers and their retainers and supporters in the cities. That is, the retainers, merchants, and even the artisans are dependent upon, as well as subordinate to, the ruling class.

Lenski is sensitive to the fact that modern Western assumptions about private property tend to obscure our understanding of political-economic-religious relations in traditional agrarian societies. This is of greatest importance in understanding how the ruler or state can lay claim to such a huge share of a society's productivity. 'At the head of nearly every advanced agrarian state was a single individual, the king or emperor. Monarchy was the rule…' If we approach such societies with the societies with the modern capitalist concept of private property in mind, it must appear that the monarch is the 'owner' of the land. But then how do we explain that the peasants in such societies are by and large not slaves but free (to a degree) and that they also have certain claim to the land and its produce? The concept of private property or ownership may simply be inapplicable. More appropriate to traditional agrarian societies would be to reconceptualize property *in terms of rights not things*, with the possibility of overlapping rights to the land, or, perhaps, to the produce of the land and the labor of the peasants. Accordingly Lenski suggests 'a proprietary theory of the state', as a way of understanding what 'property' or 'owner-ship' might mean in the concrete relational terms in which such societies apparently operated. How can royal ownership be consistent with local possession or ownership? The common or corporate 'ownership' can be understood as vested in the head of state. '*All agrarian rulers enjoyed significant proprietary rights in virtually all of the land in their domains*' (Lenski 1966: 215-16; emphasis original). It may thus be possible to understand how agrarian rulers appear to be 'owners' or rather 'part-owners', not only of their own 'royal estates', but of all other lands which they grant as prebends and/or from which they extract taxes or tribute.

It is curious that in this connection Lenski does not even raise, let alone address, the mechanism by which such 'proprietary rights in virtually all of the land in their domains' is legitimated for the monarchs of traditional agrarian societies. Ironically, Lenski focuses almost exclusively on the material level, while Karl Marx provides a far less reductionist approach, one that takes the religious dimension more fully into account. Lenski does mention in passing, with regard to the advanced horticultural system of Dahomey, that the rulers 'were regarded as divine or semi-divine and thus the owner of all property in the land' (Lenski 1966: 154-55), as well as the ancient Mesopotamian conception of the land as the estate of the society's god(s), the temple(s) as the house of the god(s) and the king or high priest as the chief servant of the god(s). But it is Marx who reflects more generally that in such societies it is by virtue of being the symbol of the society as a whole, the head of the whole body, that the god or the god's regent is the controller (and beneficiary) of the tribute taken from the members of the social body. We theologians and students of religion jealous for the importance of our subject matter can legitimately point out (over against the apparent reductionism of Lenski's comparative sociol-ogy) that the working of such a system is dependent on just such an ideology or mythology of god(s) and king and/or high priest as the representative/symbol of the whole.

Lenski's model of agrarian society, perhaps because of its part in his overall evolutionary scheme, does not take into account the fact that most concrete examples of agrarian societies are parts of larger agrarian empires. As John Kautsky explains in his *The Politics of Aristocratic Empires* (1982), the aristocratic rulers of a large agrarian empire usually comprise a different society from the peoples they rule, and the subordi-nate peoples often include different societies. Since many large aristo-cratic empires ruled their subject peoples indirectly through the native aristocracies or monarchies, the overall political-economic-religious system was usually more complex than Lenski's model allows. If we consider this point together with the previous point about how the social system was held together by an ideology of a god and the king/high priest at its center as a symbol of the whole, we can immediately see the interrelated issues of (1) the 'legitimacy' of the ruler(s), local and/or imperial, and (2) the potential conflict between the levels of rulers with different legitimating ideologies.

As illustrated by that last issue, Lenski's model does not deal with social conflict, whether 'manifest' or 'latent'. His model sets up the potential for structural conflict, by highlighting how the wealth and 'privilege' of the rulers and governing class are based on their political 'power' (although, as noted he fails to focus on the religious limitation of their power and privilege). But the potential lines of conflict go unexamined.

With these major adaptations or revisions of Lenski's model of a traditional agrarian society, that is, dominated by centralized rule, as distinguished primarily from the more diffuse medieval European feudal system but also from classical Greek and Roman city states, we can bring comparative historical sociology to bear on evidence of social structure and social relations from the wisdom of Jesus Ben Sira.

Finally, we should reaffirm that historical sociology should be historical, attentive to developments, conflicts, shifts, and so on, from time to time insofar as they may appear through the few windows provided by our limited literary and other sources.

Social Structure and Social Relations in Ben Sira

In the perspective provided by comparative sociological studies of traditional agrarian societies, the evidence Ben Sira provides of the relatively simple and compact Judean temple-state and supporting community has great credibility. The picture Ben Sira sketches in the paean of praise to the High Priest Simon reflects the basic social structure. State and society are headed by the high priest, who is surrounded and assisted in ruling by the inner concentric circle of 'his brothers', the aristocracy among 'the sons of Aaron', who are in turn surrounded and supported by the outer concentric circle of the people, 'the whole congregation of Israel' (esp. 50.1, 12). Not included in the hymnic version, of course, is the wider political-economic-cultural context in which the Judean temple-state and community fits as one tiny subordinate unit in the wider Seleucid empire. From that wide perspective the high priesthood was subordinate to, and the representative of, Seleucid imperial authority, responsible for maintaining imperial order and collecting imperial taxes.

What appears to the modern reader (accustomed to 'structural differentiation' between religion and politics and economics) in Ben Sira's hymn of praise as a distinctively religious ceremony therefore includes and presupposes (or is inseparable from) the political and economic dimensions as well. From the section of the hymn in praise of Aaron, and Ben Sira's exhortations to dutifully bring such produce to the priests, it is clear that the priestly aristocracy is economically supported by the tithes and offerings of 'the whole congregation of Israel', that is, largely the Judean peasant agricultural producers (45.20-21; 7.29-31). The high priest was the political-religious 'head of state' ruling Judea, while also serving as the chief political-economic Seleucid imperial officer over Judea.

From the rest of Ben Sira's book, checked at points against related textual or other evidence, we can then obtain information that further articulates the fundamental structure of priestly rulers and their peasant producers-supporters. The ruling high priest and priestly aristocracy are assisted in governing the people by the ordinary priests and, in Ben Sira, particularly by the scribes/sages. Supporting services for the priestly rulers and their functions are provided by the artisans, smiths, potters, and so on, who comprise the other residents of the capital city built around the temple. Since there would have been little or no trade in a traditional agrarian society for anyone except the ruling elite, the merchants Ben Sira castigates (26.29–27.2) must also basically have serviced the lifestyle of the priestly aristocracy in Jerusalem.

The High Priesthood and Ruling Aristocracy

Just as the high priest at the altar in all his cosmic glory had 'a garland of brothers around him...the sons of Aaron in their splendor holding out the Lord's offerings' (50.5-13), so the high priest as head of state stood in the midst of a priestly aristocracy both in governing the people and in receiving their economic support. As noted above, Ben Sira refers to rulers in his society in what appear to be two different sets of terms. On the one hand, he has the Aaronid priesthood established with 'authority over' and 'inheritance in' the people. On the other hand, he speaks of 'judges', 'chiefs', 'rulers' and 'nobles' as dominant in the society and as those among whom the scribes served and (apparently) as forming various courts, assemblies or gatherings for whose deliberations the scribes might be important (39.4; 38.33). What is the relationship between these two? The 'chiefs' and 'rulers' would appear to be (basically) the ruling aristocracy among 'the sons of Aaron'. Not all priests, perhaps not even all of the Zadokites, would have been among the ruling aristocracy. Some of the aristocracy may have held a particular office (שׁוֹפֵט/κριτής may refer to such an office), but we should not imagine that all members of a dominant aristocracy held a particular 'minister's portfolio' as in the cabinets of modern governments.

The proclamation of Antiochus III about the restoration of temple and temple-government in Jerusalem, nearly contemporary with Ben Sira, has ἡ γερουσία καὶ οἱ ἱερεῖς καὶ οἱ γραμματεῖς τοῦ ἱεροῦ καὶ οἱ ἱεροψάλται (Josephus, *Ant.* 12.142) listed as the favored ones relieved of tax burdens. The letter of the Hasmonean high priest Jonathan to Sparta a half-century later lists at the head of the people 'the high priest, the γερουσία of the people, and the priests' (1 Macc. 12.6). Ben Sira's references to the people governing the society fits these lists if his 'chiefs', 'rulers' and 'judges' are understood as the same as ἡ γερουσία in the Antiochene decree and Hasmonean letter.[11] That is, a much larger number of priests served in various capacities in the temple and other offices, but a few distinguished and well-born priestly families (designated as the *gerousia*) wielded political-economic control. Not only is it unlikely that the *gerousia* was a purely lay body (Hengel 1974: I, 26), but it may well have been a purely high-priestly 'council'. Ben Sira's references to the role of sages and their relations with 'chiefs' and 'rulers' suggest that the sages were not 'members' of the 'council' (or ruling class), but merely advisers (i.e. not councilors but counselors).

The central figure in the aristocracy, as well as head of the society as a whole, was the high priest. In order to understand how the whole political-economic-religious system of Second Temple Judea worked, we must devote far more attention to the religious dimension focused on the high priesthood, a dimension simply neglected in Lenski's model, as we noted above. The people are to be focused on, to fear and to serve 'the Most High', who is explicitly understood as 'the king of all'. Correspondingly, the whole temple-state apparatus is structured ostensibly to the service of God. Within that conceptualization, then, the high priest stands as the head

11. The difference is that from the perspective of Antiochus III, the Greek king of a Greek empire, or from the later point of view of a head of state communicating with a Greek city-state, the chief officials in the high priest's administration would constitute a senate (γερουσία). From Ben Sira's perspective as an insider, however, there were individuals who held certain high offices and collectively formed the leadership of Jerusalem.

of the whole (the whole people and the whole temple-state apparatus). The high priest(hood) is the people's representative to God, therefore they bring their offerings to the priesthood. The high priest(hood) is God's representative to the people, established by everlasting covenant, and given 'authority and statutes and judgments' over the people, therefore the people (are to) 'honor the priest' with their tithes and offerings as the way of 'fearing the Lord' (see esp. ch. 50 and 7.29-31). Ben Sira presents what Lenski appropriately calls a 'proprietary theory of the state', in a combination of theocratic and hierocratic terms. God is the ostensible 'head of state' and, apparently 'proprietor' of the land. But the Aaronid priesthood is God's regent and actual head of (temple) state-and-economy. In that position Aaron was granted a 'heritage' but no 'inheritance' (45.20-22).

The modern Western concept of private property gets in the way at this point. Ben Sira has a proprietary concept of state-land-people in hierocratic form. That is, the Aaronid priesthood (ideologically) has no land of its own because as the head of the whole it receives a (special) heritage of 'first fruits and sacrifices'. Ideologically, the high priest(hood) has no individual or personal wealth and power separate from his wealth and power as a public figure representative of the whole. The high priest and other members of the priestly aristocracy may well have used their public wealth and power as a means of generating what would appear as private wealth or property, for example, by charging interest on loans made from the stores/wealth they controlled (as representatives of the whole), but they were wealthy and powerful because they stood at the representative head of the whole.

This particular hierocratic understanding of the Judean state and its religious political-economy is the key to understanding both the internal relations of the temple-community and the conflicts that arose (might arise) between local and imperial rulers or between the subjects of the temple-state and the rulers, both local Judean and imperial. Insofar as the (high) priesthood is the representative of and has authority over the whole, then it would both claim support from the agricultural producers and command whatever governing apparatus was developed in addition to the priesthood itself. Both the ruler-ruled relationship and the ruler-retainer relationship will be pursued in the sections below. The potential for conflict in the local system and in the overall imperial system is also evident once we consider how essential the hierocratic ideology articulated by Ben Sira was to the working of the Judean temple-state, both in itself and as a component political-economic unit of the overall Seleucid empire. So long as the traditional Judean hierocratic ideology and institutional forms were left intact, the Judean temple state could operate in a semi-autonomous way, with the high priesthood serving its traditional function representative of the Judean people in their particular focus on God, temple and high priesthood, while simultaneously serving as representatives of the imperial regime and thus maintaining the imperial as well as domestic order. But to the extent that the ruling aristocracy in Judea appeared to compromise with or sell out to the ideological or institutional forms of the imperial regime, it lost 'legitimacy' among the Judeans. And such a compromise of Judean traditions and compromise with an alien culture affected Judeans according to their position and role in the social structure of the temple-state or temple-community. At such times rival parties could gain considerable support and influence as the bearers of tradition and representatives of God.

The Judean Peasantry

There would have been no glory for the high priest and no high priest at all without the peasant producers who supported the whole temple-state apparatus with their tithes and offerings. But peasants, like women, have generally been 'hidden from history'. While Ben Sira repeats the same information in saying after saying about sages such as himself and lauds the glory of the Aaronid high priesthood in paeans of praise, he barely mentions the ordinary people who made it all possible. Yet he does provide a few glimpses of the peasants' situation which make it possible to compare with other traditional agrarian societies. Insofar as the taxation to support the temple-state apparatus took the form of tithes and offerings from agricultural products, it was only the plowman, but not the artisan, the smith and the potter, and the scribe mentioned in 38.24-34 on whose agricultural labor the whole system rested. Comparative studies suggest that since the level of agricultural production is traditionally low, the peasants who support the rest of the society as well as themselves with food usually must comprise about 90 per cent of the population. They generally live at the subsistence level, constantly threatened with poverty and hunger since their 'surplus' produce has been expropriated by their rulers. To cite Lenski's summary, 'In short, the great majority of the political elite sought to use the energies of the peasantry to the full, while depriving them of all but the basic necessities of life' (1966: 270).

This is precisely the picture Ben Sira offers in the few references he makes to the peasant's situation. In striking contrast to the castigation of merchants, Ben Sira expresses admiration for agricultural labor, 'which was created by the Most High' (7.15). He leaves us with no illusions about the peasants' standard of living. 'Better is the life of the poor under their own crude roof than the sumptuous food in the house of others' (29.22). A survey of Ben Sira's use of the term 'poor' (עני, דל, אביון) suggests that more often than not it refers not to an exceptional case but to a wide range of people. 'Poor', 'hungry', 'needy', 'desperate' and other synonymous terms refer apparently to a large proportion of the people (4.1-9). Like peasants in most societies, the Judean producers were economically marginal, therefore chronically in need of loans if not alms, in response to which Ben Sira exhorts his listeners, who are better off, to respond mercifully (29.1-20, esp. 29.1-2, 8-12, 14-15). Because they are marginal, however, they are all the more susceptible to the predatory practices of the wealthy and powerful. 'Wild asses in the wilderness are the prey of lions; likewise the poor are the feeding grounds of the rich' (13.19). The imagery used at one point, reminiscent of the prophetic indictment in Amos 2.6-8, suggests that powerful creditors were taking advantage of the peasants who had fallen heavily into debt.

> Like one who kills a son before his father's eyes is the person who offers a sacrifice from the property of the poor. The bread of the needy is the life of the poor; whoever deprives them of it is a murderer. To take away a neighbor's living is to commit murder; to deprive an employee of wages is to shed blood (34.24-27).

The dynamics of social relations, given the basic political-economic-religious structure, led Ben Sira to exhort his hearers to 'rescue the oppressed from the oppressor' (4.9).

Some of the sayings parallel to 'the poor are feeding grounds of the rich', such as 'What peace is there between a hyena and a dog? And what peace between the rich and the poor' (13.18-23), suggest that this fundamental, structural opposition in the society had potential for more overt class conflict. From much of the Hebrew Bible we are aware of the fact that many components of the Israelite (and Judean) cultural heritage would have provided an ideological basis for popular resistance. In Ben Sira's book, however, typical for the wisdom tradition, historical memories (including those of the people's deliverance from Egypt or the Philistines, for example) are virtually excluded. Where historical reminiscences are present, as in the hymn of praise to the great office-holders, the judges and prophets are domesticated into the grand scheme of legitimation precisely for the high priesthood at the head of the society.

Artisans and Traders

As Ben Sira states, the artisan, smith and potter were essential to the operations of the capital city (38.27-32). Lenski says that the artisan class may well have been 'originally recruited from the ranks of the dispossessed peasantry' (1966: 278). In the case of a temple-community, one wonders the extent to which the ordinary priests and/or Levites may have performed some of these supportive services. Some of Lenski's principal points about the artisan class, however, appear to be based on evidence from medieval European towns, and may not apply to most traditional agrarian societies. There is certainly little evidence from the ancient Near East generally that would indicate that 'the majority of artisans were probably employees of the merchant class' (Lenski 1966: 279). Nor is there evidence of artisans rebelling against those in authority over them. In the case of a temple-city such as Jerusalem (or for that matter in any capital or royal city), the artisans would have been economically dependent on the (priestly) rulers in command of the temple, city and society.

Artisans would not have been employees of the merchants because any native merchants would themselves have been fellow 'employees' of the rulers and governing families. Other merchants were perhaps foreigners serving the needs of the ruling families in a somewhat more independent manner. Lenski's discussion of the merchant class is flawed insofar as he is drawing heavily on medieval European, even nascent capitalist evidence, and on agrarian societies which had come into contact with and been affected by mercantile or capitalist systems. Given the variety of societies he is considering, it is facile to generalize that 'from a very early date merchants managed to free themselves from the direct and immediate authority of the ruler and governing class' (Lenski 1966: 250). As has been repeatedly observed, certainly in the Ptolemaic empire which dominated Palestine just before the time of Ben Sira, trade was a virtual monopoly of the (imperial) state. It is highly unlikely that things were any different in a far smaller entity such as the Judean temple-state, but with a significant exception. The Ptolemaic regime would have been powerful enough to keep out the Greek or Phoenician traders (except for when the state did business with them!). But from Persian times on, alien traders, Phoenicians or Greeks, may well have been operating in Jerusalem, although their trade would still have been primarily in luxury goods and items desired by and paid for by the ruling elite.

Tcherikover, followed by Hengel, as noted above, fostered a picture of Jerusalem under Hellenistic rule as suddenly a-bustle with mercantile capitalism.

> Ben Sira frequently mentions merchants and their pursuit of profits, and
> these passages again reflect the new period which began in Judea under
> Greek rule, when the money economy, the opportunity to invest one's
> means in profitable enterprises, and lively and absorbing commercial traffic
> had begun to develop (Tcherikover 1979: 149).

This is an anachronism, quite unwarranted by the text of Sirach. Ben Sira
mentions merchants and traders (and buying and selling) explicitly at
only three points: the sharp criticism in 26.29–27.2, and the brief references to merchants and bartering/buying-selling in 37.11 and 42.5. As in
most ancient literature and the societies they come from, he has a negative view of trading and traders, in this case 'moralized' in terms of 'sin'.
Otherwise, Tcherikover, Hengel *et al.* appear to be projecting nascent
capitalist mercantile relations onto Ben Sira's references to 'goods'
(χρῆματα) and wealth and 'gold' and the use of other people's goods
(Hengel focuses on 11.10-19; 13.24-25; 21.8; and 31.3-9). In most
political-economic systems prior to the early modern Europe, however,
wealth and exploitation of others' goods did not involve trading, invest-
ment, or mercantile activity.

Besides the artisans of various sorts who served the needs of the priestly
governing class in Jerusalem, Ben Sira mentions '(household) servants/
slaves' (οἰκέται, עבדים, 6.11; 7.20-21; 42.5; 30[33].33[25]-40[33]).
Given the infrequency of references to wages, these seem to be household
slaves; certainly the Greek translator thought so. There is no clear indication in the text of Sirach whether they are primarily in the households of
the governing families, or also in those of the sages themselves.

Scribes and Other Retainers
The scribes, Ben Sira himself and the typical scribe-sage he writes about,
clearly belonged to what Lenski called the retainer class.[12] It is worth
noting that Antiochus III's decree exempting the principals of the temple-
state in Jerusalem from taxation closely associates 'the scribes' with the
gerousia and the priests.[13]

There must have been other types of retainers. Presumably there was

---

12. It is interesting that Smith (1978: 70) has made similar observations concerning
the Babylonian scribes, whom he characterizes as 'an elite group of learned, literate
men, an intellectual aristocracy which played an invaluable role in the administration
of their people in both religious and political affairs'.

13. There may have been two classes of 'scribes', one including only those who
performed the relatively menial tasks of recording deeds, tax receipts and other

little need for military retainers insofar as the Seleucid regime would have retained a monopoly on military force, although there were temple guards and doorkeepers in the temple compound. Ben Sira mentions 'physicians' who are 'rewarded by the king' and are admired by 'the great ones' for their skills with healing and medicines (38.1-8). The priests and Levites would have functioned somewhat as did the 'retainers' Lenski describes in other agrarian societies, that is, mediating between the governing class and the common people, including 'effecting the transfer of the economic surplus from the producers to the political (and religious) elite' (Lenski 1966: 246).

From Ben Sira's extensive reflection on the activities of his own 'profession' it is clear that the sages were retainers with scribal-legal-cultural-religious functions, some of which may have overlapped with those of the priests. According to Ben Sira's ideology of the priesthood, the function of teaching the law, originated with Moses (45.5), belonged to the Aaronid priesthood (45.17). In Second Temple Judea the (high) priesthood must have, in effect, over a period of generations, delegated that authority and function to the sages, both with regard to the people generally (37.23), and with regard to the exercise of their own governmental authority (8.8; 9.17–10.5; 38.32-33; 38.34–39.4). In 9.17–10.5 it seems particularly clear that it is the scribe who stands behind 'the wise judge' and 'the government of the intelligent one'. As noted above, it is necessary to collapse Lenski's 'priestly class' into the rulers, in the case of the high-priestly families, and into the retainers, in the case of ordinary priests and scribes/sages. In Ben Sira's Judea, the sages performed the functions that Lenski ascribes to 'the clergy' in societies of limited literacy, officials and diplomats as well as educators.

In many traditional agrarian societies 'the boundary between the retainer class and the governing class' was 'often fuzzy' according to Lenski (1966: 244). This statement should be reformulated somewhat for the temple-state in ancient Judea. Josephus claims that a century after Ben Sira, after being out of favor under John Hyrcanus and virtually at war with Alexander Jannai, the Pharisees became, in effect, the real rulers under Alexandra Salome. That would appear to illustrate Lenski's point that at times the retainers could move into the governing class. With service in the highest temple-state offices depending on belonging to the proper high-priestly lineages, however, scribes from non-priestly or ordinary priestly families

records, and the other being limited to the sages whose business was involved in the practice and dispensing of wisdom.

could not have moved into the sacerdotal governing class even if they held considerable *de facto* power. Furthermore, Ben Sira gives no indication that scribes wielded much power in his own day.

Lenski stresses the dependence of retainers on the rulers or governing class. The sages do indeed appear to be dependent economically on the priestly aristocracy in Ben Sira. Lest anyone would project back the old notion that their successors, the Pharisees and rabbis, were artisans, the sage Ben Sira clearly looks down on artisans, potters, smiths, and so on. And, like those workers with their hands, peasant plowmen would also lack the leisure for acquiring wisdom (38.24). It seems clear that when Ben Sira says, several times, that the scribes 'serve the rulers' this implies that such service is the source of their livelihood. Being economically dependent on the high-priestly regime, they are thus also 'politically' vulnerable. Ben Sira's exhortations to other sages to be cautious in their dealings with rulers and wealthy-powerful figures can be read as testimony to just such a dependency.

The sages, however, also have a certain authority of their own independent of their 'employment' by the high-priestly regime. At least in their own mind, their own authority stems from their knowledge of wisdom and their faithful teaching of and adherence to the law of the Most High (which are evidently the same thing in Ben Sira). Just as the high priesthood has its power, privilege and authority from God through an eternal covenant, so also the sages have their authority as the custodians of divine revelation. Besides being the heirs of earlier generations of sages, they are the successors of the prophets as well, speaking by divine inspiration. Nor would this have been simply a matter of their own self-image unmatched in the concrete power relations of early second-century Jerusalem. Lenski claims that such retainers can gain in power relative to their superiors when the governing class is dominated by a hedonistic ethic. Evidence external to Ben Sira indicates that some and perhaps many in the high-priestly circles were seriously distracted by the 'opportunities' of Hellenistic culture and politics. Apparently these distracted aristocrats must have given lip-service to the traditional Judean ways which were ostensibly still in force until the dramatic Hellenizing reform of 175 BCE. In just such circumstances a scribal class with rigorous loyalty to the tradition of which they were the custodians could have enjoyed greater actual power in the administration of affairs.

Ben Sira repeatedly mentions the scribes' dedication to the revered covenantal laws and divinely bestowed wisdom, from which they claim their own authority independent of the high priesthood. Viewed in the broader political-cultural context of the Hellenistic imperial situation in which they were operating, this dedication and sense of independent higher authority should alert us to the potential for eventual overt as well as latent social conflict. Insofar as the sages' professional role or function was the cultivation and administration of the traditional Judean covenantal laws as the official state law, their dedication to those laws would have been far more than a matter of individual morality. The sages had a clear sense of their own, independent of their employers, of how the temple-state should operate, in accordance with (their interpretation of) the covenantal laws. Their high-priestly superiors, however, had regular dealings with the Hellenistic imperial officials and were susceptible to influence from the wider Hellenistic culture. Recognition of this potential structural conflict may help us understand the open social conflicts which erupted when ruling class elements instituted their 'reform' in 175 BCE.

The strong personal (and 'professional') dedication to the Mosaic covenantal laws and independent authority claimed on that basis among the sages also contributed to their concern for the poor, judging from Ben Sira's 'wisdom'. His exhortations include not only admonitions of personal ethics to 'stretch out your hand to the poor' (7.32), but also what look like instructions to other sages not to 'cheat the poor' or to 'reject the suppliant' and even, more positively, to 'rescue the oppressed from the oppressor' presumably in their official or professional capacities (4.1-10). Sharply criticized are those who take advantage of the desperate situation of the poor to enhance their own wealth ('offering sacrifice from the property of the poor' and 'taking away a neighbor's living' in 34.24-27, reminiscent of Amos 2.6-8, may refer to creditors' 'foreclosing' on debts).[14]

In both their potential opposition to certain actions or policies of the high-priestly rulers (on whom they were economically dependent) and their concern for the poor, the sages display similarities to the medieval clergy described by Lenski. But their social structural position was quite different. The medieval Christian clergy was 'a specially protected class', economically and politically separate and independent, whereas the Second Temple sages were economically dependent and politically-religiously subordinate. Yet the claim to direct divine authority independent of the rulers was clearly asserted by the scribal class as evidenced in Ben Sira

14. The discussion of loans and alms in Sir. 29.1-13 may imply that one should give to the poor and not loan. It seems likely that Ben Sira did not approve of foreclosing on loans to the poor.

and other (Enoch) literature, and helped set a precedent for what the Christian church eventually institutionalized more securely.

Presumably the rulers accepted this semi-independent role of the sages because it was part of the foundation of their claim to divine authority and this made the sages able to provide the ideological basis for the priests' rule. Indirectly it served the interests of the wealthy in that the existence of a powerful class that defended the interests of the poor provided a legitimate (but non-threatening) outlet for the anger and frustration of the poor and oppressed.

Evaluation and Implication of Ben Sira's Picture of Judea

If we now place Ben Sira's picture of Judean society into comparison with the pictures of intense social conflict represented in near contemporary literature, such as certain sections of *1 Enoch* or Daniel, we must evaluate the serious differences and seeming discrepancies. Is Ben Sira's picture of a social structure that is stable and quiet despite its deep divisions a reliable picture of Judea, and its differences with other sources to be explained as representing the calm of the early second century just before the storm unleashed by the Hellenizing reform of 175? Or should Ben Sira be seen as an accurate observer of the basic social structure but himself a conservative supporter of the high priesthood (and one perhaps simply oblivious to the roots of the impending social conflicts)? Or should Ben Sira's picture of a relatively simple basic social structure in Judea be dismissed as inaccurate insofar as it must miss a more complex structure and division in the society?

The last option is the most unlikely and least compelling because it would assume or project from other literature a complex social structure unique among traditional agrarian societies of the ancient Near East. The first option made sense so long as we were assuming that the social structure of Second Temple Judea had been stably in place since early Persian times and it was only the sudden impact of Hellenistic influence and the especially dramatic reform of 175 BCE that caused deep social conflicts to emerge. But, as we are finally recognizing, intense conflicts attended the various attempts to stabilize a regime in Jerusalem at least through the reform missions of Nehemiah and Ezra in the mid-fifth century. Thus we would have to project a period of quiet stability during the fourth and third centuries despite the military campaigns and changes in imperial rule whirling around Jerusalem on all sides. The option that takes into account Ben Sira's own point of view as a conservative supporter of the high priesthood thus appears the more likely option. We believe that Ben Sira can be read as a relatively reliable witness to the basic social structure of Second Temple Judea. Despite its relative simplicity, however, that basic social structure could produce and accommodate certain conflicts, conflicts which would likely have been exacerbated by the cultural differences between the Judean traditions and the empire at large.

Just as there had been different parties or factions among the ruling class struggling for control of the Davidic monarchy earlier in the kingdom of Judah, so there were priestly and other factions competing for power for well over a century in early Second Temple times, as evident from the books of Ezra and Nehemiah. Insofar as scribes and sages had no independent economic base, they would have been associated with one or another of those (priestly) factions, and insofar as sages claimed independent, divinely given authority as the guardians of the revered traditions, they likely had their own ideas about policy and practice in the temple-state. Further, insofar as different scribes performed different functions and cultivated somewhat different forms/modes of wisdom, mantic as well as traditional/educational, different sages may have developed different interests and affiliations. Thus, although relatively simple, the structure allowed for considerable conflict between scribal-sapiental retainers and priestly rulers and between rival groups of sages as well.

We illustrate our contention with just one example. Sirach and the *Book of the Watchers* in *1 Enoch* 1–36 should be read as complementary sources rather than contradictory or alternative sources. The one clarifies the basic structure, while the other gives us access to a particular conflict that emerged. Furthermore, the basic structure discerned through Ben Sira can help us understand better the structural roots of the particular conflict evident in the *Book of the Watchers* of the Enoch tradition.

The *Book of the Watchers* was written and redacted during the third century BCE.[15] The dating of this book is complicated by the fact that three or four layers of composition can be detected. The oldest is chs. 6–11, itself a composite of two narratives. In one, Shemihaza and 200 other angels descend to have intercourse with women who then bear giant

15. The oldest ms. of the *Book of the Watchers* is 4QEn[a], dated by Milik to the first half of the second century BCE. Milik concludes from the orthography and copying errors that this ms. was copied from a third century ms. (Milik 1976: 141). He also suggests that the script may reflect scribal customs of Northern Syria or Mesopotamia. Accordingly, the *Book of the Watchers* must have reached its present form by early in the second century at the latest. A third-century date of composition/redaction is more likely. Hence it is contemporary to, or earlier than, Ben Sira.

offspring who in turn act violently and, along with their angelic fathers, are judged. In the other, Asael alone descends to teach forbidden secrets to humans, especially the arts of making weapons and cosmetics, both of which depend upon metallurgy. In the story as it now stands, others of Shemihaza's subordinate angels teach various mantic and astrological skills.

The other layers in the *Book of the Watchers* are (1) chs. 12–16, the story of Enoch's involvement in the judgment of the watchers; (2) chs. 17–36, stories about Enoch's travels to learn about world geography, including the places of judgment and the location of the mountain of God; and (3) chs. 1–5, an introduction to the *Book of the Watchers* with vocabulary taken from the stories of Balaam, a mantic diviner (Num. 22–24), a warning of future judgment, and lessons for obedience taken from the regularity of nature.

The debate concerning the intellectual antecedents of Jewish apocalyptic continues. Most scholars believe that there are connections to both traditional wisdom as exemplified by Proverbs and classical Israelite prophecy, as well as to various foreign influences. The 'foreign' influence that seems to be determinative in Enoch literature is Mesopotamian 'mantic' wisdom (see VanderKam 1984: 8; and Stone 1976).

Earlier analyses, such as that of von Rad, 'did not distinguish sharply enough between an educational kind of wisdom and the less rational sort that found expression in divination' (VanderKam 1984: 5). Enochian wisdom depends upon visions, interpretations of visions, and proto-scientific speculation, especially concerning astrology/astronomy and geography.[16] These are doubtless skills that were learned by Jewish sages in the Babylonian diaspora and developed in and for a Jewish audience around the figure Enoch. However, from a sociological perspective, the differences between Enochic, mantic wisdom and traditional, 'proverbial' or 'educational' wisdom do not imply differences in social position and role. One group of sages cultivated both kinds of wisdom; another only educational.

During the period of Ptolemaic rule, Enochian sages used their mantic

---

16. This is especially clear in Book 3, the *Astronomical Book*, which probably assumed something like its present form early in the third century, if not already in the fourth century BCE. Further examples of visions and interpretations of visions can be seen in both Books 4 and 5, both written in the first half of the second century. Compare this with the Babylonian scribes, who, according to Smith (1978: 70), 'speculated about hidden heavenly tablets, about creation by divine word, about the beginning and the end and thereby claimed to possess the secrets of creation'.

and astronomical wisdom as a way of articulating their opposition to the alliance of the high priesthood with the Hellenistic empire. The Enochic traditions that are now found in the *Book of the Watchers* combined Mesopotamian traditions (the cosmic travels and geographical reports and possibly the revolt of Shemihazah and his cohorts) with Greek traditions (Asael = Prometheus). It has already been proposed that the *Book of the Watchers* was composed as a polemic against the Greek overlords who claimed divine descent and consumed goods and brought violence upon the land (see Nickelsburg 1977; Bartelmus 1979: 175-79). It appears to be a bit of an embarrassing contradiction, that the Watchers are condemned for bringing knowledge of divination and astrology, when those are precisely the skills for which Enoch himself is famous. Presumably the Greek diviners practiced divination and astrology that was based upon illicit sources, while that of Enoch and his followers was based upon licit revelations by God and good angels.

Various Enochic compositions refer to the fact that Enoch is passing on what he has learned from his inter-stellar travel with the angels and from his dreams to his son Methuselah. This may reflect a practice among Enochic sages to pass on their wisdom in a contest similar to that of traditional Israelite wisdom.[17] The fact that the *Animal Apocalypse* (*1 Enoch* 85–90) reflects knowledge both of the traditional sources behind the *Book of the Watchers* and of the *Book of the Watchers* itself indicates that the Enochian traditions were being passed on from master to student, as well as in written documents. The *Animal Apocalypse* quite clearly implies that the group to which its author belongs arose in the beginning of the second century (just about when Ben Sira wrote). It is possible that one of the forces leading to the (re-)formation of this group was the change of imperial power and the ensuing political shakeups.[18] It is difficult to say much more.

It is clear that the Enochic sages took a rather dim view of most (if not all) of those who currently held political power. None of the Enochic compositions displays very much interest in the temple, priesthood or Mosaic Law. The *Animal Apocalypse* is positively against the second temple, and the *Apocalypse of Weeks* (*1 Enoch* 94; 91.11-17), by implication, agrees.

---

17. See Smith (1978: 74): 'I would argue that wisdom and apocalyptic are related in that they are both essentially scribal phenomena. It is the paradigmatic thought of the scribe—a way of thinking that is both pragmatic and speculative—which as given rise to both.'

18. Although, clearly, the Enochic sages were no fans of the Ptolemies either.

There is a strong possibility that already in the third century, the *Book of the Watchers* reflects the view that while the Enochian sages fulfilled a sociological role identical to that of Ben Sira and his students, the Enochic sages served a priestly party that (at least in the third and second centuries) unsuccessfully competed for influence and authority. The competition between their respective patrons is probably reflected in what seems to be competition between the Enochic sages and Ben Sira. Whereas the Enochic texts consistently lay claim to knowledge about the stars and cosmic geography and the ability to interpret dreams, Ben Sira explicitly warns against such presumption (1.1-5; 3.21-24; 34.1-8; 42.17).

CONFLICTING IDEOLOGIES CONCERNING THE SECOND TEMPLE

John M. Halligan

This exploratory essay looks at some of the multiple strands of ideologies vying for control in Palestine during the Seleucid period. Unlike the vast literary blanks during the Persian era and the patchy materials from the Ptolemaic time, we have abundant literary sources to draw upon in reconstructing the various ideologies, and I shall look in particular at the place of the temple in these.

The books of 1 and 2 Maccabees provide a kind of history in so far as it relates events affecting the Jewish society of the Seleucid period. These accounts are of course highly subjective, and the motives of the major players—Mattathias, Antiochus Epiphanes, Jason, Menelaus, Judas and others—are presented in terms of grander mythic schemes: the oppression of Israel by foreigners and Israel's deliverance through divinely chosen leaders, or the courageous martyrdom of individuals demonstrating their loyalty to the faith; the issue of fidelity to the law versus idolatry; the threat to the sanctuary, the divine home, and its repulse.

Historically, the cause of the conflict that led to the Hasmonean dynasty is probably to be traced to a fault-line that, like all geological fault-lines, eventually caused an earthquake. That fault-line ran through Palestine, dividing the Jewish leadership as well. Ptolemaic sway in Palestine, long contested by the Seleucids, ended with the battle of Panias and the advance of Antiochus III into Egypt proper. The Jewish society was divided in its allegiances to the two great Hellenic powers and a significant segment held for independence from either. Some in the last group were content with religious freedom, others aspired to political autonomy. The Seleucid kingdom itself also fractured: claimants to the throne multiplied, coalitions formed and dissolved. And Rome grew closer. The authors of 1 Maccabees in particular were absorbed also by these events, which of course they recounted in a manner validating their ideological stances.

However, another fault-line relevant to this essay is the power structure within hierocratic Judea, and the ideology that supported it. The Hellenistic period saw the growth of non-priestly power groups who needed to be accommodated to the increasingly dominant power of the ruling high-priestly dynasty. And of course this fault-line was connected to the other: political allegiance to Seleucids or Ptolemies implied a stake in the political and social power structure of Judea.

Conflicting ideologies concerning the Jerusalem temple thus reflect changing political configurations, social units, structural planes and the relationships among all of these. Order, class, status, wealth and power were the foundation stones on which the superstructure of the Seleucid Empire was built. This kingdom was also committed to an active policy of creating wealth through conquest but also through the establishment of cities and citizenship. The perplexing question for the established Jerusalem aristocracy as hegemony shifted from Ptolemaic to Seleucid will have been: what would be the new order? Some continuity of structure would remain but uncertainty concerning the ability of the Seleucids to reign effectively would persist and allegiances would bend. Seleucid attitudes would also affect the balance of power in Jerusalem, and mutated classes, status and mobility, shifts in wealth and changes in power implied instability.

The Second Temple in Seleucid Times

The origins of the Second Temple were remembered in Jewish literature in terms of imperial patronage. With Persian support, Sheshbazzar had allegedly laid the foundations for the Second Temple in 539 BCE and Zerubbabel completed the structure in five years, from 520 to 515. Appointments stolen by Nebuchadnezzar in 587–86 were apparently returned by Persian decree and funding made available for the upkeep of the sanctuary. Little else is said of the temple edifice itself during the Achaemenid period unless one takes the reference to Nehemiah's repair of the city walls as an oblique mention of the temple walls (see Goldstein 1983: 174-76, who sees Nehemiah as the builder of the Second Temple). The *Letter of Aristeas* (320), embellished by Josephus (*Ant.* 12.2.8-10) relates that Ptolemy Philopator sent gifts to the Temple in Jerusalem. But *3 Maccabees*, in a story reminiscent of 2 Macc. 3.7-30, relates that the same Ptolemy, after his victory at Raphia, was refused entrance to the temple by the priests claiming that only the high priest once a year could enter the temple proper (1.10–2.30). He was repulsed by a divine intervention and thus the temple was not violated. The theme of imperial

patronage of the temple here turns to the more common one in later
Second Temple times, of attempted violation of the temple (both successful and unsuccessful).

Possibly the measures of Antiochus IV were largely responsible for this.
For Antiochus III, who did not secure Palestine without the help of some
Jews, according to Josephus issued a decree restoring the damaged temple
and city precincts. The decree includes that no foreigner may enter the
temple of Jerusalem, in fact, no animal forbidden for sacrifice was permitted within the city (*Ant.* 12.3.3-4; for arguments in favor of the authenticity of this document, see Bickerman [1980b]). Thus the Seleucid era begins
with the king himself proclaiming the sacrosanct character of the Second
Temple. The reign of his successor Seleucus IV also passes without mention of any disturbances over the Temple.

The Jason File

The figure of Jason the Oniad makes an interesting case for analyzing the
ideology of the Temple in the early Seleucid period. According to
2 Maccabees, Jason sought to be a new kind of leader of a new kind of
society. He envisioned functioning not simply as head of the Judean
temple-state, a tiny subunit within the Seleucid Empire, but as the founder of a new form of citizenship for (certain) Jews within the realm. He
thus petitioned Antiochus IV to be authorized to draw up the list of those
who would be the Antiochene citizens of Jerusalem, those enjoying all
the privileges accorded the citizens of Antioch at Daphne, the capital of
the Seleucid empire (2 Macc. 4–5).

Whereas Roman practice allowed members of Latin and Italian towns to
become Roman citizens in full or part *per magistratum*, that is, through
military or civic service, the stratagem of Antiochus IV was to create an
empire of city-states containing imperial citizens, well educated and loyal.
The gymnasium and ephebate would be the channels for civic education
and the military training required to be an Antiochene citizen. Antiochus
foresaw an empire analogous to Rome; his years as hostage had taught
him the finer points of Roman governance (see Goldstein 1976: 104-110).
That Jason took advantage of this policy is implied in 2 Maccabees and
seems also to be historically plausible.

But what of the existing state of affairs? In their essay in this volume,
Tiller and Horsley portray Ben Sira as providing a view of the social structure of Judea in the early second century BCE. The ideology of the temple-
city or temple-state placed the 'god and the king/high priest at its center as

a symbol of the whole', operating in accordance with covenantal laws (p. 92). During Ptolemaic times this ideology had not been seriously disturbed by external pressures, but the picture changed rapidly when Antiochus IV came to power and put in motion the reorganization of the Seleucid Empire. This triggered a tectonic change in the alignment of the social units and planes of intersection.

Tiller and Horsley demonstrate that the scribes, while not a part of the ruling class, participated in its functions, and likewise, while not a member of the labor class, the plowmen and artisans, they were close enough to be sympathetic to their needs. It was the scribe's privilege to gather wisdom broadly while nevertheless being guided by the covenantal traditions dear to the Aaronide priesthood and the law of Moses. Their own authority derived from both their employer's commissioning (something they were careful to protect as their instructions to their students indicate) and the content of what they taught. Hence, the scribe perpetuated the ideology of the hierocratic class bearing the responsibility of governing the temple-state, maintaining the identity of its people, and welfare of all its faithful (see p. 93). We can thus take Ben Sira as speaking for his overlords.

But such a voice does not necessarily represent reality as everyone saw it. Ben Sira, and his masters, are not without their own ideological interests. There may have been a weakness inherent in the ideology of temple-state as given in Ben Sira more apparent to his contemporaries than modern scholars. While such an ideology assured 10 per cent of the population the dutiful support of 90 per cent, it did not, for instance, always function outside Jerusalem. While the Jerusalem authorities took for granted the priority of the temple of Jerusalem, other temples existed elsewhere: Elephantine in upper Egypt, the Oniad temple at Leontopolis in lower Egypt, Mt Gerizim in Samaria, and possibly at Lachish and at Araq el-Emir in Transjordan, while the Qumran texts, while upholding the sanctity of the temple, did not associate this with the priesthood that historically sustained its cult, and created an ideology that radically separated the two.

There were corresponding claimants to priestly control in these temples: Zadokites, Aaronites, Hasmoneans of the Yehoyarib clan, Oniads, Tobiads. (Which priestly families serviced the Samaritan and Elephantine temples the records do not make clear.) From 350 to 175 BCE the high priests in Jerusalem were Oniads by hereditary succession; from 175 to 134 BCE all were appointed by the Seleucids. Thereafter Simon Maccabee had the distinction of being both appointed and proclaimed high priest in 143–142. The stability of the high priesthood apparent in Ben Sira was quickly dissolved. In the absence of a king and in the context of imperial rule, the position of high priest, perhaps beginning in the Ptolemaic period with the demise of the role of governor, came to include military and civil leadership as well. But the various factions of pro-Ptolemaic, pro-Seleucid, Hellenists, nationalists and pietists all maintained the temple as a focal point of Jewish identity, religious and cultural. Thus the Temple was the supreme symbol of national identity (whatever that meant), of legitimacy and political supremacy. Where other temples could not be built to secure local authority, the Jerusalem temple would inevitably become the major site of ideological as well as actual conflict.

Jason is the major villain in the eyes of the author of 2 Maccabees, gaining the office of high priest while its rightful holder was still alive. Onias III was in Antioch pleading his case against the charges of Simon, the 'chief administrator of the temple', that he was not being financially honest about temple revenue. (The Tobiad Simon, we may guess, had motives of his own for the accusation.) Jason offered the regular payment of 360 talents from tithing that he must have collected in his brother's place, and another 80 from an undisclosed source. In addition he promised yet 150 more talents if he be allowed to construct a gymnasium. Where was this revenue coming from? From his own resources or those yet to be acquired? From the Tobiads, with whom Goldstein believes that Jason was in league, in particular with Menelaus, who would later turn traitor to him (Goldstein 1983: 226-27)? But I do not believe the text tells such a tale. Rather, Jason is maintaining the Oniad line at whatever cost. It is clear that the cultic side of the high-priestly office is of little interest to him, but conversely the priestly rights to the first fruits and sacrifices would afford him continued wealth and power. Jason thus seeks to secure a permanently safe political-social-religious role through imperial citizenship, yet without undermining the role of the temple.

According to 2 Macc. 4.18-20 Jason sent 300 talents through his 'Antiochenes of Jerusalem' to Tyre for the sacrifice to Hercules at the quadrennial games. But the story runs that piety prevented these Antiochenes from applying the money to the sacrifices. The inference is that Jason did not have control of some of his own closest supporters within his hierocracy. However, Menelaus outbid the absent Jason and secured the high-priestly office by bidding higher (2 Macc. 4.23-24); perhaps the figure of '300 talents' by which he outbid Jason was deliberately the same as the amount of Jason's gift; Menelaus's usurpation exercises a poetic justice. Hengel (1974: I, 273-76) suggests that Jason may have functioned as the high priest at the temple at Araq el-Emir, the site of the Tobiad cleruchy (a body of citizens holding grants of land from the sovereign). If so, he took his priesthood seriously enough. But according to 2 Maccabees, after a failed attempt to regain power, Jason fled a second time to the Ammanitis, and his misadventures are followed to a tragic conclusion among the Lacedaemonians, where he ended a man without country, mourners, funeral or tomb.

According to 2 Maccabees, Jason's attempt to secure imperial citizenship for his fellow Jerusalemites ends in ignominy because he abandoned the principle that fidelity to the covenantal laws precedes any accommodations to non-Jewish law. He gained the high priesthood through bribery, he ignored the exclusivity of the God of Israel, he polluted the cult, and disregarded the traditions of the people. Although he was of the proper family, it was not good enough; although he had considerable financial resources, they failed him; although he had a power base in the ruling class, they deserted him.

In particular, the author of 2 Maccabees accuses Jason and his followers of neglecting their temple duties, making this the reason for their downfall (4.13-17). But in securing this power base did Jason really wish to diminish the role of the temple and create a different power-base on Seleucid lines? This seems less plausible. How was the ideology endorsed by Ben Sira affected by the activities of Jason (and Menelaus)? Their policies did not require that they abandon the temple-state structure of Judea. They did weaken the status of the temple of Jerusalem and the privileged position of the land of Israel (Judah) among Jews. The Seleucid policy carried an egalitarian trait that did not rest well with the ideology of the pre-eminence of the laws of Moses. But they also strengthened the position of Jerusalem and its favored leadership with the imperial structure. But such a motive implies already a change of direction away from isolationism (and this too is hinted at in 1 Macc. 1.12). What might have prompted such a move?

It is first to be noted that such a move would require no fundamental change in the manner in which the Judean temple-state as a whole would function. It is true that the introduction of the gymnasium would bring increased exposure to non-Jewish culture but as Doran has demonstrated elsewhere in this volume, this was already the case in Alexandria and the leading intellectuals in the Jewish community had no fear that Jewish wisdom as contained in the Torah was inferior to anything the gentile world produced. Ben Sira was not a 'Hellenizer' of the cut of Jason, but he was not adverse to foreign culture. The ephebate, providing physical and military training and the study of philosophy and literature, did not pose a threat to the political structure, though perhaps it did to the aristocratic-hierocratic ideology that supported its priesthood.

How, then, may we understand historically the ideology of Jason which caused the tectonic upheaval? Was he, as 2 Maccabees suggests, the arch-Hellenizer and root of all evil that befell Judah under Antiochus IV? We may look for deeper and more rational motives. Jason probably intended to maintain the equilibrium of the high priest ruling the temple-state as the legitimate representative of God through his eternal covenant with Aaron, and, equally, as the representative of the people before God. As an Oniad he probably upheld the Oniad ideology and other structural elements could have remained stable as long as an Oniad ruled; the presence of a traditional leadership could balance the inevitable shift in political influence that was taking place. His scheme to enfranchise the members of the *gerousia* into imperial citizens in constructing a gymnasium and ephebate, and obtain for himself or the priesthood the founder's right to choose these 'Antiochenes', may have been partly designed in order to thwart the Tobiad family, but mainly created to accommodate the rising power of the wealthy non-priestly families of Jerusalem and give them a status that did not threaten the traditional high-priestly office, or undermine the veneration of the law of Moses and the centrality of the cult, for which the Oniads stood. In short, Jason's moves were calculated to maintain the power of the Oniads in that high-priestly office and the stability of the social structure. But he miscalculated.

The Qumran File

We can now examine temple ideologies from the opposite end of the spectrum. Whatever the ultimate origins of the Qumran community/communities, it is now becoming clearer that the immediate cause of their formation had to do with a conflict of priestly traditions and priestly privileges, as reflected especially in 4QMMT. Withdrawal from the Jerusalem sanctuary more probably followed a cessation of participation in the religious leadership than provoked it. Concerns about Hellenism, though often claimed for these groups, are hardly evident; rather the paramount issues in the group focused on interpretation of the law and the preservation of Israel as a holy nation. Indeed, their exact political affiliations remain unclear, as do their opinions regarding the conduct and outcome of the Maccabean wars.

The groups responsible for the Qumran texts cherished their own priestly ideology. Whether they were themselves historically representatives of a 'Zadokite' priestly line, or adopted priestly leaders from this line, or simply took the name 'Zadokite' to symbolize the true biblical priesthood (following Ezekiel), they insisted that the purity of the temple itself was threatened by the impurity of the priests who served in it. However, the question that needs to be asked is why they seceded when they did. At what point did they come to regard the ruling priesthood as illegitimate? The mere existence of an independent legal or priestly tradition does not seem to be adequate. If the tradition was new, it was invented; if old, then how had it been accommodated before their secession?

The logical conclusion of these groups was the claim that the true temple never had been built and that it, and its holy precinct, the city of Jerusalem, had to be reconstructed in the fullness of time (as in the *Temple Scroll*). In the meantime, the true cult and the true sanctuary could be found in heaven (as in the *Songs of the Sabbath Sacrifice*). And, as in the *Melchizedek Fragments*, the true messiah of the Chosen People was the heavenly high priest, Melchizedek.

We need more than religious explanations for the creation of the Qumran group(s) and their ideology. And we must not be content to explain their ideology without reference to social and political realities. Clearly, the proliferation of claims upon the temple that Jason had sought to avoid, and which the Maccabees had exploited, once again had to be suppressed by the Hasmoneans. While one priestly regime (not necessarily always the same one!) was installed, others were excluded.

Conclusions

A wider investigation of the literature of the Seleucid period would further illustrate the way in which the ideologically centralizing and stabilizing effect of the temple was quickly converted into its opposite: it became the site of contention, not so much between Jews and foreign kings, as with Antiochus IV, but between various factions, each with their own version of the true faith. At the center of almost all of these (the Enochic literature is the major exception), the temple cult and Mosaic law are indispensable to any definition of Judaism.

No single ideology of the temple could prevail, however, except through political favor and through the exclusion of others. Foreign domination might prove more successful at uniting the Judeans than domestic kings (Herod the great being the outstanding exception, though it could be claimed that he was not entirely 'domestic'). But only the destruction of that temple, perhaps, would in the end resolve the problem of who should run the temple.

JEWISH EDUCATION IN THE SELEUCID PERIOD

Robert Doran

The authors of both 1 and 2 Maccabees place education at the beginning of the troubles in early second century Jerusalem—rascally Hellenizers built a gymnasium to lead the people astray. Following the lead of these authors, histories of the Maccabean revolution portray Jason the high priest as a wildly enthusiastic Hellenizer. As Martin Hengel commented (Hengel 1974: I, 74):

> We have no detailed knowledge about the training given in the gymnasium in Jerusalem. It will, however, hardly have been different from that usual in other Palestinian and Phoenician cities. Obviously the ephebes completed naked in sports, an offence about which the Book of Jubilees becomes excited even two generations later. II Macc. 4.10 states that Jason conformed the young ephebes completely to the Greek style of life by means of gymnasium education: thus the instruction will have embraced not only sports, but also music and literature, like the reading of Homer.

If one wishes to investigate the origins of the Maccabean revolt, one needs to explore further what education meant in pre-Hasmonean Jerusalem.

The whole question of education in Israel is a vexed one. James Crenshaw (1985) and Shaye Cohen (1987a: 120-23) have approached the problem from opposite chronological directions: Crenshaw took a hard look at evidence for schools in early Israel and found little; Cohen discussed the evidence in rabbinic sources and was equally skeptical. Yet it is clear that some form of education must have taken place, whether there is evidence for a *bet midrash/bet musar* or not. Somehow people were taught to write Hebrew, Aramaic and Greek as the Qumran fragments show (see Naveh 1986). Everyday life required scribes who could write bills, deeds of sale and other documents. At the level of international politics, the family of Hakkoz sent ambassadors (1 Macc. 8.17; 2 Macc. 4.11) both to the Seleucids and to the Romans and probably had some knowledge of Greek, if not at the level of trained rhetors. One of its members, Eupolemus, is thought to be the author of Greek fragments found in Eusebius of Caesarea (Holladay 1983: 93-156). The instructions found at 1QSa 1.4-9 regarding education are interesting.

> This is the rule for all the hosts of the congregation, for every man born in Israel.
>
> From [his] youth they shall instruct him in the Book of Meditation and shall teach him, according to his age, the precepts of the Covenant. He [shall be edu]cated in their statutes for ten years...
>
> At the age of twenty years [he shall be] enrolled, that he may enter upon his allotted duties in the midst of his family [and] be joined to the holy congregation (translation from Vermes 1997: 157-58).

Here membership occurs at age 20, the age to pay the temple tax (Exod. 30.14) and to be able to go to war (Num. 1.3). Prior to that the youth would have studied Bible and the statutes of the Community. This presupposes that reading would have begun by age seven at the latest, and the writing exercises uncovered by Naveh at Qumran testify to the study habits there. This document belongs to the first century BCE, with its heightened sense of us versus them, insiders versus outsiders, and the strong need of indoctrination, but one suspects that these rules for education are not new, but codify earlier practice.

Ben Sira

The one work of a teacher that we have from the Second Temple period is that of Ben Sira (see Gammie 1990). After listing various types of wise men—the instructor of many who is useless for himself, the skillful speaker who is hated, a man wise only for himself—Ben Sira describes the wise man *par excellence*:

> A wise man will instruct his own people
> And the products of his understanding will be trustworthy.
> A wise man will be filled with blessing
> And all who see him will bless him.
> The wise man of a people will inherit honor
> And his name will live forever (37.23, 24, 26).

This is no doubt how Ben Sira saw himself—as a teacher of the people. Ben Sira, however, was also writing for an elite. H. Stadelmann (1980: 12-26) has emphasized the priestly concerns of Ben Sira's writings and argued that Ben Sira was a priest.[1] Stadelmann also distinguished two levels of

---

1.   See also Mack 1985: 105-106. For a view of Sirach as a temple scribe, see

education in Ben Sira (1980: 271-309). The first aims at the education of
the priestly learned class, as Ben Sira insists on the prerogatives of Aaron
and his posterity:

> In his commandments he gave him [Aaron]
> Authority over the agreements about judgments,
> To teach Jacob the decrees
> And to enlighten Israel with his law (45.17).

And Ben Sira prays that this pre-eminence remains forever:

> May he give you wisdom of mind
> To judge his people justly
> So that he may not forget your wealth (טובכם)
> And your power (גבורתכם) for ever (45.26).

But Ben Sira also shows concern for non-priests. The end of the great
hymn in ch. 24 stresses that the wise man has not labored for himself only,
but for all who seek out Wisdom (24.34; cf. 33.17 [30.26]). Wisdom has
been poured out on all God's creation, on all humans as he chose, but
especially to those who love God (1.9-10). Ben Sira calls out to the leaders
of the people and the rulers of the assembly to listen to his instruction
(33.18-19 [30.27]).

What is the educational process that Ben Sira recommends? Clearly,
that one lead a godly life:

> The fear of the Lord is the sum of wisdom
> And in all wisdom the Law is fulfilled.
> The knowledge of wickedness is not wisdom
> And where the counsel of sinners is, there is no understanding.
> A man who is inferior in understanding but fears God is better
> Than one who abounds in prudence but transgresses the Law (19.20, 22, 24;
> cf. 1.20, 26-27).

Stadelmann has suggested that herein lies an essential difference between
Ben Sira and the hellenistic *Zeitgeist*:

> For him, there can be no programme of civic wisdom education that freed
> itself from religion, following the Hellenistic delight in personal formation.
> Education for him remains, despite an openness to the world, 'education
> coming from religion'[2] (Stadelmann 1980: 300).

Blenkinsopp (1977: 130, 132). Gammie (1990: 364-65) suggests Sirach was of priestly
descent but did not serve as a priest.

2.   'Ein weisheitliches Volkerziehungs-programm, das sich im Zuge einer vom
hellenistischen Zeitgeist getragenen Bildungsfreude vom Glauben emanzipiert, kann es

One might note here that Stadelmann has completely overlooked the strong links between gymnasium education and the civic religion that Chrysis Pélékidis (1962: 211-56) and Jean Delorme (1960: 448-58) have shown at length. The ephebes took part in civic religious festivals, and the sights and sounds of religion were all around them. Stadelmann denigrates this civic religion too quickly.

Three passages in Ben Sira are particularly interesting for what they suggest about the educational process.

6.32-37	8.8-9	39.1-5
My child, if you wish, you can be educated. And if you devote yourself to it you can become shrewd. If you love to hear, you will receive, and if you listen, you will be wise. Take your stand in the throng of elders; Which one of them is wise? Attach yourself to him. Be willing to listen to every godly discourse, and do not let any wise proverbs escape you. If you see a man of understanding, go to him early, and let your feet wear out his doorstep. Think about the statutes of the Lord, and constantly meditate on his commandments. He will strengthen your mind, and the wisdom you desire will be given to you.	Do not neglect the discourse of wise men, but busy yourself with their proverbs; for from them you will gain instruction, and learn to serve great men. Do not neglect the discourse of old men, for they learned it from their fathers. For from them you will gain understanding, and learn to return an answer in your time of need.	It is not so with the man who applies himself, and studies the Law of the Most High. He searches out the wisdom of all the ancients, and busies himself with prophecies. He observes the discourse of famous men, and penetrates the intricacies of figures. He searches out the hidden meanings of proverbs, and acquaints himself with the obscurities of figures. He will serve before great men, and appear before rulers. He will travel through the lands of strange peoples, and test what is good and what is evil among men. He will devote himself to going early to the Lord his Maker, and will make his entreaty before the Most High. He will open his mouth in prayer, and make entreaty for his sins.

In Ben Sira 39.1-5 three facets of the educational process are described. Emphasis is placed on prayer and worship of God (39.5). Experience of court life and foreign lands is important (39.4; cf. 34.9-11). What one must acquire, though, to understand the law of the Most High is an acquaintance with traditional knowledge. To be wise one must be versed in the writings of the people—the wisdom of the ancients and prophecies. One must also

für ihn nicht geben. Bildung bleibt für ihn—bei allen Weltoffenheit—"Bildung aus dem Glauben"'.

note the discourse, conversation of notable men (6.34-36; 8.8-9). One must listen to how they compose their speeches, presumably so one can imitate them. The emphasis on discourse continues in the recommendation to concentrate on proverbs, riddles and figures. This emphasis on listening to one's elders and garnering and examining proverbs is not peculiar to Ben Sira. Timothy Polk (1983) has shown how Ezekiel uses proverbs in his speeches: the prophet both bases his arguments on them in speeches, and also shows, for example, the way in which Ezekiel rejects 'accepted wisdom' in his vision of a new world. No longer will the proverb apply that 'the fathers have eaten sour grapes, and the children's teeth are set on edge'.

This use of proverbs and sayings of the wise is, of course, not limited to Hebrew wisdom. Theognis, a Greek writer of the sixth century BCE, whose work was well known and with some of whose maxims Ben Sira may have been acquainted, begins his work to his friend Cyrnos:

> It is for your well-being Cyrnos that I am formulating these precepts which I as a youth received from good people. Be wise, and do not seek by shameful and unjust acts honor, fame and fortune. Know this. Then do not converse with base men, but always with good—eat and drink with them, sit with them and please those whose power is great. You will learn virtue from the virtuous. But if you mingle with base men, you will destroy your very spirit. So taught, frequent good people and you will some day say that I advised my friends well (*Elegies* 1.27-38).

In Plato's *Protagoras*, Hippocrates and Socrates go to the house where Protagoras is staying. There the students of Protagoras follow him around hanging on every word. The students must be prepared to give up every-thing to follow their teacher and learn from him. Plato himself elsewhere rejects simple book-learning:

> For this knowledge [philosophy] is not something that can be put into words like other sciences; but after long-continued intercourse between teacher and pupil, in joint pursuit of the subject, suddenly, like light flashing forth when a fire is kindled, it is born in the soul and straightway nourishes itself (*Letter* 7.341c).

Plato describes how the teacher must impress on would-be students of philosophy how difficult it is (7.340b-d), just as Ben Sira speaks of Wis-dom's fetters and collar (6.18-31). One should also note how the study of proverbs and figures is part of the training in argumentation. Aristotle places *parabolē* among the examples used by an orator as either inductive or indirect proof of his argument (Aristotle, *Rhet.* 2.20, 1393a23–1394a18).

In the *Topics*, one of his earliest works, Aristotle speaks of how one can be well supplied with reasonings:

> The means whereby we are to become well supplied with reasonings are four: (1) the securing of propositions; (2) the power to distinguish in how many senses a particular expression is used; (3) the discovery of the differences of things; (4) the investigation of likeness... Propositions should be selected in a number of ways corresponding to the number of distinctions drawn in regard to the proposition: thus one may first take in hand the opinions held by all or by most men or by the philosophers, i.e. by all, or most, or the most notable of them; or opinions contrary to those that seem to be generally held; and again, all opinions that are in accordance with the arts. We must make propositions also of the contradictories of opinions contrary to those that seem to be generally held, as was laid down before (1.13-14, 105a23–105b18).

Aristotle is here codifying and classifying common rules for argumentation, and one of his sources is commonly held opinions, that is, proverbs. Aristotle was later blamed, in fact, for not collecting proverbs (by Isocrates's pupil Cephisodorus Athenaeus, *Deipnosophistae* 2.60d-e), whereas Diogenes Laertius (*Lives of the Philosophers* 5.26) states that Aristotle authored works entitled *Parabolai* and *Paroimiai*. As Rudolf Pfeiffer states (1968: 83-84),

> In his first anti-Platonic dialogue, *Peri Philosophias*, he regarded proverbs as 'survivals of a pre-literary philosophy' and treated them in a survey of early wisdom, together with the 'Orphics', the Delphic maxims and the precepts of the Seven Wise Men. He liked to embellish his later writings on rhetoric and politics with proverbial quotations. One of his pupils, Clearchus of Soloi, enlarged his master's collection by writing two books of *Paroimiai* which for the amusement of his readers he cast in a literary narrative form; many others followed, who were content to arrange dry lists.

Aristotle's emphasis on collecting commonly held opinions and investigating the limits of their applicability, that is, the meaning of the terms of the propositions, resonates with Ben Sira's recommendation to not let a wise proverb slip by and to check out hidden meanings and obscurities in comparisons. Such a comparison between Ben Sira's description of the process of education and that found in Athens is not meant to suggest derivation of any kind. The educational break-through of the Sophists and the cultural position of Athens led to more technical developments in science, historiography, geography and rhetoric than took place in Jerusalem. But the process recommended by Ben Sira and found in classical

Greek writings reflects education in a traditional society. J. Messenger (1965) has described how proverbs were used in speeches in Nigerian indigenous courts in the 1950s and how the apt use of a little-known proverb could effectively sway the court. Ben Sira too is describing the traditional educational process in Judea. He writes in the traditional tongue to inculcate traditional values. But Ben Sira is also doing more than that. Not only does he go beyond simple traditional proverb collecting and group proverbs thematically and also at times form an argument, but he also, as J.T. Sanders (1983) has persuasively shown, evidences knowledge of Greek and Egyptian writings. Scholars like Alexander Di Lella (Skehan and DiLella 1987: 50) have argued that Ben Sira makes such sources authentically Jewish, but one should also pause a moment to reflect on what is going on. Ben Sira is writing in the 180s BCE, just a decade or so before Jason builds his gymnasium, for the upper classes in Jerusalem and, as part of his instruction, includes references to Greek and Egyptian literature. Presumably this means that he knows Greek and Demotic; Thomas Robert Lee (1986), followed by Burton Mack (1985: 120-37), has strongly argued for Ben Sira's awareness of Greek rhetorical style. Therefore, the one teacher we know of in pre-Hasmonean Jerusalem is someone who maintains a strong interest in Jewish traditional literature but is not averse to including in his curriculum suitable literature from other traditions (39.4), nor would he discourage the study of foreign languages. In this, Ben Sira is not that different from what is going on in Rome at precisely the same time (see Bonner 1977).

Jewish Education in Alexandria

Ben Sira's Grandson

Ben Sira's grandson translated his work into Greek. In his prologue, he makes the obligatory self-deprecating remarks, and also that he translated the work 'with much pain and diligence' especially for those 'living abroad who wished to gain learning and are disposed to live according to the Law'. He makes an interesting distinction when he writes:

> those things spoken in their own right as Hebrew do not have the same power when they are translated into another language. Not only these but even the Law and the prophets and the other books are quite different when spoken in their own language (*Prologue* 20).

He is not only aware of the difficulties of translating, but his use of the verb ἰσοδυναμεῖν conjures up the power of using the original sacred language. This sense of power inherent in the language lies behind the use of sacred formulae in healing rituals both in the Synoptic Gospels and the magical papyri (see Theissen 1985: 63-65; and Plato, *Cratylus* 390e on the relationship of nature to name). But is this just another example of *traduttore e traditore*? Is Ben Sira's grandson claiming superior knowledge because of his knowledge of Hebrew? Is this the claim of the immigrant to inside knowledge of the parent culture, or does it hint at rivalries in Alexandrian Judaism? It might be interesting to investigate the Greek translation from that point of view. For what we do know is that earlier the Greek translation of the Hebrew Scriptures—when and where and by whom still vague—is being touted as just as good as the Hebrew original. The *Letter of Aristeas* has none of the reservations of Ben Sira's grandson about a difference in power between the versions, although he does not think much of translations done by non-Jews (314-16).

What I would like to point to here are some indications of an educational process among Alexandrian Jews as gleaned from the fragments, tantalizingly brief and frustratingly difficult to place and date as they are known only third-hand from Eusebius of Caesarea of the fourth century quoting Alexander Polyhistor of the first century BCE (see Holladay 1983).

Demetrius

The concern over the Greek Bible surfaces particularly in the exegetical work of someone like Demetrius. In the late third century BCE, Demetrius tried to establish chronological and genealogical order among the biblical events and the patriarchs and also to answer difficulties which arise in reading the biblical text. How could Moses, for example, have married Zipporah, an Egyptian? Well, Zipporah really was a descendant of Abraham through Keturah's son Jokshan, and so Moses actually did not marry a foreigner. The genealogy Demetrius devises to solve this problem also helps him explain how Moses, seventh in line from Abraham, could marry someone sixth in line from Abraham since Abraham begot Isaac, Moses' ancestor, 40 years before he begot Jokshan. As Holladay comments (1983: 52): 'Perhaps the most notable characteristic of Demetrius' work is his biblicism. The LXX serves as his only source, and his knowledge of its contents is detailed and exact.' Yet Demetrius's work is also at home in the Greek world of Alexandria where scholars such as Zenodotus, Callimachus, Eratosthenes and Aristophanes of Byzantium had such a strong influence on the study of texts (see Pfeiffer 1968: 105-209; both Holladay 1983: 52 and Collins 1986: 28 draw attention to the Greek influences on Demetrius).

Demetrius blends Hellenistic culture with strong attachment to the Torah. A similar concern is found in a writer such as Aristeas the Exegete, who both links the character of Job in the biblical book with the Jobab of Gen. 36.33 and transforms the theme of the biblical book into an edifying story of endurance for the sake of religion. There is also reference to another writer, Philo, who disagreed with Demetrius. Thus the tradition of close reading of the biblical text and investigation into the characters and the chronology of events, part of the basic educational curriculum in the study of Greek classics, was also being practiced on the Greek Bible by observant Jews. But for whom? Was it also part of an educational curriculum for young Jews?

A different set of questions concerning the Greek Bible is provided by Aristobulus. Writing in the middle of the second century BCE, Aristobulus interprets seeming anthropomorphisms in the Bible. He explains what the Bible means when it speaks of God having hands and feet, standing and speaking (frag. 2 *PE* 8.10.9-10; frag. 4 *PE* 13.13.3-4):

> Therefore the lawgiver has employed a metaphor well for the purpose of saying something elevated, when he says that the accomplishments of God are his hands. And the establishment of the cosmos might well be called divine 'standing' in accordance with the elevated (level of meaning).

> For it is necessary to take the divine 'voice' not as a spoken word, but as the establishment of things… And it seems to me that Pythagoras, Socrates, and Plato with great care follow him in all respects. They copy him when they say that they hear the voice of God, when they contemplate the arrangement of the universe, so carefully made and so unceasingly held together by God.

In this last sentence one sees how Aristobulus uses non-Jewish sources. They depend on Moses, they say the same thing as Jewish writers but the Jewish sages say it more clearly and better (*PE* 13.12.10) For Aristobulus, Jews are a philosophical school 'and the whole constitution of our Law is arranged with reference to piety and justice and temperance and the rest of the things that are truly good' (*PE* 13.13.8). The universal significance of Judaism is also shown in that both Passover and Sabbath have cosmic significance—at Passover the sun and moon stand diametrically opposed to one another, and the Sabbath observance agrees with the sevenfold structure inherent in the cosmos.

Aristobulus's work is thus apologetic, but it arises out of a grammatical reading of the text which prompts philosophical questions, much as the Greeks tried to find deep meanings in Homer (see Buffière 1956). Again, to what audience is this directed? Does it correspond to a more advanced reading of the text than that of Demetrius, much as the curriculum in Greek studies moved on to a deeper level of reading after basic grammatical and rhetorical studies?

Ezekiel the Tragedian

Writing towards the end of the third century BCE, Ezekiel composed a tragedy according to classical norms, and its language 'attests a full knowledge of tragic and particularly Euripidean usage' (Fraser 1972: I, 708). R.G. Robertson (1985: 805) arranged the fragments that remain into a pattern of five acts:

Act 1 Scene 1	Moses' monologue
Scene 2	Moses' dialogue with Zipporah
Act 2 Scene 1	Zipporah's dialogue with ?
Scene 2	Moses' dream, and Jethro's interpretation
Act 3 Scene 1	Moses' dialogue with God
Scene 2	Moses' instructions to the people
Act 4	Report of the Egyptian messenger
Act 5	Elim, and the report of the messengers to Moses.

Ezekiel introduces characters unknown in the Bible—Chus and the Egyptian messenger—but follows the biblical narrative closely. Through the technique of a dream report, Ezekiel emphasizes Moses' kingship and his prophetic ability. In the last scene, the description of the phoenix near Elim (Exod. 15.27, just before the return to Sinai in the biblical narrative) raises the question of the symbolism behind Ezekiel's text. Cerfaux (1954: I, 85-88) and Goodenough (1935: 288-91) hypothesized a mystery ritual, for which there is no evidence. Collins argued that the drama ended at Elim and was not extended to Sinai, and cautiously suggested that 'the symbolism of the phoenix opens the possibility that the Exodus may be understood allegorically as a journey, not to Canaan, but to eternal life, which is completed under the guidance of Moses' (Collins 1986: 210). However, in view of the central place which both Moses' vision of kingship and prophecy occupy and the fact that Moses symbolically takes the seat of God, as well as the sign of the burning bush at Sinai where God's word shines forth to Moses, the appearance of the kingly phoenix with its connotations of fire and replacement of father by son all suggest that the climactic event in Ezekiel's tragedy was the giving of the Law at Sinai.

Whatever the case, Ezekiel has blended Greek form and legend with biblical narrative. Like Robertson, I see no reason why it would not have been staged. But for whom?

This quick glimpse of some of the works written in Alexandria gives us a sense of a vital intellectual world, a world based on the study of the Bible in Greek. The authors noted range in date from the late third to the middle of the second centuries BCE. They should not be seen, however, as isolated individuals. Their work rests upon and pre-supposes a living Jewish community, a community that must also be versed in the Greek Bible. The scholarly discussion of the Jewish community in Alexandria has concentrated often on their legal and political status—how and in what way were the Jews related to the citizen body of Alexandria? What is the precise meaning of Josephus's statements that the Jews in Alexandria were a *politeuma* (see Kasher 1985)? What has often not been discussed is that for the Jews to remain a distinct body—as they did in Alexandria for over 400 years—each new generation must have been educated in the national traditions. The interpretation of difficult chronological and philosophical problems in the Greek Bible, the re-telling of the biblical narrative in dramatic form as well as the Greek translation of the Hebrew Scriptures as such—all these suggest that there was in place among the Jewish community in Alexandria some sort of educational system based on the Greek Bible. There would have been differences of opinion in this community about Greek culture. No doubt there would have been opposition to the allegorical interpretations of Aristobulus and Aristeas. Such differences only underscore, however, the importance of biblical education in the community and that this education was being carried on in Greek.

The Jerusalem Gymnasium

The third area I wish to discuss is the gymnasium built by Jason around 174 BCE. The statements about this found in 1 Macc. 1.15 and 2 Macc. 4.7-20 are notoriously polemical in character, but the gymnasium is always singled out as the classic case of Hellenization by a group of wildly Hellenized priests. Jason's initiative is explicitly contrasted with that of Ben Sira by John G. Gammie (1990: 372):

> In no way does Ben Sira's openness to foreign culture bring him to reject the Hebraic religion or values in unrestrained embracing of Hellenistic norms of beauty and art. Thus Ben Sira's social universe was not that of Jason who was to acquire the high priesthood within two decades after the demise of Ben Sira's beloved Simon. It might be argued, however, that Ben Sira's failure to speak out forcefully against idolatry, his openness to foreign travel, and obvious attraction to Hellenistic rhetorical models did little to shore up Israel's defenses against a more extreme Hellenization such as that advocated by Jason.

In contrast to Gammie, I would like to stress two factors:

1. The texts tell us nothing about what actually happened at the gymnasium and in the ephebate except that there was a *palaistra* (2 Macc. 4.14). All the rest is commentary, a reading into the text of one's own insights. A classic example is the quote from Hengel at the beginning of this paper: since we do not know what went on in 'other Palestinian and Phoenician cities', comparing Jerusalem to them is not very helpful. What I would suggest is that frequently those readings have been guided by the bias of the authors of 1 and 2 Maccabees who first framed the response, namely that Jason was an extreme Hellenizer, and that therefore the gymnasium and ephebate in Jerusalem would be exactly along the lines of gymnasia elsewhere. Hence Hengel's suggestion quoted earlier about the Greek classics.

2. One should emphasize that education at a gymnasium embraced many things. 'The ephebeion presents several aspects: it is a military school, a school of preparation for civic life, a philosophical and literary school, a school of physical training, a school of piety towards the gods and an institution of parade and of examination' (Pélékidis 1962: 197).[3]

For too long one has stressed a simple notion of 'Hellenization' as though this was some core curriculum that one could transfer from place to place without any differentiation. What R.E. Wycherley said *à propos* of the diversity of architectural plan for the gymnasia could equally well apply, I suggest, to what went on there: 'each gymnasium had its own peculiar structure and lay-out, determined by natural features, immemorial religious associations, and the needs and ideas of the local community it served' (Wycherley 1962: 201). It is increasingly recognized that each city and culture retained its own vitality and distinctiveness under Seleucid rule. In his conclusion to a discussion of the coins issued under Antiochus IV, Otto Mørkholm (1965: 67) argued that the local coin issues evidenced a 'proof of his [Antiochus IV] eagerness to infuse new vigour into city-life' (more recently presented by Habicht 1989: II, 346-50). Bickermann (1939) has clearly shown, for example, how Sidon maintained its own local institutions when Hellenized. The process which was called 'syncretism', whereby local gods were assimilated or changed into Greek divinities actually was the reverse: the Greek name was simply an easy way for

---

3. 'L'éphébie présente plusieurs aspects: elle est école militaire, école de préparation civique, école philosophique et litteraire, école de culture physique, école de piété envers les dieux, et institution d'apparat et de revue'.

Greeks to get a hold on what was going on, but the local cult retained its own unique qualities and substance. Education, like religion, was a civic affair. There clearly was room for local pride, as in Halicarnassus, where it was made sure that copies of the works of its two famous authors, Herodotus and the obscure C. Julius Longianus, were kept in the gymnasium library (Forbes 1945: 37). At Lamia the poetess Aristodama was given citizenship in gratitude for the epic poem she had composed and performed on the history of Lamia (*IG* 9.2.62)

Unfortunately we do not have the curriculum followed at different cities. Clearly Homer was taught in many (Marrou 1956: 164-65, 187). But what of a city which already had a long and unique literary and legal history? What would happen there to the curriculum taught to its noblest youths who were to be its leading citizens? Would it abandon its ancestral heritage? One small piece of evidence to suggest otherwise would seem to be the number of local histories written for specific cities. And the opposite happened at Rome in the second century as Stanley F. Bonner (1977: 1-37) has shown. Young Romans were taught their own language, laws and literature and, alongside those, given an entrée to Greek literature and rhetoric. In an important article, Jonathan Goldstein (1981) drew interesting comparisons between the Roman and Jewish position. Given the developing literary education curriculum among Jews in Alexandria as well as the attempts by Ben Sira to include Greek and other literature under the umbrella of education for young Jews and the work of Eupolemus, I would argue that a Roman rather than an Athenian model should be applied to Jerusalem. The literary education of wealthy young men would have remained an education in the language, laws and literature of Judea, their processions would be the festivals of the God of Jerusalem; alongside this, education in Greek language and rhetoric would have taken place. This would not preclude use of a Greek translation of the Hebrew Scriptures.

One would dearly love to know the curriculum of studies at other gymnasia in the Seleucid Empire. Fergus Millar (1987b: 151) has drawn attention to how little we know 'either of the content, or the possible modes of transmission of any non-Greek culture in this area'. Babylon might have been an interesting test case since inscriptions attest to continued writing in cuneiform in the first century CE (see Geller 1983), but the names on the inscription from 109–108 BCE all are Greek, and it may have been a gymnasium for local Greeks (Haussoullier 1909: 353):

Of the Ephebes

With the bow	Dikaios son of Diodorus
With the javelin	Artemidorus son of Andronicus
With the curved shield	Castorides son of Kephalon
With the oblong shield	Demetrius son of Athenogenos
In the long race	Aristides son of Artemidorus
In the sprint	Nicanor son of Hermolaos

Of the Neoi

With the bow	Dikaios son of Nikostratos
With the javelin	Herakleon son of Herakleon

What is fascinating about this list is not only its correspondence with lists from Athens, Samos, Tralles, and so on, but also, and for my purposes more significantly, the connection between the exercises for the ephebate and at the gymnasium with pre-military exercises.

Marcel Launey made a thorough collection of the evidence which connected the gymnasium with the army and argued that, even in the Hellenistic period, the gymnasium prepared the citizen for war: 'One is...struck by the considerable enough number of documents that prove with what attention was given before, during and after the ephebate, to the most technical training of the future warrior' (Launey 1950: II, 813-74 [816]).[4] Launey's suggestion was roundly refuted by Jean Delorme (1960: 471-74), for whom the military exercises performed in the gymnasium were simply outdated: 'emptied of all practical application...an archaeological relic' (472).[5] Delorme's most effective argument, and one echoed by Bezalel Bar-Kochva (1976: 94), is that in the Hellenistic period one is dealing with a mercenary army, not a citizen army.[6] One can also find specific instances, like the Theban generals Epameinondas and Philopoemen who both are said to have discouraged soldiers from taking part in gymnastic exercises; however, one could argue that they spoke against exercises not geared towards military training but rather moving towards the professionalization of athletics. There was always to be criticism of over-emphasis on athletics to the detriment of a rounded human ideal:

4.   'l'on est...frappé du nombre assez considérable de documents qui prouvent avec quelle attention était entreprise au gymnase, avant, pendant, et après l'éphébie, la formation la plus technique du futur combattant'.

5.   'vidés de toute portée pratique...un souvenir archéologique'.

6.   The formulation of this argument should be slightly reconsidered in light of the inscription discussed by Roesch 1971.

> Of the thousands of evils which exist in Greece there is no greater evil than
> the race of athletes. In the first place, they are incapable of living, or of
> learning to live, properly. How can a man who is a slave to his jaws and a
> servant to his belly acquire more wealth than his father?... What man has
> ever defended the city of his fathers by winning a crown for wrestling well
> or running fast or throwing a diskos far or planting an uppercut on the jaw
> of an opponent? Do men drive the enemy out of their fatherland by waging
> war with diskoi in their hands or by throwing punches through the line of
> shields? No one is so silly as to do this when he is standing before the steel
> of the enemy (Euripides, *Autolykos* 282).

Yet Plutarch will still insist that 'the race in armor is presented after all the
rest of the athletic events, so testifying that military fitness is the aim of
athletics and competition' (*Moralia* 639e). Here I would simply insist that
at the gymnasium young men were being trained how to use arms. Even in
the late second century, the Athenian ephebes guarded the Museum, and
went on maneuvers on the borders of Athenian territory (Delorme 1960:
472). This education in military drill seems the one constant among the
many gymnasia.

The most grievous lack one feels is the inability to give a thorough
history of the gymnasia in individual cities. The city for which we have
the most information, Athens, shows fascinating developments in response
to changes in the city's fortune. Pélékidis has argued that the small
numbers of ephebes from 307 to 166 BCE reflects a Macedonian desire to
keep Athens weak, while the resurgence of ephebic numbers after 166
attest to Rome's clear confidence in its own arms, and Athens' position as
a centre of Roman influence in Greece (Pélékidis 1962: 159-60, 185-86).
When discussing the gymnasium in Jerusalem, one must not impose some
external criteria on what was happening there, but must see the institution
as vitally connected to Jerusalem's individual culture and circumstances in
the early second century BCE.

One always has to be careful in arguing from silence, but one intriguing
aspect of the data assembled by Delorme on the number of gymnasia in
the Hellenistic period is the almost total lack of evidence for gymnasia in
Syria and Palestine in the second century BCE. Delorme's evidence shows
a great increase in the number of gymnasia in Asia Minor during this
period, but for Syria one has evidence, outside of Antioch of course, only
for Laodicea, Babylon and Jerusalem. Damascus, Ptolemais and Tripoli
only have gymnasia under Herod the Great. One can infer that there were
gymnasia in Sidon, Tyre and also Ptolemais in the second century BCE, but
one should further note that these are all Phoenician cities and geographical

expansion of 'Hellenization' appears limited to coastal areas. If the reason for a gymnasium was Hellenization, why do there not appear to have been more in the interior centers of the Seleucid Empire?

If one can put aside 'Hellenization' and 'assimilation' as sufficient grounds to explain the building of a gymnasium in Jerusalem in the early second century BCE, what other motives are left? For his own part, Jason needed political support to bolster his own position after ousting Onias III from the position of high priest. Controlling access to the gymnasium would provide Jason with a means of bestowing favors and thus of building his own political base (the political factors behind Jason's request are also recognized by Delorme [1960: 426, 478]). What of Antiochus IV? Is it sufficient to assert with Habicht (1989: 347) that Antiochus IV was 'unaware of what the consequences of his concession could be'? When he came to the throne in late 175, he needed to shore up his southern frontier against possible Ptolemaic attack in preparation since 176. There would be threats and aggression from the Ptolemies before Antiochus IV counter-attacked and invaded Egypt in 170–169. Jerusalem, a hill-city not far from that southern border, at the time of his accession was wracked with factional strife (2 Macc. 4.1-2) and its leader was absent from the scene. In what way could stability be restored to Jerusalem? A gymnasium may have seemed the perfect solution. Gymnasia were centers of devotion to the emperor (Delorme 1960: 342-46). The very name given to Jerusalem, Antiocheia, suggests a desire to show proper deference to Antiochus IV and Seleucid authority, and this would have carried over to prayers and sacrifices on his behalf. A gymnasium would also furnish a group of men trained in the use of arms who could provide support to the Seleucid garrison in case of siege or who themselves could defend the city and free the garrison for other duties. This is not to say with Launey that the ephe-bate was geared exclusively to provide recruits for the army, nor with Delorme that such training in arms was empty of all usefulness. Rather, it was a means of securing stability in a buffer state and making it into a center devoted to the Seleucid cause. Such an explanation of the building of the gymnasium says nothing about its curriculum in literature, and certainly does not require any change in ancestral religion, laws and constitution. It is the author of 2 Maccabees who has given it this spin. One does not therefore have to posit motives of Hellenization, that is, apostasy from Judaism or an enlightened reform of Judaism, to explain why a gymnasium was built in Jerusalem.

Conclusion

I have tried to link some of the literature written by Jews in the third to early second centuries BCE to an audience and to an educational curriculum. I have also tried to rethink what education meant, particularly education in a gymnasium, in this period, and therefore to suggest that we take a little more seriously how the biases of our principal sources for the Maccabean revolt, 1 and 2 Maccabees, have skewed our understanding of what took place in second-century Jerusalem.

Part III
THE HASMONEANS

THE EXPANSION OF HASMONEAN RULE IN IDUMEA AND GALILEE: TOWARD A HISTORICAL SOCIOLOGY

Richard A. Horsley

'Sociology of the Second Temple' must mean something very different when we move from the beginning of the Hasmonean regime to its climax under Alexander Jannaeus. The territory controlled by the Hasmoneans changed from a tiny area of a day's walk in any direction from Jerusalem to all of Palestine. Jerusalem went from an out-of-the-way town in the Judean hills to the capital of one of the largest kingdoms that arose in the decline of the Seleucid empire. The Hasmoneans Judas, Jonathan and Simon had been local leaders of bands of brigands and guerrillas, whereas John Hyrcanus and his sons conquered extensive territory and beat down domestic opposition with their professional armies. The populace went from the 100,000 to 200,000 Judeans ruled by their hereditary high priests to perhaps a million people of diverse ethnic-cultural backgrounds, many of whom were supposedly Judaized by order of priest-kings whose administration consisted of a number of Palestinian strongmen of various ethnic-cultural backgrounds. This is a historical transformation as dramatic as that in eastern North America between 1720 and 1820 or that in German-speaking territory between 1770 and 1870. To use the term 'Judaism' with reference to both social-religious phenomena in tiny Judea in the first half of the second century BCE and social-religious phenomena in wider areas of Palestine in the early first century BCE would only perpetuate hopelessly vague or even false knowledge. In order to appreciate the dramatic historical changes we must generate far greater precision in our conceptual apparatus, research and historical constructions.

We tend to approach the history of late Second Temple Palestine out of a certain naivety, somewhat oblivious to the hard realities of the structural tensions and outright conflicts that dominate our literary sources. Despite the volume of recent scholarship documenting the extreme diversity of late Second Temple Palestine, we continue to use the vague conceptual apparatus of earlier theologically based constructions. For example, we use the term 'Jews' in reference both to Ben Sira, the pious sage of pre-Hasmonean Jerusalem, and to the Galileans who followed Jesus of Nazareth barely 100 years after the Hasmonean takeover of Galilee. We assume that both the Jerusalem scribe and those Galilean peasants and fisher-folk were involved in something called 'Judaism' which was focused on the twin redemptive media of temple and Torah. And we refer to the events of 66–70 CE as 'the Jewish revolt' (or the great revolt) in the sense that a somewhat unified Jewish people rebelled against Roman rule, or at least that a widespread 'Zealot' (or 'politics of holiness') movement devoted to temple and Torah fought persistently for their faith.

But in what sense could Galileans at the time of Jesus be called Jews? Is there any evidence that those Galileans understood themselves as involved in 'Judaism' and/or were familiar with or loyal to temple and Torah? Or, with regard to events of 66–70, were the parallel insurrections by peasants in different regions of Palestine driven by loyalty to or protest against the Temple and high priesthood? Did the temple and high priesthood have *legitimacy* among the peasantry?

The application of sociological questions, methods and models to the history of late Second Temple Palestine is timely and should begin to make a difference in our historical constructions. The increasing diversity of literary and archaeological evidence generated by burgeoning recent studies can simply no longer be accommodated by the vague general received conceptual apparatus with which we have been working. Indeed, much of our literary and archaeological evidence becomes more intelligible only as we adjust our conceptual apparatus to the recognition of ancient social structural realities. Moreover, historical-sociological analysis can be pursued not simply to describe social structures for their own sake, but to elucidate the dynamics of the virtually continuous social conflicts that characterize Palestine in this period.

The extension of Hasmonean rule over Idumea and Galilee has been variously understood as a fanatical national-religious crusade, a (forced or voluntary) 'conversion' to 'Judaism', a military conquest or a reunion of peoples previously cut off with their longstanding cultic and cultural center in Jerusalem. Each of these constructions either projects an inappropriate concept onto political-economic-religious events in the second century BCE and/or provides only a partial explanation. A more adequate and comprehensive approach entails, among other things, recognition that social phenomena and relations we designate as 'religious' were inseparable from those we call 'ethnic' and 'political-economic' (including imperial and military!), that the Hasmonean high-priestly 'state' was different from the Judean people and other peoples they ruled, and that nearly all of our literary sources focus on relations between the ruling elites of ancient societies. The historical-sociological analysis below focuses on events of the late second century. Yet it has important implications for our continuing attempts to understand both the origins of early Christian movements and the emergence of rabbinic circles in Galilee and their relationship with the people of Galilee.

From the Oniads to the Hasmoneans: Continuity in Fundamental Structure, Change in Basis of Power

Judea on the Eve of the Reform

From the proverbial wisdom of Ben Sira we can discern that the fundamental political-economic-religious structure of the Judean society headed by the temple-state was similar to what the sociologist Lenski studied as traditional agrarian societies. The structure consisted basically of two classes, the rulers based in Jerusalem along with the scribal 'retainers' and artisans who were their staff and dependents, on the one hand, and the peasantry located in the surrounding villages, on the other. Because the 'state' and the ruling aristocracy were sacerdotal and the ordinary priests held higher social status than the common peasants, some of Lenski's (Lenski 1966) categories must be collapsed or adjusted (see the essay by Horsley and Tiller in this volume). As the paean of praise that Ben Sira hymns to the high priest Simon II illustrates, high-priestly rule of Judean society was elaborately grounded in the mystified epic traditions of the great office holders of Israel's hoary antiquity (see further Mack 1985).

The Judean temple-state, however, was also an integral part of the larger Seleucid (and previously Ptolemaic and Persian) imperial system, which shared most of the principal features of the political-economic structure of 'aristocratic empires', as delineated by John Kautsky (1982). As the machinations of Ptolemaic and Seleucid politics make clear, the concrete political-economic power of the high priesthood was dependent on the favor and fiscal desires of the imperial regime. Because of the latter, vertical divisions could and did emerge within the ruling Judean aristocracy as factions competing for imperial patronage and domestic power. Broadly speaking, it was when the dominant faction relied overly much on imperial favor and neglected the importance of the traditional sacred legitimation that the Judean temple-state system disintegrated.

The Rise and Consolidation of Hasmonean Rule

What was missing in the Judean temple-state system under imperial sponsorship was precisely what brought that system back into operation: a
Judean military force. The 'Maccabees' were apparently not so much
leaders of a holy war of resistance to religious persecution and of divinely
inspired 'national liberation', as the later Hasmonean propaganda would
have it, as local strongmen who exploited the situation of extreme
political-religious turmoil to expand their militarily based political power
in rural Judea (so, with appropriate sensitivity to the social-historical
situation, Schwartz 1993). It is increasingly clear that, once we cut through
the rhetoric and agenda of 1 Maccabees and 2 Maccabees, the leadership
of a revolt by Judas the Maccabee began in local raids and harassment by
insurgents based in the Gophna mountains and never commanded a widespread following throughout the Judean population. The central Seleucid
government had far more important matters demanding their attention.
Judas' first victories were merely guerrilla strikes against small forces led
by low-ranking Seleucid officers, the routing of Seron taking place at Beth
Horon, an optimal site for an ambush by local insurgents familiar with the
terrain, as the Roman army found out in the summer of 66 CE (1 Macc.
3.10-26). The withdrawal of the invasionary force led by Lysias in 165 (1
Macc. 4.28-35) was almost certainly due to attempts at negotiation (see the
letters cited in 2 Macc. 11.16-33). Other Judean groups, those described as
'Hasideans' (see Davies 1977) had long since become active, and were
pursuing negotiation and compromise with the Seleucid regime.
Apparently the Seleucid forces mounted no new invasion from the fall of
165 to the spring of 163. Judas and his band, however, took the occasion
of the interlude to seize at least partial control of Jerusalem and besieged
the Seleucid garrison in the Akra (1 Macc. 4.36-41). If we read between
the lines of 1 Macc. 4.42-58, the narrative does not claim either that Judas
and his brothers purified the temple or that the priests who did purify the
temple at that point were under the command of Judas. Apparently the
priests were somewhat independent and only allied with him in some way.

Ensuing events—the continuing struggles led by brothers Jonathan and
Simon—indicate that by no means had Judas led and won a 'war of national liberation'. But he had generated a sizeable and experienced fighting
force to be reckoned with, and set a precedent both of persistent opposition
to Seleucid rule and of unwillingness to compromise with rival groups of
Judeans, even those with whom he was ostensibly in alliance. When other
important groups settled for the high priesthood of Alcimus, despite the

reconciliation by the scribes of the 'Hasideans', Judas's forces persisted in their agitations until defeated (temporarily) by Seleucid forces.

After Alcimus died in 160 CE, Judas's brother Jonathan emerged in the ensuing power vacuum as leader of one of the rival forces seeking dominance/control in Judea (do the origins of the Qumran community lie in one of those rival groups which lost in the struggle for control of the temple government in Jerusalem?). Opportunities that Jonathan could exploit in his maneuvering for power presented themselves in the emergence of rival factions among the Seleucids, from 153 BCE onwards. By playing one rival ruler badly in need of allies off against another, Jonathan achieved Seleucid blessings on his army and finally recognition of himself as the new high priest and of his jurisdiction over three districts of Samaria just north of Judea (1 Macc. 9–10). There was still serious opposition to his rule within Judea, however, and the way in which he maintained power in Judea and by which he eventually lost his life—by maneuvering between rival Seleucid factions—reveals that his authority was that of a regent dependent on recognition by the/a Seleucid regime (1 Macc. 11–12).

The third brother, Simon, finally consolidated Hasmonean power in Jerusalem, apparently by making accommodations with some of his Judean opponents. The decree of the great assembly and stela erected in the temple in Simon's third year (1 Macc. 14.28-49) provide revealing indications of the bases of Simon's power and of the rival power blocks in Judean society with whom some accommodation must have been reached. Such an unprecedented 'great assembly' and grant of powers—well into his reign—would be unnecessary for a ruler already firmly and legitimately in control of the ruling institutions. His original and ultimate base of power was apparently the substantial military force which he and his brothers had built up over the previous decades. With the extensive wealth (t)he(y) had acquired, for instance from spoils (on Hasmonean economic consolidation see Applebaum 1989: 10-11, 15), he had even created a professional army (14.32). His initial recognition as 'ruler and high priest' by 'the people' was related to, and perhaps even the same as the army, for in 1 Maccabees the term 'people' seems almost coextensive with the ordinary people and/or those fighting with the Hasmoneans (and exclusive both of priests and of their opponents; 14.35 cf. 5.30; 7.6; 12.44; 13.2, 7; and note that 'people' is not differentiated from 'the soldiers' by 12.32, contrary to Sievers 1990: 125). The circumstances by which Simon obtained Seleucid recognition of his high-priestly authority indicates that he was now quite blatantly playing the Romans off against the Seleucids, on the one hand, but was still dependent on Seleucid approval on the other (14.38-40).

The 'great assembly' was necessary, however, to formalize compromises with other power blocks and rival leadership. That it was necessary to prohibit meetings without Simon or speaking against him indicates that there had been active opposition (14.41-45). Previous high-priestly office holders (the *archontes tou ethnous*), (different factions among) the ordinary priests, and prominent 'elders from the countryside', had to be appeased and neutralized (14.28). Some of the opposition, such as the priestly-scribal faction that withdrew to Qumran, was not so easily placated. That Simon was given authorization to make appointments of officials in charge of fortresses, armories and the countryside, as well as of the temple itself, indicates that he had not previously consolidated these powers in his regime.

The decree and stela cited in 1 Maccabees 14 also thus indicate that, despite the Maccabean revolt, the fundamental social structure of Judea remained much the same as it had been at the time of Ben Sira. 'The people' lived in larger or smaller villages scattered throughout 'the countryside', with certain more powerful men having prominence as 'elders'. But political-economic power was concentrated in Jerusalem, legitimated as a temple-state staffed by ordinary priests, but dominated by a priestly aristocracy (the *archontes tou ethnous*), with the whole headed by a high priest. Whereas the Zadokite high priesthood had the legitimacy of a lineage of hoary antiquity, however, the principal base of power for the nascent Hasmonean high priests was their own, increasingly professional army. From that base Simon could now consolidate his power by placing his own men in crucial administrative as well as military positions. This consolidation of powers in the hands of Simon amid the wider context of the decline of Seleucid power set the stage for the expansion of Hasmonean rule over the rest of Palestine in the next two generations.

From the Early to the Later Hasmoneans:
Continuity in Basis of Power, Dramatic Change in Scope

Scope and Structure of Hasmonean Rule in early First Century BCE
By the time Alexander Janneus completed his conquests, the territory under Hasmonean rule equalled or exceeded the scope of the Davidic-Solomonic Empire (*Ant.* 13.15.4 [395-97]). Hasmonean control in the conquered areas was consolidated under Alexandra Salome, who also enlarged the army despite the fact that no more expansionist wars were being conducted. Before I explore the dramatic extension of Hasmonean rule to most of Palestine, however, I should note that the fundamental structure of

political-economic relations did not change, nor did the basis of Hasmonean power, the Hasmonean military. To appreciate the structure and character of the relationship between Hasmonean rulers and subject populations I shall look briefly at two bits of evidence, that of the confirmation of Hasmonean rule once the regime became subject to Roman imperial control, and that of the extensive network of fortresses and garrisons by which the regime maintained its rule.

Josephus cites a series of decrees by which Julius Caesar had confirmed the power and prerogatives of the Hasmonean regime over its principal Judean and other subjects even after the conquered Hellenistic cities had been restored to their freedom (under Roman rule).[1]

> It is my wish that Hyrcanus, son of Alexander, and his children shall be Ethnarchs of the Judeans and shall hold the office of High Priests of the Judean for all time in accordance with their ancestral customs (*ta patria ethnē*); …and whatever high-priestly rights or other [pecuniary] privileges exist in accordance with their laws (*tous idious nomous*), these he and his children shall possess by my command… That his children shall rule over the Judean nation and enjoy the fruits of the places given them… That both Hyrcanus and his sons shall be High Priest and Priests of Jerusalem and of their nation with/by the same rights and laws/regulations (*epi dikaiois kai nomimois*) as those with/by which their forefathers uninterruptedly held the priesthood… These men shall receive and fortify the city of Jerusalem… That [the Judeans] in the second year shall pay the tribute at Sidon, consisting of one fourth of the produce sown, and in addition, they shall also pay tithes to Hyrcanus and his sons, just as they paid to their forefathers… For the city of Joppa, Hyrcanus and his sons shall pay tribute, collected from those who inhabit the territory… As for the villages in the Great Plain, which Hyrcanus and his forefathers before him possessed, it is the pleasure of the Senate that Hyrcanus and the Judeans shall retain them with the same rights (*epi tois dikaiois*) as they formerly had. Also the ancient rights (*dikaia*) which the Judeans and the high priests and the priests had in relation to each other should continue, and also the [pecuniary] privileges which they received by vote of the people and the Senate. As for the places, lands (*choras*), and farms, the fruits of which the kings of Syria and Phoenicia, as allies of the Romans, were permitted to enjoy by their gift, these the Senate decrees that the ethnarch Hyrcanus and the Judeans shall have (*Ant.* 14.10.3-6 [194-96, 199-200, 203, 205-209]).

The traditional 'rights and privileges' which the Romans here confirm to the Hasmonean regime are those of ruler over and taxation of the people under

---

1.   On these decrees, see Rajak 1984. Freyne (1980: 62) takes these Roman decrees as evidence that Galileans could claim the rights of Jews.

their jurisdiction. It is not necessary to determine whether 'the Judeans' in the phrases 'High Priest of the Judeans' and 'Judean nation' are ethnically or geographically precise or limited to a particular area/populace. The reference to the Great Plain makes clear that the Hasmonean dynasty is here being confirmed in control of its wider territory (excepting the Hellenistic cities). However vague the phrase 'Hyrcanus and the Judeans' (in *Ant.* 14.10.6 [207, 209]) may seem, it is clear from the rest of these decrees that the vast majority of 'Judeans' were politically-economically-religiously subject to the Hasmonean regime. Specially noteworthy for consideration of the relations between Hasmonean regime and Galileans below is the function of 'their own / traditional laws (or customs or regulations)' in this connection. That is, all of the three times the decrees refer to 'the laws' are understood as legitimating or regulating the 'rights and (economic) privileges' of the high-priestly rulers of the Judeans (*Ant.* 14.10.3, 4, 6 [194, 195, 199]).

It seems clear from information which Josephus provides almost in passing, but which is confirmed by numerous archaeological digs, that the means by which the Hasmoneans maintained their rule over the vastly expanded territories was the (increasingly mercenary) army. Josephus reports that Aristobulus II, unhappy that his brother Hyrcanus II was to succeed their mother in power, moved quickly to take control of the military fortresses. In 15 days, says Josephus, he had gained control of 22 fortresses (already commanded by his father's 'friends'). Since this did not include the major royal fortresses of Alexandrium, Hyrcania, Machaerus and the Jerusalem citadel, it suggests that the Hasmonean regime had upwards of 30 fortresses around the various districts that they used to control and administer the local areas as well as, along the frontiers, to protect against attack (see the evidence and analysis in Shatzman 1991: 44, 95-96). We should attend to evidence of fortresses again below insofar as they may be relevant to relations between the Hasmonean regime and Galilee.

Was Hasmonean Expansion a Religious Crusade or by 'Conversion to Judaism'?

In reconstructing the history of Second Temple Judea it is important precisely *not* to move too quickly and directly from literary text to historical context and precisely *not* to formulate a broad general picture of affairs on the basis of a synthesis of accounts from various sources (without taking adequately into account the ideology of those sources).

Previous constructions of Hasmonean history as a religious crusade by the Maccabean people's armies destroying idols in its territory and forcibly Judaizing neighboring peoples depends heavily on certain passages in 1 Maccabees as read through a conceptual apparatus developed by modern Christian biblical studies. The construct of 'Judaism' as a religion is something projected back into Second Temple times by modern Europeans. That this was an especially exclusive and 'national' religion in late second-century Palestine is a further extension of this modern conceptualization developed without attention to ancient social and political forms.[2] That 1 Maccabees has its own particular political-religious ideology is, of course, now clearly recognized, enabling us to avoid imposing that ideology uncritically onto the events of Hasmonean expansion.

With regard to the Idumeans to the south and the inhabitants of Galilee to the north, the expansion of Hasmonean rule is most commonly imagined as some sort of religious 'conversion' to 'Judaism'. Such a conceptualization would appear problematic simply on the surface of the matter. The concept 'conversion' usually implies a deep sense of change in one's religious conviction by an individual,[3] not the shift in political-religious (even ethnic) status of a whole people. And 'Judaism', as just noted, is used to refer to a religion, whereas no religion separable from the political-economic-ethnic forms of communal life had yet been differentiated in Second Temple Judea.

More substantively, moreover, recent presentations of Hasmonean expansion in terms of 'conversion' to 'Judaism', whether 'forcible' or 'voluntary', are based on a broadly synthetic reading of the sources. The intricate arguments for a gradual and 'voluntary conversion' offered recently by Kasher (1988: ch. 3) are problematic and unconvincing (see the critique in Shatzman 1991: 58-59 n. 90). While accepting some of Kasher's arguments for Galilee, Grabbe has recently argued with regard

---

2.   How this peculiar modern concept of 'Judaism' as a religion determines the construction of the history of Hasmonean expansion and other ancient Judean history can be seen clearly in Hengel (1974: esp. 305-307).

3.   As in the classic study of ancient Mediterranean materials (Nock 1933), who defined conversion as 'the reorientation of the soul of an individual, his deliberate turning from indifference or from an earlier form of piety to another, a turning which implies a consciousness that a great change is involved, that the old was wrong and the new is right' (p. 7). A quick check of the entries on 'conversion' in standard dictionaries and encyclopedias (whether in biblical studies and religion or general) will further indicate how problematic the concept is for Second Temple history.

to the Idumeans that however problematic the hypothesis of forced conversion, it is plausible in this case (Grabbe 1992: II, 329; similarly Sievers 1990: 143). Grabbe comments:

> [T]he effects of the conversion...lasted. Forced conversion does not usually represent a change of mind, and, if possible, those compelled carry on their original religion covertly and revert to it openly as soon as they can. This did not happen with the Idumeans. Although we know of the occasional individual who intended to return to the ancestral religion (e.g., Costobarus [*Ant.* 15.7.9 §§253-55]), the Idumeans as a whole supported the Jews in their later wars with the Romans. For example, in the 'war of Varus' (ca. 4 B.C.E.) Idumea revolted along with Jerusalem (*War* 2.5.2-3 §§72-79). Attested in even greater detail is the participation of several thousand Idumeans in the defense of Jerusalem during the 66–70 war.[4]

As long as we are working with the broad general categories 'Judaism' and 'Jews' and 'Idumeans' (reading references to whatever groups or incidents in highly synthetic fashion as implying 'Jews' or 'Judaism' generally) such conclusions may seem warranted. Once we ask questions of political-economic structure and historical dynamics, however, such a synthetic picture begins to disintegrate. With these more precise questions in mind, a closer look at Josephus's reports of incidents involving Idumeans reveals a very different situation.

To claim that 'Idumea revolted along with Jerusalem' after the death of Herod is to go far beyond what Josephus's reports suggest. First of all, the widespread insurrections in 4 BCE were not centered in or led from Jerusalem. The protest of the Jerusalemites to Varus, according to Josephus's accounts (*War* 2.5.2 [73]; *Ant.* 17.10.9 [293]), that they had not been involved in the revolt, has some credibility, for Josephus makes clear here as well as earlier in his accounts that those besieging the Romans in Jerusalem were from the countryside. The insurrections put down by Varus were themselves based in the countryside in Galilee and Perea as well as Judea itself, even though the former two had attacked

---

4.   Kasher (1988: 63, 65) makes even more of Josephus's accounts of Idumeans' actions in the great revolt: 'The sincerity of the Idumeans' conversion and their considerable integration into Jewish life may also indirectly be seen by their activist stand during the Great Revolt against the Romans. They proved themselves faithful sons to the Jewish nation and fought with uncompromising devotion, a fact which may serve to show the depth of their national and religious integration... This demonstrates once more the degree of their integration into Jewish society and the fervor of their Jewish nationalism...'

royal armories to obtain weapons and supplies (*War* 2.3.1-2 [56-65]; *Ant.* 17.10.1-2 [271-84]). Josephus also mentions 2000 veterans of Herod in Idumea (*War*. 2.4.1 [55]; had they been settled there?) assembled in Judea fighting against Herod's troops under Achiab, a cousin of Herod (*Ant.* 17.10.4 [270]). Then, after Varus had suppressed the insurrections in Galilee, Perea and Judea, 10,000 more rebels surrendered to Varus on the advice of Achiab. Josephus calls the latter *ioudaioi* in one report (*Ant.* 17.10.10 [297]) and locates them in Idumea in the other (*War* 2.5.3 [76]). Perhaps these last hold-outs were fugitives from Varus's suppression of widespread insurrection in the Judean countryside. If they were Idumeans, they were acting parallel to the peasantry in the other districts of Herod's realm, not revolting 'along with Jerusalem'.

Moreover, whether or not those 10,000 were Idumeans involved in outright rebellion, the motives of the rebels from the various districts of Palestine may be indicated in Josephus's reports of the massive demonstration in Jerusalem at Pentecost. Panicking at the insistent demands by the crowds at Passover, Archelaus had already turned his troops loose against the demonstrators in the Temple courtyard, who had included many peasants from the countryside. Further angered by the high-handed actions and harassment of Caesar's *epitropos* of Syria sent in to handle Herod's estate, huge crowds gathered in Jerusalem at Pentecost (late May), predominantly from Judea, but also from Galilee, Idumea and Perea. In both accounts Josephus states explicitly that they came more out of indignation at the actions of Sabinus and the Roman troops than for the customary ritual (*War* 2.3.1 [39-44]; *Ant.* 17.10.2 [250-55]). Thus according to our principal source for such events, the insurrections in 4 BCE were popular outbursts of long pent-up resentment of Herodian tyranny touched off by Archelaus's and Sabinus's repressive measures. There is nothing in Josephus's accounts to suggest that these rebellions were somehow motivated by 'Judaism', much less that Idumeans protesting at Pentecost were making common cause with 'Jerusalem'.

The second argument offered for the solid conversion of the Idumeans to 'Judaism' is the participation of several thousand in the defense of Jerusalem in 69–70. The great revolt of 66–70, however, cannot be understood simply as a two-sided conflict between 'the Jews' and the Romans. Josephus's accounts make it clear repeatedly that the revolt was also a civil war, indeed a class conflict between the priestly aristocracy and Herodian nobility, on the one side, and the ordinary people, on the other. Moreover, the principal fighting forces who continued resistance to the Roman siege of Jerusalem had originated from among the peasantry in different districts of Palestine, and battled among themselves even during the siege. The Idumeans, furthermore, appear as distinctive among those rival groups, with their own indigenous social structure, apparently a traditional tribal structure headed by chieftains (Josephus's *archontes*; *War* 4.4.1, 9.5 [228-35, 517-20]). We cannot take the speeches by Jesus the chief priest and Simon the Idumean chieftain as good evidence for the Idumeans' views of Jerusalem and the temple since they are written from the point of view of the wealthy and powerful Judean priest, Josephus—the very historian who claimed that from the time of Hyrcanus the Idumeans had continued to be Judeans.[5] According to Josephus's accounts, finally, the Idumeans were invited into Jerusalem by 'the Zealots' (a coalition of peasants fleeing the Roman reconquest in north-west Judea) to aid them in their struggle against the priestly aristocracy. Tiring of the purge of the nobility, most of the Idumeans withdrew from the city, some remaining with the party of John of Gischala. Later, after Simon bar Giora took control of Idumea by treachery, against the resistance by the tribal militia, some Idumeans joined his army. But when they attempted to surrender to the Romans, Simon bar Giora thwarted their plan (*War* 4.4.1-6.1 [228-35, 326-33, 345-53], 4.9.3-8, 10-11 [517-26, 566-72]). It would be difficult to claim that the Idumeans were fighting faithfully for the temple and Torah of 'Judaism' in the events of 68–70, or that the spasmodic involvement of some contingents of Idumeans is evidence of the permanent conversion of Idumeans generally to Judaism.

Not only are Josephus's reports of events in 4 BCE and 68–70 CE not susceptible of interpretation in terms of religious conversion, but he also provides evidence that some Idumeans were not effectively 'converted' at all. The case of Costobar provides evidence that indigenous Idumean traditions were still being cultivated and Judean traditions resisted nearly a century after Hyrcanus supposedly effectively converted the Idumeans to 'Judaism'. Grabbe dismisses Costobar as an 'occasional individual who intended to return to the ancestral religion', and Kasher, while recognizing this evidence that conversion had not been imposed on all the Idumeans collectively, claims 'there is reason to believe this was just a small group...

---

5. For some reason, Stern (1974: I, 356) fails to consider that the very text he cites as evidence that 'at the end of the period of the Second Temple the Idumeans felt themselves to be Jews in every respect', *War* 4.4.4 [270-75] is a speech written in good Hellenistic historiographic fashion by Josephus himself and hardly a valid source for Idumeans' own feelings.

and something of an exception', but offers none (Grabbe 1992: II, 329; Kasher 1988: 62-63). Costobar, however, was not simply 'an occasional individual'. He was a scion from one of the most distinguished among the Idumean noble/aristocratic families, whose ancestors had been priests of the Idumean god Koze, and he possessed his own ancestral estates in Idumea (*Ant.* 15. 7.9-10 [253, 264]). His family was thus parallel to another high ranking and most powerful Idumean family, that of Antipater, Herod's father. Thus it may not be surprising to find that Costobar had cast his lot with Herod in the struggle for the domination of Palestine and that Herod rewarded him for his loyalty by appointing him governor of Idumea and Gaza and by giving Costobar his sister Salome in marriage. According to Josephus's report, Costobar, from one of the most powerful families in Idumea and descendant of the priests of the Idumean god, did not think it right that the Idumeans should be adopting the customs of the Judeans or be ruled by them. But this was nearly a century after Hyrcanus had supposedly successfully insisted that the Idumeans observe 'the law of the Judeans'. Moreover, Costobar was dismissed and eliminated by Herod not for failing to enforce the laws and customs of the Judeans in Idumea, but for his questionable loyalty to Herod in having protected the sons of Baba, prominent figures of great popularity in Jerusalem who had been supporters of Antigonus, Herod's last remaining Hasmonean rival. Clearly Palestinian politics were a matter of shifting coalitions and loyalties among prominent Judean and Idumean families and their power and influence (see further *Ant.* 14.1.3-4 [8-10]; *contra* Kasher 1988, such links between powerful Idumean families do not suggest integration into *Jewish* society). Observance of the laws of the Judeans was of secondary importance at most. With regard to how complete the 'conversion' of the Idumeans was, if a prominent figure such as Costobar, already assimilated into the world of Hellenistic power politics, was still surreptitiously loyal to Idumean traditions, can it not be surmised that Idumean villagers were equally or even more so?

The available historiographical evidence of relations between Judea and the Idumeans is thus not susceptible of interpretation in terms of conversion. Indeed, the very concept of conversion (to a religion or way of life) seems inapplicable to a situation in which the religious dimension was inseparable from the political and economic dimensions of life.

In a series of recent studies, Shaye Cohen has been struggling with similar difficulties in the use of the concept 'conversion' in relation to the different meanings and nuances of the term *ioudaios/oi* and *ethnos*, among others. His observations may be helpful in clarifying the issues. In consideration of material primarily from Diaspora situations he argues that 'conversion to Judaism' (as distinct from some more partial demonstration or respect for Judaism) involved three components: 'practice of the Jewish laws; exclusive devotion to the god of the Jews; and integration into the Jewish community' (Cohen 1989: 26). As should be clear from the preceding discussion of Josephus's accounts of the relations between the Idumeans and the Judeans, however, the Idumeans apparently did not meet any of the three criteria: although they supposedly agreed to live according to the laws of the Judeans, at least some, as illustrated by the family of Costobar, resisted for generations; again, as illustrated by the prominent priestly family of Costobar, at least some Idumeans continued to worship their own traditional god(s); and they were clearly not integrated into the Jewish community, having remained a separate *ethnos* with its traditional social structure. Thus the Idumeans did not become ethnic *Ioudaioi*, but retained their own ethnic identity. In the case of the Idumeans (and surely of the inhabitants of Galilee as well) the question of the degree of change of religion or way of life is inseparably bound up with the way in which they became subject to a state that operated according to the traditional 'laws of the Judeans'. It is necessary to re-examine the evidence and re-reconstruct the history.

Hasmonean Expansion in the Vacuum of Imperial Power

While the most dramatic expansion of Hasmonean rule over most of Palestine happened under John Hyrcanus and his sons, Hasmonean expansion into districts bordering the tiny area governed by the temple-state prior to the Maccabean revolt had begun under Jonathan and Simon. The Seleucid ruler Demetrius had transferred the three districts just north of Judea, Aphairema, Lydda and Rathamin, from Samarian jurisdiction to Jerusalem high-priestly rule (1 Macc. 10.30, 38; 11.34). To the west toward the Sea, Simon had taken and fortified Joppa and Gazara, and settled Judeans there (1 Macc. 13.43-48; 14.3-7, 34).

Extensive expansion began under John Hyrcanus, but not until after one last effort by the declining Seleucids to resubject Judea to its control. During the lengthy siege, Hyrcanus ejected from Jerusalem all but the able-bodied defenders, which could not have endeared him to ordinary Jerusalemites and the Judean populace at large. Hyrcanus also plundered David's tomb of 3000 talents, using 300 to buy off Antiochus VII Sidetes, and the remainder to hire mercenaries, which Josephus claims was unprecedented (*War* 1.2.5 [61]; *Ant.* 13.8.4 [249]; at least since the Jewish Persian governors such as Nehemiah! Cf. Neh. 2.9). Josephus also reports that Hyrcanus amassed great wealth by his exploitation of Judea, thus providing a secure economic basis for the expansion of his rule into new territory (*Ant*. 13.10.1 [273]; see further Applebaum 1989: 18-22).

While Josephus places Hyrcanus's destruction of Shechem and the temple on Mt Gerizim early in his reign, the excavators of the site date the destruction of Shechem after 112 (Wright 1964: 172; Bull and Wright 1965). This date would be much closer to the subsequent year-long siege and destruction of Samaria toward the end of his reign. Judging from the severity of the devastation in both cases (according to Josephus's accounts, *War* 1.2.7 [65]; *Ant*. 13.10.2-3 [281]), Hyrcanus was apparently eliminat-
ing any possibility that a rival center of political-religious power could re-emerge in Samaria or Gerizim. It is even credible that Hyrcanus had the inhabitants of Samaria enslaved, for there is no reference to *protoi* of the Samaritans active in political affairs until well after the city was restored following the Roman takeover in Palestine (*War* 1.7.7 [166, 213, 229, 302-303]; *Ant*. 18.4.1 [88-89]; 20.6.1-3 [118-36]). With the destruction of both temple and capital city, Hyrcanus apparently intended to rule the whole district up to Scythopolis and Mt Carmel directly from Jerusalem. The effects of this conquest, however, was finally to create an irreconcil-able alienation between Judeans and Samaritans that erupts occasionally into the historical record in incidents such as the Samaritans' strewing bones in the temple courtyard and armed attacks which eventually impli-cated even the respective aristocracies under Cumanus in mid-first century CE (*Ant*. 18.4.1-2 [30]; 20.6. 1-3 [118-36]). That popular traditions con-tinued among the people in Samaria is dramatically evident in the move-ment led by the prophet who promised his followers he would find the sacred vessels Moses had deposited on Mt Gerizim (*Ant*. 18.4.1 [85-87]).

The Hasmonean expansion that has been inappropriately dealt with in terms of conversion was over the Idumeans and Galileans. Because of their implications for subsequent developments, including the ministry of Jesus, the great revolt, and the emergence of rabbinic leadership in Galilee, these cases require closer scrutiny and analysis.

Relations between the Hasmoneans and the Idumeans

The Idumeans appear still to have retained a traditional tribal structure into the second century BCE (see Rappaport 1967: 222). Significantly, in con-trast to the temple-state of Judea, no central capital city ruled over the whole area. Rather, regional towns, principally Hebron, Adora and Marisa, held prominence in relations to the surrounding villages, with a certain degree of Hellenistic influence evident in Marisa. It is interesting to speculate that Idumean villagers may have developed 'an identity of interest' with their Judean counterparts as 'oppressed native village populations' (Kasher 1988: 27, 46-47) but we have little or no evidence to that effect.

The accounts of Judas's attacks into Idumean in 1 Maccabees 5 and 2 Maccabees 10 and 12 should be evaluated critically and in close comparison.[6] The accounts of raids into Idumea in 1 Macc. 5.3, 65-67 do not fit the stated agenda of the series of attacks led by Judas and Simon to rescue kindred/'Israelites' (Judeans) under attack by hostile neighboring nations (5.1-2, 9-17). The accounts in 2 Maccabees 10–12, which have Seleucid officials rather than the neighboring nations as the principal instigators of the conflicts, stand in a parallel sequence of several expeditions into neighboring lands, suggesting that a common source lies behind 1 Maccabees 5 and 2 Maccabees 10–12. That 2 Macc. 10.15, in the account where the principal agenda is not such harassment by the Gentiles, mentions Idumeans 'besieging' Judeans makes such harassment credible. Judas's attack against the strongholds of Idumea was not a rescue mission of fellow Jews under attack, however, but a punitive strike against the neighbors to the south who were also apparently harboring Judean opponents of Judas (refugees from Jerusalem?). 1 Maccabees 5.65-67 and 2 Macc. 12.32-38 must then refer to a second attack into Idumea. Both accounts save Judas from any responsibility for what must have been a serious defeat, but they do so differently. 1 Maccabees has Judas conveniently absent on the expedition into Gilead, returning to retaliate against the Idumeans, while 2 Maccabees blames the defeat on idolatry (12.39-45). However serious the damage done behind the account in 1 Macc. 5.65-66, these were not conquests but punitive or preemptive strikes at Hebron and Marisa, although it is conceivable that Hebron and its villages were from this point periodically under effective Hasmonean domination. In any case, the initial relations between the Hasmoneans and the Idumeans involved sharp hostilities, apparently from both sides.

Josephus has three brief accounts of John Hyrcanus's treatment of the Idumeans.

---

6.   Kasher (1988: 25-33), after seemingly subjecting 1 Macc. 5 to critical analysis, but without comparisons with 2 Macc. 10–12, then trusts the narrative as basically historical record. Sievers (1990: 49-57) charts the parallel accounts that must depend on a common source, and notes some of the factors that account for the differences. Schwartz (1991) provides the most critical assessment of the ideology and rhetoric of 1 Maccabees.

He further took numerous cities in Idumea, including Adoreon and Marisa (*War* 1.2.6 [63])

Hyrcanus also captured the Idumean cities of Adora and Marisa, and after subduing all the Idumeans, permitted them to remain in their country so long as they had themselves circumcised and were willing to observe the laws of the Judeans. And so, out of attachment to the land of their fathers, they submitted to circumcision and to making their manner of life conform in all other respects to that of the Judeans. And from that time on they have continued to be Judeans (*Ant.* 13.9.1 [257-58]).

Now Hyrcanus had altered their constitution/form of government (*politeia*) and made them adopt the customs and the laws of the Judeans (*Ant.* 15.7.9 [254]).

To these should be compared two other references to the Idumeans:

Judeans and Idumeans differ, as Ptolemy states in the first book of the History of King Herod. For Judeans are those who are so naturally from origin, whereas the Idumeans...were not Judeans by origin, but Phoenicians and Syrians, having been subjugated by the Judeans and having been forced to undergo circumcision, so as to be counted among the nation [or, to contribute to the nation, *syntelein eis to ethnos*] and keep the same customs/laws (*nomima*), they were called Judeans (Ptolemy the Historian in Stern 1974–84: I, 146; trans. adapted).

As for Judea, its western extremities...are occupied by the Idumeans and by the lake. The Idumeans are Nabateans, but owing to a sedition they were banished from there, joined the Judeans and shared in the same customs/laws (*nomima*) with them (Strabo, *Geogr.* 16.2.34 [Stern 1974–84: I, 115]).

Those who argue for 'voluntary conversion' of the Idumeans to 'Judaism' rely on the second sentence cited from the Strabo passage over against all the other texts. To do so they must take it out of literary context, for the latter testifies to the extremely mixed background of the peoples of 'Judea'. But there are two other major problems for their preferred reading of this sentence. Strabo has the first part wrong—the Idumeans were not Nabateans banished due to a sedition, but were descendants of the Edomites displaced (north-westward into what had been southern Judah) by the invading Nabateans (Arabs)—giving us reason to doubt the reliability of the second part. Moreover, the second part is vague, not specifying precisely how they came to 'join' the Judeans. Insofar as the citation from 'Ptolemy' is said explicitly to come from a history of Herod, it indicates observers still aware of the striking difference between the Idumeans and the Judeans over a century after the supposed 'Judaization' of the former, according to Josephus.

Both of Josephus's principal accounts about John Hyrcanus's treatment of the Idumeans come in the midst of his summary reports of Hyrcanus's expansionist military expeditions against Shechem and Gerizim to the north, cities and their territories across the Jordan to the east, and eventually the city of Samaria. There seems no reason to doubt that military action was involved as John Hyrcanus took control of Idumea. Hyrcanus's actions, moreover, followed upon the earlier strikes against Hebron and Marisa by Judas. It is worth noting the marked increase in the numbers of Idumeans mentioned in Egyptian papyri in the late second century BCE, possibly a reference to refugees (Rappaport 1969). That the Idumeans were subjugated by Hyrcanus is independently suggested by the book of *Jubilees*, especially chs. 36–38.6.[7] On the other hand, the relatively gentle treatment of the Idumeans stands in stark contrast with the utter destruction of Samaria by Hyrcanus and his sons. It may be surmised that the reason for the punitive destructive measures against Samaria was to eliminate the principal historical rival of Jerusalem for power and influence in Palestine. Since no corresponding center of power had emerged in Idumea, there was no need of such extreme measures.

That the Idumeans remained in their territory, were circumcised or observant of the laws of the Judeans, is not susceptible of reduction to a religious dimension. It is abundantly clear from a story Josephus tells about the tense situation in Galilee in 66–67 CE that circumcision held broad social-political significance, and was not simply a religious and/or ethnic matter. Indeed the political and religious dimensions were inseparable (see *Life* 112–13, 149–54). It is likely that the Idumeans (and the Galileans and/or Itureans to be discussed below) already practiced circumcision (see Kasher 1988: 56 n. 35; Tcherikover, Fuks and Stern 1957–64: I, 4; Stern 1974–84: I, 2-4; II, 620-25). Understanding circumcision simply as a cultural/religious practice leads to the hypothesis that Hyrcanus was demanding circumcision primarily of Hellenized Idumeans, primarily in the 'city' of Marisa, who had not previously undergone circumcision. If, on the other hand, we recognize that circumcision was likely an important symbol of membership in a religious-political group or community, then the point of having the already circumcised Idumeans submit to circumcision (again, by the Judeans) was likely as symbol of their incorporation

---

7. That *Jubilees* pertains to the subjugation of the Idumeans in the 120s by Hyrcanus rather than to Judas the Maccabees's attacks in the 160s has been persuasively argued by Mendels (1987: 75-88).

into the social-political community (i.e. the social-political 'covenant')[8] based in the Jerusalem temple and ruled by/subject to the Hasmonean high priesthood.

Moreover, Josephus uses 'the laws (or customs) of the Judeans' in a comprehensive sense, traditional regulations of all aspects of social life, political-economic-religious-familial. If the account in *Ant.* 15.7.9 [254] were our only source available, we would conclude simply that Hyrcanus had forced a change of polity on the Idumeans. This is a pattern familiar from some ancient empire building. The Persian imperial regime had encouraged the revival of local laws among its subject peoples. But other ancient kingships imposed their own polity or laws on subjected peoples. This appears to be what Hyrcanus did with the Idumeans. Whatever else it may have meant for the Idumeans, observing 'the laws of the Judeans' would have included the political-economic-religious relations of subordination to the Hasmonean high priesthood in Jerusalem, as indicated in the language of Caesar's decrees cited above.

If we have eyes to see, Josephus offers us glimpses of how the Hasmonean regime, and later the Herodian as well, actually governed the Idumeans. Herod's father Antipater was not the first powerful Idumean figure to become prominent in the Hasmonean regime. Alexander Jannaeus appointed his father Antipas as *strategos* of all Idumea, including Gaza; and we know from comments about Antipater elsewhere that these men were not only 'Idumean by birth (*genos*)', but 'in the front rank of the people (*ethnos*) by ancestry, wealth, and other advantages' (*Ant.* 14.1.3 [10]; *War* 1.8.9 [123]). Two generations later, once (the Idumean) Herod had become the Romans' client king, he in turn appointed Costobar, scion of another powerful, aristocratic Idumean (priestly!) family, as the governor of Idumea. That is, the Hasmonean rulers in Jerusalem made political alliances with powerful Idumean families, through which the district was then controlled. Insofar as Idumean society still maintained a certain patriarchal tribal structure, the rest of the society could be expected to follow the lead, or be subject to the power, of the most prominent families. As mentioned above, one receives the impression of a tribal structure still somewhat intact in Josephus's reports about the Idumeans in 68–69 CE. Josephus characterizes them as 'a turbulent and disorderly people (*ethnos*)'

---

8.   Note that *Barn.* 9.6, precisely in a context of pointing out that other non-Judeans were also circumcised, refers to circumcision as the symbol of being part of the covenant/community/polity.

whose multiple 'chieftains' (*archontes*; Thackeray's translation is appropriate) can muster a popular militia 'hastily from the countryside (*chora*)', whether to respond to the call of Judean fellow peasants for help against the dominant aristocracy in Jerusalem or to defend their own territory against the ambitious popular Judean king-on-the-rise, Simon bar Giora (*War* 4.9.4 [230-33]). It is surely significant that throughout his treatment of Idumeans, whether of leading figures from prominent families or of the ordinary folk, Josephus refers to them as a people (*ethnos*) distinct from the Judeans (e.g. *War* 1.6.2 [123]). In the latter account, all the Judean peasants-turned-Zealots have to do to solicit an army of Idumeans is to appeal to their chieftains!

Relations between the Hasmoneans and the Galileans

Since both the 'Jesus movement' and Gospel tradition behind emergent Christianity and the emergence and consolidation of the rabbinic movement took place in Galilee, the watershed constituted by the Hasmonean takeover of the area is of great importance for subsequent history. Most scholarship in recent generations has simply assumed that Galilee in the first century CE was Jewish even though their 'Judaism' was not as rigorous as the Pharisees and early rabbis would have liked. When one probes for evidence, however, there turn out to be precious few indicators. It would appear that many of our assumptions about the Galilee of the Jesus movement and early rabbis are rooted in the theologically influenced conceptual apparatus with which we are accustomed to dealing with the rise of 'Christianity' out of 'Judaism'. But that is precisely what has been thrown into question by recent recognition both that religion is inseparable from political-economic life in traditional societies such as those in ancient Palestine and that there was a considerable diversity of social-religious phenomena in ancient Palestine. How the importance of the Hasmonean takeover of Galilee is understood and estimated depends heavily, first, on who the inhabitants of Galilee were at the time and, second, on what the structure and dynamics of Hasmonean rule in Galilee were.

The Inhabitants of Galilee Prior to Hasmonean Takeover

There are three different views on who were the inhabitants of Galilee prior to the expansion of Hasmonean rule to the area. One is that they were Gentile, either since the Assyrian conquest and deportation of Israelites or by gradual shifts in population over the centuries of Assyrian, Persian and

Hellenistic rule, or at least since the Itureans controlled the area just prior to the Hasmonean takeover. The hypothesis that the inhabitants were (forcibly) converted to Judaism often accompanies this first view, so that Galilee then became 'Jewish' in late Second Temple times (a view popularized by E. Schürer's influential work). The alternative longstanding view is that Galilee had become heavily if not predominantly Jewish over the centuries prior to the Hasmonean 'annexation'. With this view goes the hypothesis that those 'Judaized' by the Hasmoneans were only the Itureans or other non-Jewish inhabitants at the time (the view now adopted in Kasher 1988; Grabbe 1992).

These longstanding alternative views have been based on the same texts, albeit in different readings based on different presuppositions. For example, the report of Simon's expedition to Galilee to rescue several thousand Jews (1 Macc. 5.21-23) is read by some to mean that Galilee was already Jewish, but read by others to indicate that there were only a few Jews in Galilee, concentrated in the west toward Ptolemais and Arbatta. The key passage in Josephus, where he is dependent on Timagenes as quoted by Strabo, is *Ant.* 13.11.3 [318-19]:

> [Aristobulus] made war on the Itureans and acquired a good part of their territory (*chora*) for Judea and compelled the inhabitants (*tous enoikountas*), if they wished to remain in the country, to be circumcised and to live in accordance with the laws of the Judeans (*tous ioudaion nomous*)... (Strabo, quoting Timagenes) 'he acquired additional territory for [the Judeans] and brought over to them a portion of the nation of Itureans whom he joined to them by a bond of circumcision'.

If one either trusts the Timagenes statement or does not differentiate between the Itureans and the inhabitants of the country, then it appears that the Itureans themselves were being Judaized. Those who believe that Galilee was already heavily Jewish then read this passage as referring basically to Upper Galilee, since the Itureans were then apparently based in Lebanon just to the north. If one considers that Josephus is intentionally differentiating between the Itureans and the inhabitants of the country, then the inhabitants here being Judaized must have been other Gentiles of some sort. Since this is the key text for the Hasmonean expansion into Galilee, I must return to it below.

In yet a third view of the inhabitants of Galilee, Freyne has claimed recently that Galilee had, in effect, always been Jewish since earliest times, that in the centuries prior to the Hasmoneans Galilee's 'religious and ethnic loyalties [had] transcend[ed] administrative and political boundaries', and that it was eagerly awaiting the opportune moment to be reunited with Jerusalem which had always been its 'cultural and cultic center' or matrix (Freyne 1980: 26, 38). On this view, the Hasmonean takeover was relatively insignificant, merely providing that 'opportune moment' for Galileans to become reunited with Jerusalem. (But see the qualification in Freyne [1992: 898]: 'Galilee was unmistakably Jewish, at least by the time of Pompey's intervention…')

However, in the earlier history of Israel, the Israelite tribes in Galilee were Naphtali, Issachar and Zebulun; the tribes of Judah and Benjamin, which later formed the kingdom of Judah, being in the southernmost area. After David set up his capital over all Israel in the non-Israelite (Jebusite) stronghold of Jerusalem, the Israelite tribes rebelled twice against Davidic rule from Jerusalem (2 Sam. 15–19; 20). After being resubjugated by David's professional army and acquiescing in Solomon's rule and forced labor needed to build the Temple, the ten northern Israelite tribes rebelled again, successfully, against the Davidic monarchy in Jerusalem. Thereafter for 200 years under their own kings, then for several hundred more years under foreign empires, the northern Israelite tribes and/or their ancestors, lived under quite separate political jurisdiction. It is difficult to discern how Galilee would have become Jewish at some point or how it would have formed an attachment to Jerusalem as its cultural and cultic matrix.

Moreover, texts and other 'evidence' offered by Freyne and others that Galilee was 'Jewish' in Hellenistic times, even supportive of the early Hasmoneans, appear to be read through the eyes of the view to be proven. In particular, the reading of several texts adduced in support of this view appear to be problematic.

The account of Simon's military mission to rescue 'brothers' under attack in Galilee cannot be taken at face value (see Sievers 1990: 49-57; Schwartz 1991: esp. 21-27). This highly schematic account has been patterned after biblical passages such as Josh. 9.12; Ezra 4.1; Neh. 2.10, 19; 3.33; 4.1-2 ('the nations roundabout') and Deut. 20.13-15 (Judas's treatment of towns in Gilead). The parallel sequence of places named indicates that 1 Maccabees 5 and 2 Maccabees 10–12 are following a common source. But 2 Maccabees (12.2; 10.14) represents as Seleucid officials' repression what 1 Maccabees portrays as Gentile persecution, and given the patterning of 1 Maccabees 5 after traditional Deuteronomistic patterns, it must be at least as tendentious as 2 Maccabees in this case. Furthermore, and most telling, 2 Maccabees lacks the reference to an expedition to Galilee. Little wonder that 1 Maccabees' account of a rescue mission to Galilee, with its lack of detail uncharacteristic of 1 Maccabees generally and its similarity to Judas's expedition into Gilead, has long since evoked scholarly suspicions (see Wellhausen 1905). Even if such an expedition into Galilee took place, the account still suggests that there were only a few thousand Jews in Galilee, and that in the extreme southwestern corner near Ptolemais and Arbatta.

The letter from Demetrius to the Judeans in 1 Maccabees 10 mentions 'three districts added [to Judea] from Samaria and Galilee' (10.30), but subsequently clarifies that these three toparchies, Aphairema, Lydda and Ramathaim, are 'from the *chora* of Samaria' (10.38; 11.34). This hardly supports a contention that Galilee was 'essentially Jewish' at this time (Freyne 1980: 40).

Freyne argues that the report of the Seleucid general Bacchides marching into Judea via the road to *Galgala* and encamping at *maisaloth ten en arbelois* and capturing it in 1 Macc. 9.2 suggests that 'the Galilean peasants of the region had given some sign of their support for their Judean brothers' (1980: 39). Only by reading this passage through Josephus's paraphrase of it in *Ant.* 12.11.1 [421], however, can it be taken as a reference to Galilee. But what Josephus has done is transparent: assuming that 'Judea' was the territory claimed by Jerusalem rulers in his own time (cf. his similar insertion of 'Judea' at *Ant.* 13.5.11 [174] for 'his own country' in 1 Macc. 12.35), he read *Galgala* as Galilee (thus generating the extremely awkward juxtaposition of 'coming to Judea' and 'encamping in Galilee') and read the dative plural *arbelois* as a reference to Arbela. (Josephus then embellished the brief reference in 1 Macc. 9.2 with a bit of 'local color' from the famous later exploits of Herod in ferreting out the brigands holed up in the caves near Arbela, *War* 1.16.2-3 [304-13]; *Ant.* 14.15.4 [415-30]). Bar-Kochva (1989: 552-59) has recently offered both a telling critique of alternative suggestions and a convincing explanation for this problematic passage in 1 Macc. 9.2 (*arbela* in the text could have resulted from the original Hebrew *har-bet-el*, the hill country of Bethel, cf. 1 Sam. 13.2; Josh. 16.1). This suggestion locates Bacchides's encampment and military action just to the north of Jerusalem in Judea proper, precisely where he was headed to confront Judas.

Along with criticism of our sources in such texts, caution is necessary in drawing inferences from certain passing references. For example, the report in 1 Macc. 12.47-51 that when Jonathan advanced on Ptolemais he left two-thirds of his troops in Galilee who subsequently stood their ground against Seleucid troops suggests nothing about Jonathan having 'support' from Galileans. And Josephus's comment (*Ant.* 13.5.6 [154]) that Demetrius's generals believed that Jonathan was an 'ally' of Galilee and that 'the Galileans' were 'his own' (people) is not good evidence for the Galileans' longstanding political-religious loyalties (Freyne 1980: 41).

Ironically, some of the passages mentioned as evidence for Galileans being Jews turn out on closer inspection to illustrate the basic structure of political-economic-religious domination that the Hasmoneans were reassembling over Judea and beginning to extend into other areas of Palestine. In *Ant.* 12.3.3 [138-44] Josephus cites a letter from Antiochus III to the governor of Coele-Syria and Phoenicia including the provision: *politeuesthosan de pantes hoi ek tou ethnous kata tous patrious nomous.* Freyne (1980: 36) takes this to mean that 'the right to live according to the Jewish law was confirmed to all the Jews under Ptolemy the governor, and this must have included Galilean Jews also'. Throughout the letter, however, the focus is on the Judeans in and around Jerusalem and the temple. Specially noteworthy, however, is that here, in an official Seleucid communication parallel to the later decrees of Caesar regarding Hyrcanus and his predecessors and successors, *hoi patrioi nomoi* pertains to how the nation is governed. Moreover, immediately following that key clause is another provision remitting taxes precisely to the imperial regime's client rulers in Jerusalem and their immediate retainers and dependents: *hē gerousia kai hoi hiereis kai hoi grammateis tou hierou kai hoi hieropsaltai.* The early Hasmoneans Jonathan and Simon successfully inserted themselves at the head of exactly that state structure, which was soon to be free of imperial oversight. Furthermore the beginning steps of expansion of their rule over territory beyond Judea is indicated in the letter of Demetrius cited in 1 Maccabees 10: the three toparchies from the Samaritan *chora* annexed to Judea are to 'obey no other authority than the high priest' (10.38). The various texts cited as indications that Galilee was Jewish prior to the Hasmonean takeover turn out to provide no solid evidence for such a hypothesis. But some of them do indicate the political-economic-religious apparatus of the temple-state that the Hasmoneans had taken over prior to expansion of their rule into districts such as Galilee.

In the debate over the inhabitants of Galilee at the time of the Hasmonean takeover, especially considering the lack of textual or archaeological evidence for much of a distinctively 'Jewish' presence there, there would seem to be another possibility: perhaps much of the population of Galilee was neither Gentile nor Judean, but descended from the ancient Israelites. Although there is precious little evidence for Galilean history from the Assyrian conquest to the Hasmonean takeover, the continuation of former Israelites on the land would appear to be inherently probable given what is known of the policies and behavior of ancient imperial regimes and subject peoples. The ancient Assyrian and neo-Babylonian imperial rulers deported and replaced the governing and administrative elite of conquered peoples, but left the masses of peasants intact on the land. Such a practice by the Babylonians is clear from the account about Jerusalem/Judea in 2 Kgs 24–25. Apparently we should read the accounts of the Assyrian conquest of Galilee in 2 Kgs 15.29 and of Samaria itself in 2 Kgs 17 similarly. This is confirmed by Assyrian imperial records mentioning 27,290 deportees from Samaria, a figure which would correspond roughly to the ruling elite and its religious-political-military governing apparatus (i.e. perhaps 5 per cent but not likely more than 10 per cent of the total population). While the Assyrians pointedly replaced the governing class in Samaria itself, there is no evidence that they would have brought anything more than an administrative apparatus into Galilee. Since the Persian imperial regime even restored previously deported native elites to power, as in the case of Judea, it is unlikely to have settled Galilee with non-Israelites. Further, while the Hellenistic emperors founded cities in the areas surrounding Galilee, they did not interfere much with local village life and no foundations were made in Galilee itself. In the absence of any evidence for the transplantation of foreign peoples into Galilee during these many centuries of successive imperial overlords, it seems appropriate to conclude that most of the inhabitants of Galilee were descendants of ancient Israelites—probably what was left of the tribes of Naphtali and Zebulun.

The hypothesis that the inhabitants of Galilee were basically the descendants of Israelites also helps clarify the situation in Galilee just prior to the Hasmonean takeover, in particular Josephus's report, dependent on Strabo's citation of Timagenes, that the Itureans dominated the area. The Itureans, based in southern Lebanon, will have come to dominate Galilee in the vacuum left by the demise of Seleucid imperial power in Palestine—somewhat parallel to the way in which the Hasmoneans had consolidated and expanded their sway from Judea into Samaria and Idumea. Thus Josephus's report that Aristobulus battled against and took *chora* from *the Itureans*, but imposed 'the laws of the Judeans' on *the inhabitants* of the *chora* would be an appropriate clarification of Timagenes's ambiguous report that he had acquired additional territory and brought over 'a portion of the Iturean nation' (*Ant.* 13.318-19). Military action was surely involved. But this was neither a conquest nor a conversion of the Itureans, but a displacement and replacement of their domination of Galilee by the Hasmoneans. As John Hyrcanus had done with the Idumeans, Aristobulus then did with the inhabitants of Galilee: he incorporated them into the Hasmonean/Judean state, in which they were required to live in accordance with 'the laws of the Judeans', if they wanted to remain in their ancestral homes in the Galilaean *chora.*

The Structure and Dynamics of Hasmonean Rule in Galilee

The Galileans, however, must have been different from the Idumeans in an important respect. Whereas the Idumeans' ancestors had not been part of early Israel, hence probably did not share Israelite cultural traditions, the Galileans, if they were descendants of Israelites, surely did share Israelite cultural traditions with the Judeans. It is clear that Israelite traditions such as the exodus and Mosaic covenantal principles were operative as popular traditions for many generations after the rise of the Jerusalem and Samaritan monarchies. Much has been made of the Israelite prophets drawing on those traditions, whether in the resistance movement led by Elijah and Elisha or in the oracles of an Amos. I have argued elsewhere that precisely such popular traditions, what anthropologists label 'little traditions' as opposed to official, and often written, 'great traditions', informed the emergence of both the popular messianic movements and the two types of popular prophets in late Second Temple times.[9] Thus the Galileans subjected to the Hasmonean high-priestly rule will have found some of 'the laws/customs of the Judeans' somewhat familiar. On the other hand, precisely because there is a difference between the 'little' and the 'great' traditions, including the political power that accompanies the latter, and because in this case the 'great' tradition came to the Galileans after centuries of separate shaping as the official state 'laws of the Judeans', there will have been some serious differences (see further Shatzman 1991: 83-87, 94-97). Indeed, insofar as 'the laws of the Judeans' were the articulation of the political-economic-religious structure of the relations of domination between rulers and ruled, they will have been strange to the Galilean descendants of Israelites.

Again social-structural questions need to be kept in the forefront in analyzing the fragmentary evidence for Galilee under Hasmonean rule. In Judea itself there would have been a fundamental structural division in

9.   For a suggestive treatment of the relationship between the 'little' and the 'great' traditions in agrarian societies that has considerable relevance to late-Second Temple Palestine, see Scott (1977). On the other hand, the applicability of this distinction between little and great traditions may be doubted for a society which has considerable continuity of culture with considerable interaction between the two, ostensibly different traditions, as argued by Sangreen (1984).

society between the village communities in which the vast majority of people lived, on the one hand, and the capital temple-city supposedly representing the community of the whole of Judea, but headed by the ruling priestly aristocracy, on the other. The subjection of Galileans (or Idumeans) to Hasmonean rule compounded the class difference with a historically deep-rooted regional (and perhaps quasi-ethnic) difference as well. Both levels must be considered in analyzing the structure and dynamics of Hasmonean rule in Galilee.

Minimal attention to ensuing historical events in Palestine reveals a general sense of the principal Hasmonean agenda. In the decades after Aristobulus took control of Galilee, Alexander Janneus was engaged in almost continuous wars of conquest, including areas on the frontiers of Galilee. Thus even if one assumed an utterly docile population in Galilee itself, the Hasmoneans would have established and maintained fortresses and garrisons in Galilee. This is exactly what the sources indicate. That Sepphoris was garrisoned (and as later probably already the principal administrative town) is suggested by Josephus's report that Ptolemy Lathyrus attacked but did not take the town (*Ant.* 13.12.5 [338]). In the later struggles between the Romans and the last of the Hasmoneans for control, particularly between Herod and Antigonus, Josephus assumes that there were a number of strongholds, including Sepphoris, that served as the basis for control of the area (see esp. *Ant.* 14.15.4 [413-14]). In the midst of these struggles, Marion, whom Cassius had installed as ruler of Tyre, captured three fortresses, presumably along the Galilean frontier with Tyre. A reference to 'walled cities' in *m. 'Arak.* 9.6 is suggestive in this regard, including the fortress of Sepphoris and the citadel of Gush Halav (Gischala) and Jotapata among them. Thus it would appear that the Hasmoneans established fortresses and garrisons at least along the outer frontier of Galilee as well as in the principal administrative towns (Freyne 1980: 49-50).

To administer the area, moreover, to gather tax revenues as well as to maintain internal and external security, the Hasmonean regime would have placed officers in Galilee. As Hasmonean officers settled in the area, far from a 'native aristocracy' emerging, a Judean aristocracy would have consolidated its power in Galilee (Freyne 1980: 49-50). Since it is unlikely in the extreme that the traditional agrarian economy was suddenly monetarized, the finds of large numbers of Jannean coins at points in the area (such as Meiron in Upper Galilee) do not mean that the population was (suddenly) Jewish, but simply that the area had come under Hasmonean administration.

For the general situation on the level of the village communities one can only extrapolate from later rabbinic evidence as measured against comparative sociological and anthropological studies. In most traditional agrarian societies, villages were semi-autonomous communities. Josephus's frequent references to a city or town 'and its villages' (or 'Hebron and its daughters', 1 Macc. 5.65) fits this model. Rabbinic texts repeatedly mention a village assembly (*knesset* = *synagoge*) and its leaders, such as the *hazzan*, the *rosh-ha-knesset* (= *archisynagogos* in the New Testament), or the *gabbaim*. In most matters the village ran its own affairs according to time-honored customs and traditions (cf. the origins of English common law), the central government's agents intervening primarily for taxes and trans-local problems. Assuming that the Galileans were largely descendants of Israelites, then Galilean village communities would have run their community affairs according to the Mosaic covenantal principles and traditional covenantal laws and customs. In matters such as observance of the Sabbath or other common Israelite traditions (e.g. circumcision), the Galileans would have paralleled popular Judean and official Jerusalem customs that were also rooted in Israelite traditions. However, dues owed to the Temple and high priesthood not in the ancient common Israelite tradition—but apparently included in 'the laws of the Judeans', judging from the official Seleucid and Roman decrees cited above—would have been, to the Galileans, a new demand by a new ruler. Insofar as the temple-state itself had developed during the centuries that Galilee had been administered under a separate imperial province from Judea, all of the 'laws of the Judeans' that pertained to the temple-state and its priesthood would have been new to Galileans. Indeed, assuming that 'the laws of the Judeans' were basically the Torah (along with other, oral priestly and/or scribal laws), which was also the product of the early Second Temple priesthood under Persian sponsorship, the whole framing of the common covenantal traditions would have been new to Galileans.

I have discerned to this point how the Hasmoneans would have administered and maintained internal and external security in Galilee, on the one hand, and how the Galilean village communities would have continued to run their own affairs in accordance with Israelite covenantal traditions, on the other. Structurally speaking, however, if the Galileans were to conduct their communal lives 'according to the laws of the Judeans' in any more intensive a way, if they were to be integrated into the community of loyalty to the temple and Torah, then some agents of 'secondary socialization' or 're-socialization' would have to intervene across the fundamental division between the two levels of community, rulers/temple and ruled/ village. The only possibilities for such agency emerging would be for the rulers to delegate some of their officers or 'retainers' to undertake such a program, or for some of those officers or retainers to take such a task upon themselves. Josephus happens to provide information on both of these two possibilities.

Judging from Josephus's accounts of the reign of Alexander Jannaeus (*Ant.* 13.12.1–15.5 [324-94]; *War.* 1.4 [84-106]), that is, for the first full generation of Hasmonean rule in Galilee, the ruler himself would have been completely preoccupied with wars of conquest and then, perhaps as an effect of those wars, virtual civil war with his own Judean people and/or retainers (scribal elements such as the Pharisees). It is difficult to imagine Janneus having directed much by way of a 'Judaization' campaign in Galilee or Idumea. Moreover, it was Jannaeus who appointed as governor of Idumea not a Judean thoroughly acquainted with 'the customs of the Judeans' but a prominent Idumean, Antipas. Only during the next decade, under his wife-successor Salome Alexandra Salome, were foreign conquests ended and the conflict with the Pharisees resolved such that attention could have been given to some possible program of pressing Judean laws and customs more actively on the Galilean (and Idumean) population. Thereafter, in rapid succession, the struggle between the rival Hasmonean factions for control of the state, the Roman conquest, and the overlapping Hasmonean and Roman civil wars would have preoccupied and exhausted the disintegrating Hasmonean regime. Thus if anything happened by way of Judaization in Galilee (or Idumea) it would have been under Salome Alexandra and/or by independent action by retainers of the government such as the Pharisees.

Josephus portrays the Pharisees as heavily involved in the politics and administration of the Hasmonean state. In fact, he provides a clear window onto their responsibilities and function in his accounts of how they were pushed out and then restored to their positions. In connection with interpreting 'the laws of Moses' the Pharisees had been promulgating additional regulations (*nomima*) for the people which had become a certain body of 'tradition' (*paradosis*) that had the status of state law. According to Josephus, Hyrcanus at one point broke with the Pharisees and rescinded their regulations as state law (leaving only the laws of Moses as favored by the rival party, the Sadducees; *Ant.* 13.10.6 [293-97]). The Pharisees must have been among those who bitterly opposed Alexander Jannaeus, and suffered for it. But under Alexandra Salome, they were restored to

their position of power in the administration of the state, and their regulations were restored as state law (*War* 1.5.2 [110-12]). That is, with regard
to the question of who, if anyone, would have been the agents pressing
'the laws of the Judeans' more aggressively upon the recently subjected
Idumeans and Galileans, the Pharisees would have been the obvious ones.
And since they had been in disfavor, perhaps even in overt conflict, with
Alexander Janneus, the point at which they would have been able to
devote time and energy to the 'Judaization' of Idumea and Galilee would
have been under Alexandra Salome. The fact that 100 years later the
Pharisees are portrayed in the synoptic Gospel tradition as representing
Jerusalem's interests in Galilee and advocating their special 'tradition of
the elders' is suggestive in this connection.

Of course, that the Pharisees may have been involved in such activity in
Galilee under the Hasmoneans is only a surmise. There is no evidence for
this under the Hasmoneans. But that is just the point. It seems historically
unlikely that much by way of 'secondary socialization' or 're-socialization' of the peoples subjected to 'laws of the Judeans' toward the end of
the second century BCE was mounted by the Hasmonean regime or its
retainers. Both Idumeans and Galileans would have continued to conduct
their village life according to their own cultural traditions and local customs. 'The laws of the Judeans' would have governed their relations with
the Hasmonean regime in Jerusalem, and in that connection perhaps also
impinged upon certain facets of local self-government.

Conclusions and Implications

From this investigation of the relations between the Hasmonean regime
and subjected peoples, particularly the Idumeans and the Galileans, a
thesis is emerging. Those relations, far from being susceptible of understanding in terms of religious conversion, must be dealt with in terms of
the political-economic-religious structure of an ancient temple-state that
expanded its territory and power during a period of imperial weakness. In
the case of the Hasmoneans, the new incumbents of the high priesthood in
Jerusalem were, to start with, illegitimate occupants of the office whose
power depended on the military forces built up during the resistance
against the declining Seleucid imperial regime. Beyond the confined
ideology of 1 Maccabees there is no indication that Hasmonean expansion
was a religious crusade. The Davidic-Solomonic imperial ideal may well
have influenced Hasmonean ambitions, but from the regime of Hyrcanus

onward the Hasmoneans employed non-Judean mercenaries in their professional army and established an increasingly Hellenized administration.
They seized the opportunities of Seleucid decline to expand their own
domains in Palestine. To understand this as the expansion of a religion
does not fit the situation or the sources. It is clear from the Seleucid and
Roman decrees that 'the laws of the Judeans' were understood as pertaining to the polity or constitution of the state and its relations with its
subjects. Thus when subject peoples were required to live according to
those 'laws of the Judeans', it pertained to the relations of the people in
their village communities to the Hasmonean state. There is no direct evidence of any attempt to press the subject peoples to apply 'the laws of the
Judeans' in their conduct of local community and family affairs. Of
course, insofar as observing the laws of the Judeans in relations with the
central government impinged adversely on the conduct of local affairs,
then structural conflict would have developed.

Two incidents in particular can be used to illustrate the resulting relations between the Jerusalem temple-state and the subordinate peoples as
the Hasmoneans bequeathed the situation to subsequent generations. The
first is the case of Costobar already examined above. The control of
Idumea was managed partly by alliances the Hasmoneans and later Herod
made with heads of powerful Idumean families, such as Antipas and
Costobar. But whatever the official policy was with regard to Idumeans
living according to 'the laws of the Judeans', Costobar's family illustrates
that it was not pressed upon local life in terms of suppressing indigenous
Idumean religious practices and social customs. In the case of Costobar,
the conflict came to a head for some reason, but even there the conflict that
meets the eye is a rupture in the relationship of personal-political patronage and not one between Idumean traditions and Torah and temple.

The second case can be taken from the Gospel of Mark's portrayal of
the conflict between Jesus and the Pharisees and the scribes representing
Jerusalem's interests in Galilee. The 'controversy story' in Mk 7.1-13
starts out as a conflict between local Galilean custom and Pharisaic/Judean
custom which the representatives of Jerusalem are portrayed as attempting
to press upon the Galileans (Mk 7.1-5). But the story moves quickly to
relocate the conflict between the basic (Mosaic/Israelite) covenantal commandment of God and 'the traditions of the (Pharisaic) elders' which
under Hyrcanus and then Alexandra Salome had been state law, and
focuses upon how the temple-state's economic demands made upon local
resources by 'the traditions of the elders' impinged adversely upon local

need as expected to be managed according to the basic covenantal 'commandment of God' (Mk 7.9-13).

Whatever 'Judaization' might mean when applied to the Hasmonean takeover of Idumea and Galilee, it was clearly not very thorough and effective in terms of 'the laws of the Judeans' becoming the regulations of local community life. The relations between the Hasmoneans and these subject peoples must be understood in terms of the structural conflicts involved. Those structural conflicts were not resolved by the Hasmoneans and persisted into early Roman, Herodian times. To illustrate, I refer again to the cases of the Idumeans and Galileans involvement in events of 4 BCE and 66–70 CE. The fundamental conflict was not between the Romans on the one side and the Jews on the other, but between the Judean rulers, Herodian and high-priestly, and their Roman sponsors, on the one hand, and the peasant forces from the various districts ruled from Jerusalem, on the other. In 4 BCE, a popular Galilean insurrection paralleled other popular insurrections in Judea and Perea. In the course of events from the summer of 66 through 70, Galileans resisted Jerusalem control and direction, Idumeans came to the rescue of Judean peasant forces locked in conflict with the high-priestly rulers and their Herodian allies, and (small numbers of) both Galilean and Idumean insurrectionaries joined with two popular Judean insurrectionary movements in the final resistance against Roman reconquest, after the high-priestly and Pharisaic elements had joined the Romans. Some of these groups at points were fighting from or driven for refuge into the (fortress) temple. But it would be difficult to argue that they were fighting primarily for the Torah and the temple. Yet it is fairly clear that they were fighting against the rulers based in the temple and the leading Pharisees whose function may still have included interpretation of the Torah.

The Origin, Expansion and Impact of the Hasmoneans in Light of Comparative Ethnographic Studies (and Outside of its Nineteenth-Century Context)

James Pasto

The goal of this essay is to treat the rise and subsequent influence of the Hasmoneans outside of the web of political and theological concerns that shaped the *modern* study of Judaism. This is not to say that my study is independent of *all* political and theological concerns, but only that it will remain independent of the *specific concerns* that have thus far shaped the study of the Hasmoneans and Judaism in antiquity. These include treatment of the Hasmoneans as a manifestation of an ancient Jewish 'nationalism', which, depending on the values of the scholar, is either praised as the triumph of a proto-Zionist Jewish recovery of a native past, or touted as a manifestation of an incipient Jewish particularism in the face of a proto-Western, Greek inspired enlightenment. This broad view, in turn, shapes some specific claims and perspectives. Some argue that the Greek cultural-political formation of the *politeia*, and its capacity to incorporate new members, stimulated the creation of an abstract notion of 'Judaism' capable of functioning as the basis of an achieved, rather than the hitherto ascribed Jewish identity. The Hasmoneans made use of this new notion of a conversion to Judaism in order to incorporate the populations of newly conquered regions. Others argue that the Hasmonean polity was an extreme reaction against Greek 'universalistic' notions of ascribed identity and pan-regional corporate unity, and instead an enhancement of the particularistic and fanatical tendencies in Judaism. The latter argument is sometimes taken to the radical position that such Hasmonean-stimulated particularism-fanaticism became an essential feature of all subsequent Jewish religion, and also gave rise to all forms of nationalist violence and racial intolerance in Christianity and Europe. The Hasmonean revolt is also seen as one of the formative developments for Christianity. The various and so-called pro- and anti-Hellenistic parties set the grounds for subsequent Jewish sectarianism and Jewish attitudes to non-Jews. Those

Jewish groups hostile to Greeks become the precursors for the Jewish-centric, legalistic rabbinic Judaism, while those more open to Greek ideas become the precursors to the universalistic, freedom-seeking Christianity.

I will argue that all of these positions are understandable only in the *modern* context of the Hasmonean revolt. That is, they are reflections of nineteenth- and twentieth-century notions of Judaism and Hellenism in terms of universalism versus particularism, reform versus traditionalism and nationalism, and Judaism versus Christianity, set within a broader European narrative of cultural progress. A reading of the ancient data *outside* of this discursive frame suggests a quite different understanding of the Hasmoneans in particular and Jewish–Greek contact in general. New perspectives on this may in turn also provide alternative perspectives for understanding Christian origins. I will engage the primary data on three levels. First, in terms of the prior discursive framework and narrative that shaped the dominant models used to explain Hasmonean origins and expansion. I will treat here key terms, methods and concepts used in the study of Judaism—including the term 'Judaism' itself—that may be problematic in their current formulations. Second, I will present comparative sociological and anthropological data for use as heuristic models for alternative narrative frameworks for understanding the primary data. These will replace the previous and hitherto dominant nineteenth-century models and narratives. Third, I will suggest alternative readings of the primary data on the Hasmoneans as well as on other related aspects of Jewish history. While my approach will result in an essay that is somewhat broader ranging than the title suggests, it is nevertheless unified by its central focus on the origin, expansion and impact of the Hasmoneans in light of comparative ethnographic studies.

Contexts and Methods

The Nineteenth-Century Background of the Hasmonean Expansion: The Present in the Past

The examination of the *ancient* historical and social context of the Hasmonean expansion needs to begin with a greater awareness of the social context in which the modern study of Jewish history began. This is to say that we must begin by investigating the present political and theological concerns that have shaped the representation of the Hasmonean period. We need not debate the point that present concerns pervade the study of the past (Jewish or otherwise), just as we need not thereby ascribe to a complete 'presentism' that would deny the possibility of representing the past as anything else than a metaphor for the present (see for discussion Peel 1982). A work of scholarship can, at one and the same time, be both a critical analysis of primary data as well as a critique of the political, religious or social present. One need only think of Strauss's *Das Leben Jesu* to recognize that all critical scholarship possesses what Wilk calls a 'dual nature'. It 'simultaneously engages in a fairly rigorous pursuit of objective facts about the past and an informal and sometimes hidden dialogue on contemporary politics, philosophy, religion, and other important subjects' (Wilk 1985: 308). Recognition of this principle in the disciplines of Jewish, biblical and Christian studies is simply to fall in line with other disciplines where there has been an ongoing attempt to account for the political and social contexts in which many of the accepted notions of these disciplines arose.

It is not difficult to show that some generally accepted constructions of ancient Jewish history arose within a specific nineteenth-century European social-political context. A prime example is the notion of radical rupture between a pre-exilic Israel and a postexilic Judaism, with its attendant distinguishing tropes of respective universalism versus particularism, prophecy versus theocracy, freedom versus constraint, and so on, which first appeared in the work of W.M.L. de Wette (Pasto 1999a: ch. 2). De Wette's 'invention' of postexilic Judaism is seen on closer examination to reflect the political present of nineteenth-century Germany. The notion of exilic rupture, the differentiation between an Israel and a later Judaism, the treatment of the latter in terms of degeneration, particularism, theocracy and tyranny, and the whole in a narrative of Christian succession, served at one and the same time to situate contemporary Protestants as the representatives of Hebraic antiquity and Christian modernity, Protestantism as the moral basis of German national identity and institution building, and German Jews as an allochronic, primitive population in need of Germanization and Christianization. De Wette wrote the political present through his writing of the historical past, in this case a Jewish past turned into a 'biblical' past via Christian theologies of succession and their achieved political hegemony. The Jewish past, in this sense, was good to think about the German Protestant present —but only as fractured past of pre-exilic Israelites and postexilic Jews all made good by Jesus and Christianity.[1] Such a reading of de Wette's scholarship does not in any way discount his critical contributions to the

---

1.   For detailed arguement on de Wette and other German scholars, see Pasto (2002; 1999a: 104-148). On de Wette's scholarship generally, see Rogerson (1992).

literary analysis of the Old Testament; they merely call into question the *historical frame* he placed his literary analysis within. Presumably, there are other historical narratives that can account for the composite nature of the Old Testament, and presumably the historical and archeological data on the 'exile' are understandable outside of de Wette's German Protestant narrative (see Pasto 1998).

While the model of exilic rupture does not touch directly upon the Hasmonean context, its accompanying tropes of a postexilic Judaism marked by contradictory combinations of universal versus particular, and so on, did figure prominently in subsequent constructions of the Hasmonean period—especially in relationship to Hellenism's impact on Jewish polity and society. De Wette's model had minimized the place of 'Hellenism' in postexilic Jewish history, in part because his own model was designed to emphasize the Hebraic elements in Christianity, and hence German Protestantism, against the phil-Hellenism of his times. Other scholars were not so averse to configuring Greek elements in Christianity or Germany, and there began to emerge a more complex model of Hellenistic influence on Judaism as a key development in the formation of Christianity. As Greece and Hellenism were portrayed as the bearers of a proto-European enlightenment and liberation, so Greece and Hellenism became the magnet for the supposed universalistic and liberal elements in Judaism—against the pull of the presumed reactionary tendencies of particularism and legalism. De Wette's contradictory tendencies (universal, particular, free, legal) became contrasting *types* of Jewish religion: first Hellenistic Judaism versus Palestinian Judaism, and then as well Apocalyptic Judaism versus Pharisaic Judaism. The former of both sets were situated as the universal and free types of Jewish religion and provided the matrix for Christianity; the latter were represented as particularistic and legalistic, the precursors to rabbinic Judaism.

There was also a treatment of the various sects in Judaism. This line of study emerged in part out of an investigation into the identity and influence of the Hasideans, as described in 1 and 2 Maccabees, and their relationship to the Pharisees and Sadducees. As Efron has shown, the treatment and description of these groups was never far removed from present political and theological concerns in Europe and especially Germany:

> Nationalist and revolutionary tendencies collided with religious elements. Demand for the separation of the ecclesiastical authority from the state filled the Western skies and slogans calling for religious tolerance became increasingly widespread. According to the prevailing atmosphere, the concepts were applied to the [Jewish] past (1987: 5).

One of the concerns of the prevailing atmosphere was the 'Jewish Question', that is, debates on the process and goal of Jewish emancipation. By and large Christian scholars viewed Jewish 'emancipation' in terms of assimilation: the emancipation of Jews would bring about the dissolution of a separate Jewish identity in Germany. Jewish scholars, by contrast, tended to treat emancipation in terms of Jewish corporate persistence, albeit in terms of a transformation of Jewish notions of self-reference and social organization. Both sought precedents in the Jewish past for their respective views, and both projected the dynamics of contemporary Jewish groups into the conflicts between Jewish groups evident in the data of the Hasmonean period and afterward. Accordingly, as Efron notes, Jewish 'sectarian' dynamics revolved around issues of 'national' versus 'religious' identity, and were treated in terms of 'reform', 'emancipation' and 'enlightenment'. In this way, the discussion of Jewish sectarianism, in and beyond the Hasmonean context, was a discussion of the present political and social concerns by using the past as a field of representation and as a charter for present action (see Heschel 1998, 1989).

This tendency is present as early as the work of J.D. Michaelis, more apparent in the work of scholars such as Geiger and Wellhausen. E. Meyer, however, was the first actually to speak of the Hellenizers as representing a 'progressive' and 'reform' Judaism against the reactionary position of the pro-Hasmoneans (1921–23: II, 128), a model made into the common currency by Elias J. Bickerman (1979).

As Efron notes, Victor Tcherikover attempted to get around the over-determination of present political concerns by treating the Hasmoneans in terms of their contemporary social dynamics. Nevertheless, subsequent scholars continued to treat Jewish groups in terms of 'national' versus 'religious' differences, and some persist in treating 'Hellenism' as a progressive and enlightened force against a negative, particularistic and fanatical Judaism. The premier example here is Hengel. In his grand *mis*treatment of events in the Hasmonean period, Hengel speaks of three Jewish responses to Greek hegemony and 'enlightenment': a 'radical "reform Judaism"', a Jewish 'zeal for the law', and a 'Jewish national consciousness'. Hengel presumes that 'the radical reformers were influenced by the ideas of Greek enlightenment' and 'sought to restore the original "reasonable" form of worship', while a regressive Jewish nationalism and ethno-centrism constituted the program of the Hasmoneans and their followers. The success of the latter resulted in a 'fixation' on the Torah, intellectual stagnation, and the '*connection between nation and religion*' which would henceforth give

'Judaism' its 'ethnic' characteristics (1974: I, 198, 292, 305-309; see the criticism in Collins 1989).

Hengel's statements reflect a development of the nineteenth century, which I would describe as the tyranny of Christianity and Greece over Judaism: that is, a tendency to treat Hellenism as enlightened, progressive, and the necessary dissolution of a particularistic, fanatical Judaism as the preparation for Christian origins (see Butler 1935). Yet viewed outside of this discourse, the Greeks were not benevolent messengers of cultural enlightenment but conquerors and colonizers. Neither were Jews ardent 'nationalists' bent on 'statehood', 'fundamentalists' resistant to 'progress', or 'reformers' seeking 'emancipation'. All such conceptualizations are understandable *only* in the context of the growth of the modern nation-state; to read this pattern of response into the ancient Near East in the context of Greek expansion is anachronistic at best, propaganda at worst. This is not to deny, by any means, that the Greeks viewed themselves as the bearers of civilization, which they promoted as a specific form of cultural transformation. Nor is it to deny that some Jews responded to this through accommodation, others through resistance and a reassertion of prior traditions. It is rather to assert that these ancient dynamics can and must be conceived *apart* from a narrative framework of enlightenment and emancipation, universalism versus particularism, religion against nation, and Christian-Hellenistic triumph. We must instead work toward developing an alternative frame of representation, one that is based on the application of both a critical evaluation of prior critical historiographies, and the application of alternative sociological/ethno-historical methods to our primary data in order to create alternative models.

The broad methodological presumptions here, then, are two; both based on R.R. Wilk's description of scholarship's 'dual nature'. First, we must engage in a 'negative' criticism of disentangling our primary sources from the secondary and tertiary narratives within which they are embedded. A variety of additional methods are available here, drawing upon studies in post-colonial historiography, Orientalism and ethnographic allegory (Prakash 1995; Clifford 1988), as well as ongoing studies in the construction of Judaism in modern scholarship (e.g. Levenson 1993). Second, we then engage in a 'positive' criticism of treating the sources for the possibility of historical reconstruction, by which I mean we 'study the past in order to make positive statements' about what we 'believe happened or did not happen' (Cohen 1999: 347). Here, a useful maxim is that 'texts [data] give evidence for what they imply; not [or not only] for what they say' (Thompson 2000: 147). We can then place this basic textual methodology

within the broader framework of an *Annales*-type approach, where emphasis is given to events and continuities as well as to structures, processes,
and transformations.

Terminology

As a translation of the original Greek *Ioudaismos*, most scholars understand *Judaism* to mean the 'religion' and/or 'culture' of Jews or 'Judeans'
(see below). Some view its literary appearance as an indication of the historical emergence of a more abstract, less concrete and localized, Jewish
identity (e.g. Cohen 1999: 109-39). Others emphasize that the appearance
of the term does not signal the presence of any singular or monolithic
Jewish religion (Chilton and Neusner 1995; Davies 1996). All, however,
treat *Judaism* in these and other regards as though it were a widely used
term in our Second Temple sources. This is not the case, however. *Ioudaismos* appears in 2 Macc. 2.21, 8.1 and 14.38, and then again in *4 Macc.*
4.26 and Gal. 1.13-14. These five references in three sources constitute the
total presence of the term *Judaism* in the literary and archaeological data,
Jewish and non-Jewish, for the Second Temple period! It appears in no
other sources! Note here that neither Josephus nor Philo use this term,
though both treat Jewish history, culture and religion at length and in
abstract terms, and both wrote and were well versed in Greek literary
forms. On these grounds it seems difficult to justify using the term
'Judaism' as a coeval, native (self-referencing) term to designate Jewish
corporate identity, religion or 'tradition' in the Hasmonean period. In fact,
the term remains sparse in subsequent Jewish literature as well: it appears
in two later Greek inscriptions, and, as the far from equivalent, but still
rare, *yahadut*, in rabbinic literature.[2] Conversely, 'Judaism' is more commonly used in gentile Christian literature, becoming *only there* the premier
term in reference to Jewish customs and traditions. This pattern parallels
that of the term *Ioudaizein* as discussed by Shaye Cohen (1999: 175-97):
rare in Jewish literature, it achieves currency only in Christian sources.

---

2.   Tomson (1986: 134 n. 53) notes the use of *Yahadut* in *Est. R.* 7.3 (variant reads
Yehudatan), though the context is again loyalty in the face of conflict, and a possible
parallel to *Hellenismos* in the use of *'Armayuta'* in *m. Meg.* 4.9 citing a targum (see
also *b. 'Abod. Zar.* 70a; and the *gayyuta'* of *b. Ket.* 11a). Ben Yehudah's dictionary
lists a number of occurrences of *yahadut* in medieval Jewish literature, though he
interprets this term to mean *segulat adam yehudi*, i.e. Jewish identity, 'Jewishness' not
'Judaism' in the abstract sense. It was only in the modern period that Jews begin to use
the term Judaism to mean 'Jewish religion'.

In any case, there are reasonable grounds for suggesting that 'Judaism' may be an *incorrect* translation of *Ioudaismos* as it appears in 2 Maccabees and *4 Maccabees*; that it may therefore mean something other than the religion or culture of Jews/Judeans. Rather, following at a tangent the lead of Jonathan Goldstein, I suggest that the usual translation of *Ioudaismos*, 'Judaism', is simply a *transliteration* of that term, and that it should instead be translated as something along the lines of 'collaborating with the Judeans', 'being loyal to the Judeans', and other such expressions. On what grounds? Goldstein has argued that the authors of 2 Maccabees and *4 Maccabees* coined the term *Ioudaismos* in imitation of the Greek *Medismos* in the sense that the latter was used during and subsequent to the wars with Persia. Greeks (*Hellenes*) portrayed their struggle against the Persians (*Medes*) as a defense of Greek culture and society under attack by 'barbarian' Medes, and in this context referred to Greek collaboration with Persia as *Medismos*. While *Medismos* could and often did mean the adoption of Persian dress or customs, these were linked to political collaboration. *Medismos* refers to both cultural practices and political loyalties (Goldstein 1983: 192 n. 21, 230 n. 12; cf. Graf 1984; Cohen 1999: 179, 182). Goldstein suggests that the author of 2 Maccabees is doing something similar with the terms *Ioudaismos* and *Hellenismos*, only reversing the context and changing the terms: here it is pro-Persian Judeans portraying their struggle with the Greek Antiochus as a defense of Judaic culture and society against 'barbarian' Greeks, and accusing Judeans who support the Greeks of going over to the Greeks, or *Hellenismos*. Accordingly, the author also used *Ioudaismos* to induce 'his literate Greek audience to remember the struggle of the loyal Hellenes against the "barbarian" Persians and against the "Medism" of Greek collaborators with the Persian empire' (Goldstein 1983: 192 n. 21).

Paradoxically, Goldstein does not go on to suggest that *Ioudaismos* be translated as 'collaboration with the Judeans' or similar expressions, but instead translates it as 'Judaism'. Yet, the former seems like a viable option. Thus, we could alternatively translate 2 Macc. 2.21 as: 'the story of Judas Maccabeus and his brothers... [in their] wars against Antiochus Epiphanes ...and the appearances which came from heaven to those who strove vigorously on the side of the Judeans [ὑπὲρ τοῦ Ἰουδαϊσμοῦ φιλοτίμως ἀνδραγαθήσασιν] against the barbarian hordes, and recovered the temple ...freed the city and restored the laws...' This works as well for the charges against the elder Razis in 14.37-44: 'In the last time of crisis he had been accused of collaborating with the Judeans, and he had indeed risked with all zeal both body and life for siding with the Judeans' (ἧν γὰρ ἐν τοῖς ἔμπροσθεν χρόνοις τῆς ἀμιξίας κρίσιν εἰσενηνεγμένος Ιουδαϊσμοῦ καὶ σῶμα καὶ ψυχὴν ὑπὲρ τοῦ Ιουδαϊσμοῦ παραβεβλημένος μετὰ πάσης ἐκτενίας). *4 Maccabees* 4.26 can be read similarly, where Antiochus IV attempts to 'compel everyone in the community to eat defiling foods and to renounce their oath of allegiance to the Judeans' (αὐτὸς διὰ βασάνων ἕνα ἕκαστον τούτου ἐθνοῦς ἠνάγκαζεν μικρῶν ἀπογευομένος τροφων, ἐξόμνυσθαι τὸν Ιουδαϊσμόν). We can and should understand and translate *Hellenismos* in a similar fashion, reading 2 Macc. 4.11-13 as a related sequence of shifts in cultural practice and political loyalties to the Greeks. Accordingly, v. 11 states that Jason 'set aside existing royal concessions' and '...introduced new customs contrary to the law', that is, he attempted to make changes in both the political and the cultural orientations of Jews/ Judeans. Verse 12 parallels this by indicating the political (the building of a gymnasium) and the cultural consequences (wearing of the Greek hat) of Jason's actions. Verse 13 summarizes these, alternatively translated, in stating 'there was now a rush to collaborate with the Greeks [political allegiance] and an increase in the adoption of foreign ways [cultural imitation]' (ἧν δ'οὕτως ἀκμὴ τις 'Ελληνισμοῦ καὶ πρόσβασις ἀλλοφυλισμου).[3] These alternatives do not violate the original Greek, and follow that of *Medismos* by all of its translators. Moreover, they arguably make more sense of the text in their context: a conflict between Greeks and Jews, *Hellenes* and *Ioudaioi*, in which cultural practices were closely intertwined with political actions, and where loyalty to one or the other of dualistically expressed groups was a primary issue.

Cohen has noted a similar dual meaning of the term *Ioudaïzein* in Jewish-Greek literature (as well as its similar paucity there) and its proliferation in Christian Greek literature. He also notes a shift in the meaning of *Ioudaïzein* in Christian literature that finds its parallel with

3.　This reading is indirectly supported by *4 Macc.* 8.8 where Antiochus asks the seven sons of Eleazer to abandon their ancestral customs for a political appointment: 'Trust me, then, and you will have positions of authority in my government if you will renounce the ancestral tradition of your national life. And enjoy your youth by adopting the Greek way of life and by changing your manner of living' (καὶ μεταλαβόντες 'Ελληνικοῦ βίου, καὶ μεταδιαιτηθέντες ἐντρυφήσατε ταῖς νεότησιν ὑμῶν). The immediate context of the king's words here is not a war (though this is the general context) but an offer to the brothers to give up Judean customs for Greek customs. If the terms 'Hellenism' and 'Judaism' were understood to mean 'Greek way of life' and 'Jewish way of life', then this would have been an ideal place for the author to use them in his narrative.

one for *Ioudaismos*: a move toward treating the terms as markers of Jewish—or perceived 'Jewish-like'—identity and only secondarily as signs of political loyalty. Cohen notes that *Ioudaïzein* is used in this more abstract sense in Galatians, and that the same can be said there of *Ioudaismos*, as well as for subsequent Christian literature where the use of 'Judaism' (*Ioudaismos* or the Latin *Iudaismus*) becomes promiscuous and all but impossible to translate as 'Judaism'.[4] This points toward an important sociological and semantic shift, but one that is tied to the dynamics of *Christian* not Jewish identity. The problem here is that the two are often confused in the tendency to treat the Jewish past as signs pointing to the Christian future. We must avoid this tendency. Later Christian meanings cannot determine Jewish texts. *Ioudaismos* in 2 Maccabees and *4 Maccabees* does not indicate the emergence of an abstract Jewish/Judean identity. My discussion above points rather to the opposite conclusion: *Ioudaismos* indicates a very specific, concrete identity in a particular context of cultural-political conflict; it is only in Christian literature where *Ioudaismos* comes to refer to an abstract Jewish way of life. This calls into question the claim that Jewish identity underwent a shift from concrete to abstract at this time—at least on the evidence of this term. However, the term 'Judaism' is too well-established to be abandoned and it will be used in this essay.

Another term, 'Jew', is also due some attention, though my focus here is on 'Jew' only as it occurs in Greek literature, that is, on *Ioudaios*. Unlike *Ioudaismos*, *Ioudaios* has been given some attention as to its translation, its meaning, and shifts of its meaning in time and space. Some have noted the broad and shifting semantic range of *Ioudaios*: that it can refer, in different, or even in the same, texts to an inhabitant of the territory of Judea in contrast to inhabitants of Galilee, to *Ioudaioi* and *Galileans* together in contrast to *Hellenes*, or to people living outside of Judea who follow the laws and customs of the *Ioudaioi* but are not inhabitants of Judea (see Williams 1997; Lowe 1976). Significant attention has been given to the last of these three meanings, notably by Cohen, who argues that it indicates 'a significant development in the history of Judaism' that began in the Hasmonean period, when an ethnic-geographic [Jewish] self-

---

4. Where 'Judaism' means the (false) religion of the 'law': e.g. Ignatius, *Mag.* 10.3; *Phil.* 6.1; Tertullian, *Adv. Marc.* 1.20 speaks of Paul's zeal 'against Judaism' (*adversus Iudaismum*). Subsequent Christian writers use *Ioudaismos* in this sense as well, including Origen (*Contra Cel.* 1.2), Epiphanes (*Haireses* 30.2; 41.240a), and Basil (*Homilies* 2.41).

definition was supplemented by religious (or cultural) and political definitions, because it was only in this period that the Judean ethnos opened
itself to the incorporation of outsiders (Cohen 1999: 70). For this reason,
in part, Cohen (and others) suggest that *Ioudaios* can have two translations: 'Judean' in the sense of an ethnic inhabitant of Judea, and 'Jew' in
the sense of a person professing the Jewish 'religion' or way of life.

I agree that *Ioudaios* can have two meanings, yet I hesitate in translating
these alternatively as 'Judean' and 'Jew'. First, it is inconsistent with our
treatment of other peoples of the time. Thus, we make no distinctions
between 'Greeks' and 'Greekians' or 'Romans' and 'Romanians' (or other
such terms), though the Greek and Latin terms may refer to inhabitants of
a territory or to those who practiced a way of life associated with Greeks
and Romans. Second, we have here the problem of a historiography of
translation more than of the meaning of the terms themselves: the English
distinctions between 'Judean' and 'Jew' are built upon discursive practices
that already differentiated the referent of 'Jew' in terms of limited and
expansive, or national and religious, identities, and always in terms of
Christian origins as the triumph of universalism over particularism.[5] This
makes the problem of translation that of a modern meaning and context,
not an ancient one. Third, there is also a playing out of current inter-
Jewish identity conflicts around the meaning and status of the term 'Jew',
both in respect to conversion as well as citizenship in the state of Israel
(Cohen 1999: 8-10).

This distinction between 'Judean' and 'Jews' (even as reflected in
Cohen 1999: 90-91) is too much an echo of a Christian and German
tyranny of meaning, and too deeply enmeshed in current inter-Jewish
identity debates, to serve as a useful, critical understanding of the ancient
data. Indeed, the connotation of *Iouodaioi* expanded over time to include
people outside Judea and not born of Judean parents, but this is no different than what occurred in other groups at the time, and thus there is
no good reason to use differentiating terms. A related issue here is the
broader one of corporate identity, typically and unfortunately, articulated
in terms of 'ethnicity'. The Greek word *ethnos* originally referred to a
swarm or any group with shared interests, but came to apply to people
sharing common territory, ancestry and customs. That this term is *incor-
rectly* rendered into the English 'ethnicity' is apparent when we think of

5. See esp. Ewald (1864), who used *Judäer* and *Judäerthum* to designate the
postexilic and pre-70 CE people of Israel, and *Juden* and *Judenthums* (Jews and Judaism)
for the post-70 'Talmudic', and decidedly inferior, remnant.

the variety of referents it covers in common usage. Thus, Serbs, Croats and Muslims in the Balkans are treated as 'ethnic' groups in terms of current political conflicts, while 'Muslims' are elsewhere treated as a 'religious' group analogous to 'Christians', 'Buddhists' and 'Jews'. Conversely, 'Jews' are often treated as an 'ethnic' and a 'religious' group in the United States, while in Israel 'Jew' serves as 'religious' or 'national' designation encompassing multiple 'ethnic' groups (Moroccans, Germans, Yemenites, Russians). The point here is that such terms have a way of over-determining the social groups they are used to describe, so that scholars sometimes think of corporate terms as mutually exclusive when they are not. This is especially likely in discussions of Jewish history where, as I noted, differences between 'national', 'ethnic' and 'religions' identities were first formulated in terms of options and oppositions rather than complementary categories.

In terms of Jewish history and Hasmonean origins, we might best be served by distancing ourselves from the concept of 'ethnicity' as a major category for social formation and self-reference, especially if this is configured in the destitute frame of inclusive versus exclusive forms of identity and set against the category of 'religion' (see Neusner 1995). I would rather think in terms (following Comaroff and Comaroff 1992), of Jewish identity, as well as other contemporary groups, as a *totemic* identity, that is, 'the subjective classification, by members of a society, of the world into social entities according to cultural differences', that *never* changes into an 'ethnic' identity, that is, 'the stereotypic assignment of these groupings—often hierarchical—to niches within the social division of labor', until recently, since the latter is a development of modern class societies (Comaroff and Comaroff 1992: 52). The presence of contrasting notions of identity as fixed yet mutable, ascribed (such as by 'birth') rather than achieved (such as through 'conversion') is common in ordinary social relations. Accordingly, there were no shifts or contradictions in Jewish identity between 'religious', 'national' and 'ethnic' self-understandings. Jewish totemic identity categories rather remained fixed in form; what changed were signs that distinguished Jew from non-Jew. Even the political incorporation of Idumeans and other groups did not alter the fundamental totemic nature of Jewish identity, but rather necessitated the ideological incorporation of these groups within the primary totemic genealogy (as we shall see below). None of this effaces real, social differences, among Jews in antiquity, but it does point to a different form of social formation and social classification.

The Dynamics of Culture Change

Cohen views the incorporation of the Idumeans in terms of a 'conversion' to Judaism, a development he links to shifts in Jewish self-reference and corporate formation. By 'conversion' Cohen means 'a process by which gentiles change their theology and adopt exclusive allegiance to the one true God, the god of the Jews' (1999: 129). The possibility of such conversion, according to Cohen, emerged with the adoption of the *politeia* as a form of political organization, thereby making a hitherto ascribed, territorial-ethnic based identity into an achieved, political-affiliation based identity. Cohen argues that this allowed, for the first time, the incorporation of new members (1999: 109-39).

I disagree with this position. First, as a general sociological observation, all social groups have means, whether formalized or not, of adopting or incorporating strangers, typically through intermarriage or enslavement. The Jewish Bible's presentation of the early 'Israelites' as a mixture of various intermarrying and federating populations—Canaanite, Hittite, Moabite, Judahite, and so on—fits the population dynamics of the Near East visible in the data long before Greek hegemony and before the literature was written. Moreover, Bartlett has accounted for the Nabatean incorporation of the eastern Idumeans (Edomites) without the need to resort to Greek cultural-political influences. Cohen here seems to me to have fallen under the tyranny of Greece over Judaism that I noted above. The data he cites, such as the parallels between Achean and Judean absorption of new populations, might better be seen as evidence for a reconceptualization and even formalization of older Jewish adoption processes, but not as marking a new development in Judaism.

Second, in regards to 'conversion' more generally, it is useful to understand what we mean by this term. Nock defines conversion as 'the reorientation of the soul of an individual, his deliberate turning from indifference or from an earlier form of piety to another, a turning which implies a consciousness that a great change is involved, that the old was wrong and the new is right. It is seen at its fullest in the positive response of a man to the choice set before him by the prophetic religions' (Nock 1933: 7). 'Conversion' in this sense fits what we know of the various mystery cults of antiquity, and there are some examples of this kind of conversion to a Jewish way of life (Nock 1933: 20, 48). However, this is a very different context than that of the Hasmonean expansion, where a voluntary reorientation of the soul made after careful consideration was less likely a factor than the shifting political-economic dynamics of Seleucid expansion, strategies for local allegiance, and centuries of Judean-Idumean-

Iturean acculturation. Both of these points suggest a more complex view of inter-cultural dynamics, in which 'conversion' is one aspect of a broader culture change that includes 'transculturation', 're-enculturation', 'acculturation', 'assimilation', 'transsimilation' and 'incorporation'.

Transculturation is a process whereby individuals are temporarily or permanently detached from one group, enter another and come under the influence of its customs, ideas and values. The effects will depend on the overall social and political dynamics of group interactions, their economic relations, the level of hostility or imperial centralization, and the dominant values toward culture-sharing and individual determination.

Acculturation is the selective adoption of customs, beliefs and practices by a group that does not result in the loss of corporate identity, but rather allows the acculturating group to maintain its previous identity. Assimilation is the absorption of an individual or group into another, usually dominant, group, and thus means the loss of a previous corporate identity. In this sense, acculturation can and often is a two-way process, while assimilation is unidirectional (see Teske and Nelson 1974). Transsimilation, my own term, is somewhat in between acculturation and assimilation. It refers to the process by which an individual or group loses a previous sense of corporate identity through the adoption of out-group customs, beliefs and practices, but without taking on the identity of the out-group. Instead, the transsimilating group constitutes itself as a self-styled 'new' people. This may be the result of longer processes of acculturation, or the deliberate policy of an imperial power. Note, that whereas acculturation implies an ongoing 'inventing tradition', and assimilation an 'abandoned tradition', transsimilation suggests an 'invented tradition'—although a refashioning of native and non-native traditions may occur in all three.

Transculturation is a typical process except where a group is so isolated as to have no contact with others, and imperial contexts necessarily enhance transculturation. This was certainly the case in the Near East well before the Greek and Roman incursions. Political incorporation is attested in the data in successive Assyrian, Babylonian, Persian, Greek and Roman conquests, as well as through numerous local conquests. Acculturation in these contexts would vary. Tadmor (1992) has noted the gradual 'Aramaization' of Assyria despite Assyrian political domination, and there is also the more familiar adoption of Greek names, titles and political formations by the Jews and other local Near Eastern peoples. But acculturation here went two ways as Seleucid and Ptolemaic elites adapted Near Eastern models of divine kingship to their royal ideology, while Greeks, Egyptians, Assyrians and others adopted a variety of Jewish customs. In some cases this resulted in a full and immediate re-enculturation, as in the 'conversion' of the royal family of Adiabene though the activity of the merchant Ananias (*Ant.* 20.2.1 [15-20]); in others a generational movement from an initial transculturation to a full re-enculturation (assimilation) as described by Juvenal in his fourteenth Satire. These examples have parallels in the re-enculturation of individual Jews such as Tiberius Alexander, Dositheus of Alexandria and Antiochus of Antioch. These cases indicate that in 'converting' one not only adopts a new divinity and associated practices, but one also declares a political allegiance to the deity and its community. Group assimilation is attested to as well, though the specific dynamics are less clear. What is clear is that this results in the loss of a self-referencing identity, though the population may survive. Examples here are the absorption of the Moabites and eastern Edomites by the expanding Nabateans, and the absorption of the eastern Edomites (Idumeans) by the Judeans. The Nabateans, in turn, as well as many other local groups were later assimilated into Roman, Abbasid, and other later political-cultural identities.[6] There is no evidence for formal conversion rituals in the above cases.

There are also examples of transsimilation. One may be the emergence of the Mithraic cult, in which Persian symbols and beliefs were adopted and adapted by non-Persians to constitute a distinct corporate group. A better example, discussed below, is the development of a gentile Christian identity, where various Greeks, Romans, Egyptians and others abandoned their 'ancestral' customs and identity, adopted and adapted a number of Jewish customs and beliefs, and formed a new social identity 'neither Greek nor Jewish'.

To conclude here, I would note two points: one specific, the other general. First, the tyranny of Greece over Judaism has also been a tyranny of Greece over western Asia more generally. One consequence here is that we tend to minimize or even ignore the Persian cultural influences in western Asia and on Judaism in favor of what may be an over-exaggerated Hellenism. It is only with some difficulty that we can understand Jewish

6. By this I mean that they cease defining themselves as 'Greeks', 'Egyptians' and 'Syrians' either at all, or in terms of deities, customs or symbols linked to their ancestors. Rather, as the Christians and Muslims they became, they tended to articulate their pre-Christian and pre-Islamic pasts in negative terms. This changed somewhat with the rise of modern nationalisms. This was quite different from the case of Jews, who did not negate their own past, and who continued to articulate themselves as a people in continuity with their primordial ancestors.

traditions of the period—calendar, legal concepts, apocalyptic texts, resurrection and holy war—apart from Persian influences. With the same difficulty we ignore the place of Jews within Mesopotamian-Mediterranean power dynamics, the influence of Babylonian Jewish families in Palestine, and the political leanings of the Hasmoneans toward Persia. Thus, we could just as well, and perhaps even more so, speak of Jewish 'Persianism' or 'Babylonianism' as we do Jewish Hellenism. Second, social processes and cultural interaction are more complex than the concepts we use to describe them. Accordingly, we must emphasize process over event and acculturation over conversion.

Unity and Diversity: Why There Was a 'Normative' Judaism
Many scholars now question the existence of a common and 'normative' Judaism. This is not a new development. Nineteenth-century scholars did not treat Judaism as a monolith, but in terms of the multiple contrasting types and tendencies I noted above. G.F. Moore was reacting to this theological construct when he constructed a monolithic Judaism in its place, and scholars have been reacting to Moore ever since (e.g. Porter 1927). The growing trend has thus been to move away from treating 'Judaism' as a monolithic, immutable religion, as well as away from treating differences in Judaism in terms of equally monolithic and immutable 'Palestinian' versus 'Hellenistic', and 'legal' versus 'prophetic/apocalyptic' Judaisms. The issue is still disputed, but a substantial number of scholars are moving toward a position that rejects or minimizes a common, 'normative' Judaism before the second century CE, by which they mean a 'Judaism' that was formulated and recognized as a standard, largely invariable practice for all those calling themselves 'Jews'. Such a normative Judaism, according to this argument, did not emerge until the rabbinic Judaism of the Mishnah and Talmuds, thus not fully before the sixth century CE. Prior to this, and especially prior to the Mishnah and the war of 68, Judaism was a loose collection of Judaisms; there were shared customs but no shared system of self-representation and no institutions capable of encompassing all Jewish groups: each 'Judaism' configured itself as the 'true Israel' against all others, with the result being that we have many Judaisms but no Judaism—before rabbinic Judaism (e.g. Neusner's 'field theory', expounded in Neusner 1987). A more extreme position sees even these Judaisms as a product of ancient and modern literary fabrication, and accordingly rejects any extensive Jewish corporate presence at all before rabbinic Judaism. What scholars have called 'Judaism' or even 'Judaisms' was in fact a proliferating Palestinian 'sec-

tarianism' built upon shared but variant biblical notions of the 'new Israel' and a matrix of population disruptions and transfers (Thompson 1999).

There are good reasons to reject these positions and argue that there was a normative Jewish tradition at this time (see Schmidt 2001, though the views expressed here differ from his). By a 'normative Jewish tradition'. I mean a shared tradition of myths, rituals, beliefs and strategies, which might be otherwise known as a shared 'big' tradition. This common but oft-disputed anthropological term (see Sangreen 1984) does not imply a monolithic tradition or a tradition carried out by everyone the same way everywhere, but rather a shared corpus, written or otherwise, of practices and customs that most members of the group consider authoritative and definitive of what it means to be a member of the group. It does imply, however, counterparts in 'little traditions' that represent variations in custom and practice, that are nevertheless linked to the great traditions through a common cultural idiom. Such little traditions not only reflect cultural and social differences, but may be articulated in political terms as well.

John Guilick's notion of 'sect' is important here for it helps us to view sects as expressions of both little and big traditions, and moves us away from Troeltsch-dependent notions of sects as 'dissident' or 'heretical' groups fighting against the worldliness of the normative 'church' (Guilick 1976; cf. Eister 1967). Guilick distinguishes 'sect' from 'religion' rather than 'church', a distinction that lies on *the basis of general ideas versus specific action*. Religion represents the general principles that speak to the underlying unity of a society. Sects 'represent a spectrum of behavior in which the non-religious concerns of group dynamic are, in a great variety of ways, combined or connected with religious concerns' (Guilick 1976: 164). While the sect is defined against those in power, it is not defined on the basis of a *rejection* of social and political power. Guilick's sects are not protests against worldliness, but opposition to particular religious-political orders. They seek political power to establish their views as normative.

From this alternative perspective the normative, big tradition is *sectarian* in the sense that its leadership represents a particular little tradition, but still 'normative' in so far as they promote their status and interpretations of the big tradition as the standard for the group(s) they claim to represent. Of course, the actual normative status of the ruling, sectarian group increases according to the relative hegemony of the central institutions, collective literatures and alliances. These internal factors may be enhanced through the big tradition of an imperial power, if it provides further means—edicts, military assistance, propaganda—of authorization for the local ruling groups. This was clearly the case with Judea, beginning at least with the Persians and increasing through Greek rule to its culmination in the Herodian client kingdom. Thereafter, formalized and centralized Jewish institutions go into sharp decline. It is thus primarily in the pre-70 CE period that strong and central Jewish institutions (temple, army, bureaucracy) came into being and flourished, and therefore, it is *primarily in this period that we would expect to find a normative big tradition* in terms that I have described them, and *not in the post-70 period* when centralized Jewish institutions declined (see Holmberg 1990: 90).

It is thus interesting that Josephus's first discussion of Jewish sects occurs against the background of the established Hasmonean kingdom. Moreover, whether we translate his *haeresis* as a 'philosophy', 'school', 'sect' or some other term, Josephus describes his Pharisees and Sadducees as both *little traditions* in the sense that they held different views regarding free will, the after life and the interpretation of native laws, and as *sects* in Guilick's sense of socially organized religious groups that sought to gain political control in order to promote their own particular religious views. Pharisees and Sadducees both remained within, and indeed contended to control, a common, normative, big tradition, for in my terms it is inconceivable to think of sects apart from a shared big tradition. Thus it is problematic to treat Pharisees and Sadducees as completely different Judaisms, especially in Neusner's systemic terms.

Important data supporting a 'normative' Jewish tradition are the various edicts cited by Josephus in his *Antiquities of the Jews* and promulgated by Greek and Roman authorities. First, these establish the territory and authority of the Jerusalem leaders, guaranteeing them the right to fortify Jerusalem (14.10.5 [200]), make laws according to their 'ancestral customs' and to decide questions 'concerning the Jews' manner of life' (14.10.2 [194]). Second, they focus on specific elements of Jewish life: 'a commitment to the synagogue, to the Temple tax and thus the Temple and its worship, to the Sabbath, to the food laws and to living in accordance with their tradition' (Trebilco 1991: 34), that is, the 'big tradition' of Jewish practice. Third, they guarantee the right of *local* Jewish communities to live in accordance this 'big tradition' in most cases by virtue of the treaties made between Greek/Roman authorities and Jewish authorities in Jerusalem. Thus, Hyrcanus, strongman-king of Judea, sends an envoy to Roman governors of Asia, asking them to allow his 'fellow-citizens' in Ephesus to observe Jewish ancestral customs such as Sabbath, food regulations and festivals (*Ant.* 14.10.13 [225-27]), and he sends similar envoys on behalf of the Jews in Laodicea (14.10.20 [241-44]), Miletus (14.10.21 [244-46]), and Pergamum (14.10.22 [247-55]). Other edicts, while not specifically mentioning Hyrcanus or other Jerusalem authorities, nevertheless imply that the preservation of *local Jewish rights* are based on the friendship and alliance between the *central Jewish authorities* and Rome, for example, the Jews of Delos (14.10.8 [213-17]), Halicarnassus (14.10.23 [256-59]) and Sardis (14.10.24 [259-60]). A later decree of Augustus links the right of Jews in Asia and Libya to practice their customs to the loyalty of Hyrcanus to Rome (*Ant.* 16.6.1-2 [160-66]). Note here the linkage between the practice of customs and political loyalty, which I have already mentioned as a typical feature of this social-political context. We are not dealing with nation-states and national identities where borders define political loyalty and identity. Rather, identity is based on adherence to specific customs, understood against those who practice different customs. The customs are in turn articulated in terms of their representation by central authorities, on behalf of communal divinities, as the protectors of both customs and the communities who practice them. While these communities may configure themselves in relation to a shared homeland, their identity and formal rights are not configured in terms of their place of habitation, but on their daily practices: this determines their identity and political loyalty.

Note here too the centripetal potentials of this configuration: regional Jewish communities would have much to gain in identifying with the central authorities in Jerusalem, as this would allow them to maintain their local autonomy against the hardly friendly (or enlightened) Greek and Roman big and little traditions around them. Such autonomy would include, as we know, an avoidance of military conscription, a greater control of communal funds, and some degree of freedom from local courts, as well as allow variations in practice, such as synagogue style, ritual practices, art and theatre. These would be protected by formal treaty as long as the local community adhered to the shared big tradition, which, presumably, already constituted an important and venerable portion of their way of life. In this sense, then, the stronger the normative authorities, the greater the chance for local communities to preserve a local autonomy that would include the kinds of variation in Jewish practice that we know existed. Conversely, the central authorities would stand much to gain by protecting local Jewish autonomy, as would provide them a means of prestige and income, as well as opportunities to extend their patronage and influence into other territories. On these grounds, then, *Jewish normativity and Jewish diversity are complementary, not contradictory, features of the social reality of the time.*

Some further examples from Josephus are instructive here. As reported in *Ant.* 16.2.3-5 [27-65], the Jews of Ionia sought Herod's intercession against the local Greeks, who were forcing them to appear in courts on festival days and had confiscated money collected as offerings to the Jerusalem temple. These actions are understandable from the point of view of the Greeks, who were no doubt seeking to enhance their local, normative authority. Herod responded, and Nicholas's defense included a description of the antiquity and benign nature of Jewish customs, but emphasized as well the 'decrees of the Senate and tablets deposited in the Capitol' that guaranteed Jews the right to practice their ancestral customs (16.2.3 [48])—a guarantee based on the loyalty of the central Jewish authorities to Rome. The data is clear for what they imply: the capacity of the Jerusalem central authorities to exert power helped preserve local Jewish autonomy; local Jewish autonomy depended on support from the central Jewish authorities; both were linked by shared customs of a common big tradition, in this case via the temple.

A second example concerns the actions of Agrippa I and Herod of Chalcis. Both were effective kings in good standing with Roman authorities, and both successfully petitioned Claudius to issue a new edict, in the wake of riots caused by Gaius's attempt to set up a statue in Jerusalem, guaranteeing the rights of Alexandrian Jews (*Ant.* 19.5.1-3 [278-92]). Agrippa intervened effectively again a few years later, when men in Dora, a city in the sphere of Phoenicia, set up a statue in a 'synagogue of the Jews'. He petitioned Petronius to write a letter defending Jewish local rights, which the governor did bringing about the removal of the statue (19.6.1-4 [300-11]). In both of these examples, local, extra-Judean autonomy is preserved through the patronage of central Jewish authorities. Contrast these examples with the ineffectiveness of the anonymous, post-monarchical 'leaders of the Jewish community' when they attempted to petition the government of Nero on behalf of the Jewish community at Caesarea (*War* 2.12.2-3 [266-70]). Herod, certainly, would not have allowed such rough treatment of Jews by the Roman governor as occurred here, and he had the power and prestige to intervene.

Lest we suspect that this is a construct of Josephus, we find supporting evidence in the data of Cicero's account of the trial of Valerius Flaccus, Roman Governor of Asia Minor. Flaccus had issued an edict preventing the export of funds from Asia Minor, and had seized gold collected by Jews of Apamea, Laodicea, Adramyttium and Pergamum for the temple in Jerusalem. The Jews of these towns, in turn, charged him with violating their right to send such donations to Judea. Note that Cicero emphasizes that it is just this Jewish right to honor the Jerusalem temple that is at issue here (*Pro Flacco* 28.67, 69), and he states, and it is presumed, that Jews from Italy and all Roman provinces customarily sent gifts to the temple (28.67). This is both interesting and instructive: what we have here is a case of Jews in Asia Minor willing to violate Flaccus's ban on exporting gold in order to obey what was presumably a shared Jewish custom to do so. That is, they were willing to defy an edict of the Roman big tradition in order to observe an edict of the Jewish big tradition. This is significant for it shows the power of the Jerusalem big tradition in Asia Minor. More-over, the absence of any reference to the Jewish authorities in Jerusalem—who at this time, incidentally, were divided and weakened—shows that the normative big tradition exists apart from central political authorities. Cicero does report that Jews in Rome intervened to support those in Asia Minor (*Pro Flacco* 28.66), an indication of trans-regional Jewish identity and cooperation. This evidence also shows again the link between customs and political loyalties, and raises the question as to what these Jewish communities had to gain by challenging Flaccus—apart from the ill-will of local populations and Roman governors. The answer is, most likely, the preservation of their local autonomy and customs, which are, however, incomprehensible apart from a big tradition common to Jews in Asia Minor, Judea and Rome.

A final example comes from Philo, whose education included the study of Greek grammar, geometry, music and especially philosophy. Philo had a thorough command of Greek language and literature, and he took part in Alexandrian Greek city life including banquets, theater, boxing and horse-racing. Philo also produced a large number of philosophical works that presented the texts of the Jewish big tradition in terms of a Greek big tradition (Plato's philosophy). Yet, despite the clear influences on Philo from the Greek big tradition, he remains rooted in the big tradition of Judaism. His Abraham is still the ancestor of the Jewish people and an observer of Mosaic laws, and his Moses is still the lawgiver and prophet of Israel. Moreover, Philo is quite explicit in stating that allegorical interpre-tations of the Sabbath, temple worship, and the observance of other cus-toms, are no substitutes for their practice (*Migr. Abr.* 89–93). Accordingly, he identified himself as a 'Jew' who followed 'our ancestral customs' (*Somn.* 2.123), and is probably our prime example of a local Jew preserv-ing and defending the big Jewish tradition by virtue of his articulation of a Jewish little tradition in terms of a local big tradition. In fact, what Philo does, in my terms, is transform a Greek big tradition (Platonic philosophy) into a Jewish little tradition (Philo's philosophy), while preserving the primary status of the Jewish big tradition, *and its practice*, in the process —a subordination of a Greek big tradition to the Jewish big tradition. It points to acculturation, not assimilation; to the persistence, not attenuation, of a distinct Jewish identity. While any 'Platonist' could allegorize Jewish scriptures, Philo's allegorical 'system' is not that of any Platonist. Rather, it is that of a 'Platonist' who circumcised, observed the Sabbath, made a pilgrimage to the Jewish temple, and acknowledged the Mosaic laws as the product of divine will. It is thus probably for this reason that Philo was part of a delegation protesting the planned desecration of the Jerusalem temple by the Emperor Gaius, which he described as representing 'all Jews everywhere' (*Leg. Gai.* 370).

While rejecting a monolithic and immutable 'Judaism', I disagree with those who would in turn fragment a coherent Jewish identity-tradition into multiple and discordant 'Judaisms', or worse, dissolve it into an amorphous, anonymous, biblical sectarianism. There are many good contemporary theological and political reasons for thinking of Judaism as discreet and fragmented, but little evidence deriving from the data. I see rather a common Judaism committed to the synagogue, the temple tax (and thus the temple itself), circumcision, the Sabbath and avoidance of idolatry, with multiple, local 'judaisms'[7] (*sic*) evincing variations articulated in terms of local non-Jewish big and little traditions, that is, in art, architecture, philosophy, and ritual practices.

A Re-evaluation of Hasmonean Origins, Expansion and Impact

Village Strongmen as a Social Type in the Imperial Context and the Hasmoneans as Local Strongmen
Schwartz (1993), following Tcherikover, has suggested that the early Hasmoneans were 'village strongmen' whose initial goal was not political independence from the Seleucid system but advancement within it. In this way he sees them as initially similar to the Tobiads, who also appear as local strongmen working within the Ptolemaic imperial system. Schwartz emphasizes the shifting nature of local political factions in Palestine, from the Tobiads through the Hasmoneans to the Herodians, as well as the ongoing and determining context of Greek and Roman domination.

A more recent example of a 'strongman' is Aqiili Agha, who 'spent

---

7. This deliberate use of the lower case judaism follows that of 'islam' by El-Zein (1977), as a way of distinguishing local variations within a common big tradition of 'Islam'.

most of his career either a servant of the Ottoman regime or a rebel against it' (Zenner 1972: 178). Born in Egypt in the early 1800s to an Arab father and a Turcoman mother, he and his 'tribe' of Bedouin initially served in the army of Ibrahim Pasha and were settled in Gaza immediately after Pasha's conquest of Palestine in 1831. Later, Aqiili and his troops joined a local peasant revolt, the failure of which resulted in his dismissal from Pasha's army and his appointment as head of an irregular cavalry unit stationed in Galilee. His subsequent intervention in a local dispute in 1845, and his defense of the leader of the Latin Church in Nazareth shortly thereafter, cost him his command. He then fled to the hills and began to raid local settlements until Ottomans restored him to his command to curb his raids; he returned to Nazareth and later gained some international fame by escorting an American expedition to the Trans-Jordan and the Dead Sea.

The situation in Ottoman Palestine at this time became one of shifting factions of local families, Bedouin, Ottoman officials and the European powers. All attempted a strategy of divide-and-rule to control the region, and in this spirit Aqiili continued his tactics of cooperation and rebellion with the ruling powers. With the assistance of a brother, he united a number of Bedouin 'tribes' and peasants in the area, building a coalition of villages and troops. He became the effective ruler of Galilee in 1854, a position tolerated by the Ottomans due to their pre-occupation in the Crimean war and their need to transfer imperial troops to the front. The Ottomans gave command of Galilee to their military leader in Damascus, and his invasion of Galilee with Kurdish irregulars in 1857 ended in his defeat by Aqiili. The Ottomans had no choice but to confirm his rule. In 1860 he was recognized by the European powers, a factor he hoped would help him against the local Ottoman authorities. His troops protected the local Christians in Galilee after a war between Druze and Maronites sparked massacres of Christians in Lebanon and anti-Christian riots in Damascus. He was repeatedly forced into exile on a number of occasions, alternatively fleeing to allies across the Jordan, but returning again and again through a continuing tactic of flight, banditry and accommodation.

Though Aqiili styled himself as a protector of local villages shielding peasants against marauding Bedouin and Ottoman forces, he forced the villagers to pay 'protection money' for his services. He made alliances through intermarriage with local leaders, and utilized the ethnic, religious and regional diversity to maintain his authority. The presence of incipient factionalism allowed him to play off groups against one another to his own advantage, acquiring allies by posing as the protector of local interests. His political success was due in large part to his relative geographic distance from power centers in Damascus and Jerusalem, as well as his exploitation of anti-Ottoman sentiment among the local population. The ruling authorities had more to gain by accommodating him than by opposing him.

The Zenon papyri portray a number of Aqiili-type strongmen in Ptolemaic Palestine, that is, 'well-to-do landowners, living in areas relatively remote from centers of government authority, who were influential enough locally and zealous enough of their own prerogatives to resist successfully official interference in their villages and farms' (Schwartz 1993: 306; see also Tcherikover 1979: 63-66, 127-42). Among these, Tobias was perhaps the most successful in maintaining his relative independence while influential enough to have his authority incorporated into the local Ptolemaic administration. His success assisted his descendants in maintaining their local influence and autonomy, until their power began to wane when the later Tobiads alienated other Judean factions through their pro-Seleucid Hellenization (in my sense of *Hellenismos* noted above). However, while the literary data suggest inter-Judean differences over the adoption of Greek practices and the type of political accommodation to be made with Greek powers, nothing suggests that such differences represented 'reformers' versus 'nationalists', or 'progressives' versus 'traditionalists' as expressions of the fundamental dynamics involved. Those dynamics were rather a shifting political scene marked by a Seleucid expansion and the growing influence of Rome on the region, two factors destined to interrupt a long period of Ptolemaic quiescence and Judeo-Ptolemaic harmony. Judean leaders in Palestine had been left, relatively, to themselves during the reigns of the previous Ptolemaic kings, while the Judeans in Egypt are generally portrayed as supporters of the royal government. The Seleucid expansion south in the context of ongoing and developing military conflicts stimulated efforts to centralize and consolidate rule in Palestine, a key part of which would necessarily involve the establishment of Hellenic cults in place or beside local traditions. This meant an incorporation of the Judean communities into the Seleucid regime well beyond the Ptolemaic framework. The adoption of Greek customs, in this context, has nothing to do with notions of reform or enlightenment, though it may have been couched in Greek terms of a civilizing mission to the barbarians. In any case, it is possible that Jason's 'reforms' had as much to do with reading the political winds blowing from the north as reflecting a desire on the part of Judeans to Hellenize. It could just as well have been an attempt to forestall Seleucid conquest and occupation, as seems to be the case with the Samaritans who agreed to follow Seleucid practice after they saw the 'suffering and misfortunes' of the Judeans brought on by resistance (*Ant*. 12.5.5 [257]).

The Hasmoneans come onto the scene as allies of Onias and anti-Seleucid factions, and the defenders of local, Judean tradition. However, this does not amount to a 'nationalist' movement nor a 'anti-modernist' reaction, even if they were likely seeking to return to the relative auton-omy (and stability) of the Ptolemaic status quo—only now with them-selves as its representatives and chief beneficiaries under the new rulers (see Schwartz 1991; Hyldahl 1990). They may certainly have presented this as a choice between collaboration with the Greeks (*Hellenismos*) or loyalty to the Judeans (*Ioudaismos*), but as such this refers primarily to a choice in a political conflict, and may be more a product of the propaganda efforts of the victorious Hasmoneans than a reflection of language as it was practiced during the conflict. In any case, a close reading of 1 and 2 Maccabees indicates that the initial actions of Judas and his brothers were guerrilla raids *against Judeans* outside of the Jerusalem center who were collaborating with the Seleucids. They attacked Judean allies of the Seleu-cids, tore down altars used in Greek sacrificial rites, and circumcized Judean boys who had not undergone the ritual due to Seleucid restrictions (1 Macc. 2.42-48; 2 Macc. 8.5-7). In a manner similar to Aquiili Aga in his context, Judas and his brothers negotiated when possible to avoid battle with imperial forces, and made strategic alliances with foreign allies to enhance their influence as local leaders to be reckoned with. They plundered Arabian tribes to gain supplies for their army (1 Macc. 12.31-32), and raided neighboring peoples when necessary to undermine imperi-ally sponsored, local alliances formed against them (1 Macc. 5.1-3, 65-68; 2 Macc. 10.14-17). Their overall goal appears rather limited: they sought to negotiate a settlement with the Seleucids that would give imperial sanction to the influence and power they had achieved by force; this would necessarily curtail further attempts at *Hellenismos*. The Seleucids, by recognizing the de facto success of these local strongmen, and with Rome now growing large on the horizon, would avoid a continued regional instability that would further undermine their authority. Note that John Hyrcanus, who remained more of a super-strongman than a king, contin-ued this strategy of resistance and cooperation. He resists Antiochus VII by force, but when defeated he submits and accompanies the king against Parthia (*Ant*. 13.8.4 [250]). Later, when the opportunity presents itself, Hyrcanus solidifies this control by subduing neighboring people (*Ant*. 13.9.2 [265]) and renewing Judean alliances with the Romans.

This alternative view situates the early Hasmoneans as local strongmen, who advanced to power within a broader and shifting political context and sought to maximize their political autonomy. Like Aqiili Aga they gained influence by playing off local and imperial factions against one another, all the while maintaining the willingness and ability to use military force. When necessary they engaged in direct battle with the enemy, but relied mainly on guerrilla tactics and disruptive raids to destabilize the local administration; they sought alliances with anti-Seleucid forces in Rome and Sparta in order to strengthen their position. As a result of this the Seleucid authorities were forced to negotiate with them as the only local force that could bring order to the region. They may certainly have had visions of an independent kingdom, but only in the terms of the times, and not as a 'national movement' and not against an alternative emancipation into the progressive, enlightened sphere of the Seleucids.

Conquest and Incorporation: Ashanti Expansion as a Comparative Example

Josephus discusses the conquest of Idumea in *Antiquities of the Jews* 13 and 15. In the former passage he says that 'Hyrcanus also captured the Idumean cities of Adora and Marissa and after subduing all the Idumeans permitted them to remain in their country so long as they had themselves circumcised and were willing to observe the laws of the *Ioudaioi*', which they did out of 'attachment to the land of their forefathers' and 'from that time onwards they have continued to be *Ioudaioi*' (13.9.1 [254-58]). He does not mention circumcision in the latter passage, however, but only notes that Hyrcanus made the Idumeans adopt the 'way of life' (*politeian*), customs and laws of the Judeans. Two other sources speak of these events. Ptolemy the Historian claims that the Idumeans were originally 'Phoenicians and Syrians' who were conquered by the Judeans and 'forced to undergo circumcision' (Stern 1974–84: I, 146). Strabo, in contrast to both Josephus and Ptolemy, says nothing about either circumcision or coercion: he claims instead that the Idumeans were Nabateans who were banished from their own land due to sedition, and 'who joined the Judeans and shared in the same customs with them' (*Geogr.* 15.2.34).

There is enough ambiguity in these accounts to suggest a situation of more complexity than any one account, and that the vision of Judeans forcibly circumcising Idumeans may be a fanciful one. Cohen (1987b: 423-24; 1999: 116-17) and Kasher (1988: 55-57) argue that the circumcision was already an accepted practice among the Idumeans, consequently the claims made by Josephus and Ptolemy to a forcible circumcison are either mistaken or instead refer to the cessation of the practice under the Seleucid restrictions and their reintroduction by the Hasmoneans. Forcible, in this sense, would not mean acts of forced circumcision on the spot, but the coerced reassertion of local custom abandoned under duress of the Seleucids. Cohen and Kasher also point out the likelihood of some considerable Idumean sympathy for the Hasmoneans, both as popular leaders (strongmen in my terms) as well as defenders of local autonomy and traditions against the Seleucid Greeks. They argue that Ptolemy the Historian took a hostile stance toward Judean resistance, and so presented them as local tyrants. Josephus followed this hostile source for apologetic reasons, but it is more likely that Strabo's account is closer to the truth: the Judean conquest resulted in a federation with the Idumeans based on common traditions such as circumcision, albeit led by Judea. I support these arguments, but disagree in respect of this incorporation/federation as 'conversion', or as a new development in Judean identity-tradition. I see instead a more complex dynamic of generational transculturation, in which the incorporation of the Idumeans (and Itureans) was one of many events in a process of long duration: an ongoing transculturation, acculturation and assimilation that is reconfigured in the context of the conquest and political incorporation of the Idumeans into the Judean kingdom as political incorporation and re-enculturation.

In support of this I want to review briefly another comparative model: the growth and expansion of the Ashanti kingdom, and their incorporation of Akan and non-Akan peoples. The Ashanti kingdom rose to prominence in West Africa (modern Ghana) during the early eighteenth century (see Arhin 1967; Morrison 1982; Wilks 1975). What began as a series of defensive wars against the neighboring Denkyeras, led by local strongmen and chiefs, developed into the Ashanti conquest and domination of related Akan and non-Akan peoples. This expansion was given greater momentum through the impact of European trading in Africa, while much of its success and durability were due to specfic geographic and cultural factors: (1) the location of the Ashanti capital Kumasi at the center of trade routes between the north and south, as well as the richness of the region in gold and kola nuts, both important trade items; (2) the energy and political savvy of the Ashanti leaders; (3) centuries of pre-European transculturation among Akan and non-Akan populations, including the development of shared traditions of origin and custom. These factors aided the Ashanti leaders in their campaigns of conquest and policies of consolidation, both of which had the goal of creating a degree of 'ethnic and cultural homogeneity of the Ashanti and the conquered' local populations against the

Europeans (Arhin 1967: 79). As noted, acculturation had been occurring among neighboring peoples for centuries, and many peoples round about them practiced customs and traditions similar to the Ashanti. Ashanti leaders used notions of common kinship and common customs as political propaganda to unite local groups against European rule, while at the same time legitimizing Ashanti domination of these groups to their own advantage. This was especially true for the other Akan groups, and 'Ashantization' was most effective among these populations. Note, however, that the assimilation of Akan peoples did not mean 'cultural indoctrination' or a singular reculturation event or ritual, since the Ashanti and other Akan groups already shared similar customs. Akan assimilation was instead built upon a prior acculturation facilitated by a political integration made possible through conquest. In this sense, it brought to culmination an ongoing process over *la longue durée*.

There are obvious similarities with Judean expansions. Both were rooted in the attempts of local strongmen to increase their own status and power against an encroaching, foreign power. Both sought to incorporate local totemic groups, both to enhance the position of their own people, and to unite local people against outside conquerors. Both, moreover, were indigenous populations sharing significant customs with the people round about them. I might also mention here, as well, the significance of Jerusalem, which, like Kumasi, was a known and venerable city occupying a strategic position along important military and trade routes. Domination of the regional politics, and leverage in trans-regional interactions, would be impossible without control, or destruction, of this center. The main factor of Ashanti success was the propaganda that they shared ancestors, traditions and customs with the peoples they conquered; the Judeans also emphasized, and perhaps also invented, shared local traditions and customs, and thus presented their political conquests as the necessary reunification of related people against outsiders.

Hasmonean Inclusivism and Universalism: Judeans, Idumeans, Nabateans and the 'Abrahamic Alliance'
The book of Genesis claims that Judeans (as Judahites) and Idumeans (as Edomites) shared a common ancestor. Edom/Esau is grandson of Abraham and the son of Isaac, twin brother to Jacob, 'father' of all Israel (Gen. 25.19-26). Further genealogical links are suggested in Genesis and *Jubilees*,[8] and

8. Among the kings of Edom listed in both the Bible and *Jubilees*, there is mention of a Shaul of Rehoboth (Gen. 36.7; 1 Chron. 1.48; *Jub*. 38.21-22). Among the

perhaps in *Pseudo-Philo* (Zeron 1980). Genesis assumes that Jacob and Esau, as descendants of Isaac, were circumcised on the eighth day, though it represents circumcision as a sign of the covenant, with attendant rights to land, between Yahweh and Abraham's descendants through Isaac alone. *Jubilees* 15.25-26, however, suggests that the Edomites practiced circumcision in the fashion of the Ishmaelites, that is, at puberty (15.28-31). *Jubilees* 15.33-34 also contains a strong polemic against the abandonment of circumcision under circumstances that reflect the events described in 1 Macc. 1.48, as well as what appears to be a criticism against circumcision performed at any time other than the eighth day (15.25-27). There is also an attempt to link the eighth-day circumcision ritual to Judean hegemony over Esau (*Jub.* 15.30-32), that is, as a sign of the hegemony of the Abrahamic covenant with Isaac. *Jubilees*, in fact, might be seen as outlining a kind of ancestral, Abrahamic religion, transposing a number of 'Mosaic' (Judaic?) customs into Abrahamic equivalents, albeit centered on Judah. This may point to actual historical variations in respect to a common ritual of circumcision, along with an achieved or assumed relationship of such customs to political hegemony (Millar 1993: 35). In any case, it suggests totemic identities articulated in terms of shared genealogies against parallel but different totemic groups.

The Idumeans were not the only group with whom the Judeans claimed kinship. Josephus explicitly links 'Arabs' in general (*Ant.* 1.12.2) and then the Nabateans in particular, with Abraham through the descendants of Ishmael (*Ant.* 1.12.4). In the former passage he also links the Arab practice of circumcision at age 13 to Ishmael's circumcision at that age as described in Gen. 17.25. Nowhere else, however, does Josephus indicate that the Arabs/Nabateans practiced any other customs that were similar to those of the Judeans, though proximity and regional transculturation would suggest that this was likely (Goodman 1998). However, Josephus does make use of a curious choice of terms when, describing parallel events to 1 Macc. 5.24-27, he has the Nabateans urge Judas and Jonathan to 'march speedily against the foreigners (*epi tous allophulos*) and to try to

---

descendants of Simeon there is a Shaul as well. In Gen. 46.8-10 and Exod. 6.15 he is called the son of a Canaanite women. However, *Jub.* 44.13 calls him the son of a 'Zephathite woman'. There is a Valley of Zephathah mentioned in 2 Chron. 14.10 that seems identical to the Valley of Gerar in Gen. 26.22, where a well of Isaac's called Rehoboth is located. That there were marriages between early Israelites and Edomites is probable, that later Judean and Idumean royal families intermarried is certain from Josephus. See Mendels (1987: esp. ch. 6).

save his countrymen' (*tous homoethneis*; *Ant.* 12.8.3 [336]). Zeitlin (1974: 450) has suggested that Josephus consistently uses the term *allophulon* to mean a non-worshiper of Yahweh, that is, 'gentile', and *homophulon* to mean fellow worshipers of Yahweh (*homoethnon* is used to refer to someone sharing the same country or *ethnos*). This passage might suggest that Josephus regarded the Nabateans as kinsmen and not 'gentiles'. Here we should also mention Josephus's rendition of Esau's marriages in Gen. 27.41 and 28.8. Seeing that 'Isaac and his family' were upset by his marriage to Canaanite women, Esau took Ishmael's daughter as a third wife to 'gratify them' (*Ant.* 1.18.4 [276-77]), an indication of the boundaries of kin and non-kin: Israelites, Edomites and Ishmaelites are related peoples. Note here as well that the statement in *Jubilees* that 'they have made themselves like the gentiles' (15.34) applies specifically to those Israelites who give up circumcision, but is not used to refer to the sons of Ishmael (and Esau) who practice *a different circumcision ritual*. While the latter may not be Judeans/Israelites, neither are they gentiles, that is, they are kinsmen with Israel.

Josephus derived the descent of the Nabateans from Ishmael perhaps in part from the list of Ishmael's descendants in Gen. 25.12-15, where the Hebrew *nabit* is rendered in the Septuagint as *Nabaiot* (see Bartlett 1979: 63). However, he does not link the *doma/Idouma* of the same passage with the Idumeans, which would imply that the Idumeans were descendants of Ishmael (Millar 1993: 23-45, esp. 35), a point that suggests this tradition is based on more than just a similarity of names. Instead Josephus, like 1 Maccabees, links the Idumeans with Esau the son of Isaac. The result of this is that we have Idumeans who are considered as descendants of Isaac and Esau, yet observe the practice of circumcision according to Ishmael— a point that brings to mind Strabo's comments that the Idumeans were originally Nabateans who were banished due for sedition, and then joined the Judeans 'and shared in the same customs with them' (*Geogr.* 16.2.34). It is not at all inconceivable that the Idumeans of this time were composed of old Edomite and new immigrant Nabatean populations, since, as I noted, Bartlett has argued convincingly for an assimilation of the eastern Edomites into the Nabateans, and transculturation was the rule rather than the exception in this region. This would account for both the Idumean descent from the biblical Esau, and their Nabatean-like practice of circumcision, and it would suggest that the supposed enforced circumcision of Idumeans by the Judeans rather involved a shift in the kind of circumcision performed—a shift that was significant considering the relationship between ritual and identity that the practice denotes. Moreover, such a shift would have been to the advantage of the Idumeans in the sense that now, as descendants of Isaac and Jacob, they were entitled to the rights attendant in that descent, an advantage taken by the Idumean strongman Antipater and his descendents (see below). The case of the Itureans is also instructive here. While Josephus again speaks of forced circumcision, he also presents the alternative account of Timagenes: Aristobulus brought over to the Judeans part of the Iturean nation 'by the bond of circumcision' (*Ant.* 13.11.3 [319]). Kasher (1988: 71) suggests the likely possibility that Josephus is referring to Iturean groups settled in Galilee as part of an earlier Iturean expansion. In any case, Timagenes's report implies that Aristobulus joined Judeans and these conquered Itureans together *on the basis* of their common (Abrahamic) practice of circumcision, though again implying Judean hegemony.[9]

The data cited above point in the direction of traditions of kinship among Judeans, Arabs and Idumeans based on shared ancestry signified by a shared, though not uniformly practiced, ritual of circumcision. These, in turn, may have been linked by a tradition of common descent through Abraham. The letters reportedly sent by the Judeans to Sparta and Pergamum explicitly indicate that belief in a common Abrahamic descent did serve as a basis for political alliance (1 Macc. 12.19-23; *Ant.* 12.4.10 [226]; 14.10.22 [255]), while the genealogical and ritual traditions I cited from Genesis and *Jubilees* may suggest that the Hasmoneans promoted this Abrahamic alliance, locally among Idumeans and Nabateans, as 'propaganda' for a regional alliance against the Seleucids and as a means of incorporating the Idumeans into the Judean kingdom. Nevertheless, Hasmonean hegemony was likely not built up from scratch in the Seleucid period. Inter-regional contact and transculturation had been ongoing for centuries, as was competition for what became Idumean territory. There were conflicts between Arabian traders in the south and the northern hill people as early as the twelfth century BCE, and control of these southern

9.   A point of note here is that the Judeans chose to link themselves with the Idumeans and Itureans through circumcision, but did not do so with the conquered populations in the Ascalon or Azotus. There is no evidence that circumcisions were practiced in these regions, nor are there traditions of shared kinship with its earlier inhabitants (i.e. Philistines); hence there were not grounds for promoting an Abrahamic alliance as the basis of Judean hegemony. It is perhaps for this reason that Judean rule was tenuous in these cities, and endured in Idumea and Galilee. The case of Pella may speak against this, unless we accept the reading in alternative manuscripts that Jannaeus refused to spare them 'even though the inhabitants promised' to accept circumcision.

trade routes may explain the penetration of earlier Israelite and Judean material culture in this region (see Finkelstein 1988). Nabatean expansion west was a replay of this in the Persian and Hellenistic periods, and since Idumea straddled the Petra–Gaza trade route, it constituted a kind of buffer zone between competing Judean and Nabatean trading strategies. The Nabateans had made repeated attempts to secure this region; perhaps by influencing or conquering Idumeans themselves (Bowersock 1983: 22-26), while Judean expansion is also understandable in terms of economic advantages. The competition in the region did eventually lead to conflict between the Judeans and Nabateans, and it is possible that the Idumeans may have already leaned toward the Judeans for protection against a Nabatean expansion that was swallowing their eastern kinsmen. Judean expansion into Idumea, and its incorporation of the Idumean population, was therefore more than just a dynamic of their response to the Seleucid incursions, but the end result of centuries of interaction and acculturation, geographic constraints and economic strategies, that is, a product of the region's *longue durée*.

On these grounds, and that of the other evidence cited, there seems little reason to think of the Hasmonean incorporation of the Idumeans (or Itureans) as 'conversion' in the singular and above noted sense of the term. Nor should we see this as the product of changing notions of Jewish notions of self-understanding stimulated by the acculturation to Greek notions of *politeia*. The Judean conquest of Idumea suggests instead a political incorporation based on shared customs and interests; a culmination of long-term dynamics rather than an unprecedented event, exacerbated by—the ultimate failure of—Seleucid expansionist policies and the political vacuum in the region before the Roman conquests in the east. Moreover, since there is no evidence of an overwhelming Judean military presence for the conquest and control of Idumea, and fairly strong evidence for later Idumean participation into Judean society, it is reasonable to consider that the hegemony of Judea was effectively based on more than just force. Certainly the Idumeans knew they had more to gain through their incorporation into Judea than not, since their survival was otherwise being rendered problematic in the face of Nabatean expansion. Moreover, the Idumean leaders were likely aware that with the collapse of the Seleucid sphere, and the continued decline of the Ptolemaic influence in Palestine, the only possibility for regional rule was through Judea. Whoever held control of the Judean temple, city, and later the kingship, not only ruled the subjects in his territory but also, if only symbolically, Judeans in places such as Italy, Asia Minor, Egypt and Persia as well. This was far more than a strongman in Ammon, Idumea, Gaza or Ascalon could ever hope to accomplish. Thus, the road to status, wealth and power for any local families, Judean or otherwise, became and was to remain Judea and Jerusalem. The incorporation of the Idumeans, and the subsequent ascendancy of Idumean—Herodian—strongmen, is only understandable in this context.[10] And it bears giving emphasis to the fact that it was the Idumeans, after all, who came to rule in Judea, and perhaps who gained the most out of the Hasmonean conquest and incorporation.[11]

This brings me to a concluding point. While there are data pointing to the emergence of central Judean authorities in the Persian period, the Hasmonean kingdom seems the more likely locus for a strong normative Judaism in the terms I have used above. As Davies (1992a: 156) notes, it is with the success and consolidation of the Hasmonean family that we see the establishment of complex bureaucratic institutions, a military complex, an official scripture, liturgy and calendar, a legal system, and other elements of political-cultural centralization. All were built upon previous Palestinian, including Israelite and Judahite, traditions, but they were now formulated in terms of both Hasmonean political consolidation and Hellenistic literary-historical-political norms. Yet, I would note here against Davies that it is not so much that 'Sabbath observance, circumcision, diet, tithing regulation, festivals…now became part of the official religion of the Judeans' at this time only. Rather, it is that these widely and variously practiced Judean customs were now reformulated and regulated

---

10. There was also the tradition, which was probably fairly widely known, that Judah/Judea as the favored grandson of Abraham was destined to dominate all of the related 'tribes' in Palestine and possibly beyond; Gen. 49.8-12; *T. Sim.* 7.1; *T. Naph.* 5.5, 8.2; *Jub.* 31.7; Suetonius, *Lives* 8.5; Tacitus, *Hist.* 5.13.2.

11. Cohen (1999: 111-12) and Richard Horsley in this volume, suggest that the Costobar incident (*Ant.* 15.7.910) indicates the tenuousness of the Idumean adoption of Judean identity and hegemony. They are possibly correct here, but I think they fail to consider the following arguments. First, that this is an isolated incident that must be weighed against other accounts that show the Idumeans well integrated into Judea. Second, Costobar's 'return' to his Idumean divinities and traditions was a function of his political strategy. A polity independent of Judea and Jerusalem would necessarily be articulated in terms of non-Judean customs, as my previous investigations have shown. It tells us nothing about the actual ongoing nature of Idumean identity, and may be similar to the revival of 'Celtic' identity by contemporary Europeans. Third, almost 100 years had passed since the incorporation of the Idumeans, a considerable period of time when one recalls that the Islamization of the Berbers took place over a similar period of time. While the Berbers remained a distinct group, they did so within Islam. See also Cohen's discussion of Herod's 'Jewishness' (1999: 12-24).

in terms of Hasmonean sectarian (in my terms) understanding, and promoted as such via the power of their centralized institutions. In this they were aided, as I noted, by the centripetal effects this centralization would have in the context of a larger and hostile imperium: dispersed Jewish communities (Judaisms) would stand to gain by identifying with this particular formulation of the Jewish big tradition, refashioning their own practices more in line with the new sectarian norm, so as to benefit from its patronage. However, it seems likely that it was Herod, the Idumean strongman successor to the Hasmoneans, who was the most successful in establishing a strong, central Jewish big tradition.

Herod was *the Great Normativizer* of Judaism, the Solomon of the first century whose influence stretched from Egypt to the Euphrates (and beyond). His bureaucratic expansions, support for Judean traditions, and building projects brought both Judean normative capacities, as well as the Judeans as a whole, to their heights (demonstrated well by Richardson 1996). It is thus one of those ironies of history (though still an understandable dynamic of the geographic and cultural dynamics of Palestine) that though the rise and expansion of the Hasmoneans set the stage for the height of Judean kingdom and people, it did so via the hand of a conquered Idumean.

Conclusions, Summaries and New Directions: Jews, Greeks and Contest of Cultures in the Ancient Near East

The Hasmoneans have sometimes been portrayed as fanatics and fundamentalists, whose resistance and counter-conquests become expressions of an essential religious fanaticism and chauvinist nationalism. Such a view reflects the tyranny of Greece over Judaism that I noted above: it assumes the benevolence of the Greeks and the civilizing nature of their rule, and it reflects the context of the nineteenth century with its universalistic Hellenism set against a particularistic Judaism in need of dissolution. Notably, similar arguments were made against the Ashanti. Arhin (1967: 65, 80-81) speaks of the 'barbaric or nonsense theory' of Ashanti expansion in which their conquests and assimilations were treated as an indication of Ashanti (and African) savagery rather than a political strategy—and that their defeat by the British was the defeat of civilization over savagery. Descriptions of the Hasmoneans in such terms, then, may also be described as a 'barbaric or nonsense theory' of Judean expansion, just as portrayals of them as national liberators might be dubbed the 'romantic or liberation theory' of Judean expansion. Neither view fits the data read outside of nineteenth-century notions of European-Christian enlightenment, superiority and hegemony, or the dynamics of religion versus nationalism, reformation versus tradition. The Hasmoneans, instead, were savvy but small-time strongmen and kings whose rise to power and local conquests are explainable within the social, political, economic and geographic dynamics of the region, and in terms of changing patterns of power and domination throughout the Mediterranean littoral. The Hasmoneans *were* more successful than many other local peoples in achieving a degree of political autonomy, and the Judeans *were* more successful than virtually all other contemporary peoples in marinating and enduring identity-traditions, but in most other ways they were typical of the Hellenistic-Persian, Asiatic cultures around them.

This touches on two critical points toward any future critical historiography of Judaism. First, we must abandon the view that Jews were strange or peculiar in the eyes of their neighbors; this is another product of the nineteenth-century context of ancient Judaism. While ancient authors did make statements about the oddness of Jewish customs, these must be viewed in context. For one, we find many such statements made about other contemporary people, and a strong case for the 'strangeness' of the Egyptians could also be made based on the Greek and Roman literary sources as well (see Yavetz 1993: 14). For another many of these statements, as Cohen (1999: 25-68) has shown, simply don't match the data we have, but more likely reflect the biased views of their authors: intellectuals of the very empires that were subjugating Jews. The real problem, however, is that these ancient chauvinist views have been carried forth in a modern scholarship nurtured in a nineteenth century that emphasized the distinctiveness of Jews in order to dissolve them into an incipient national, German identity (see Moore 1921). That context is gone, but the view of Greco-Roman normalcy and Jewish peculiarity persists.

Second, we must abandon the view that Jews were undergoing some kind of cultural identity crisis in the face of Greek and Roman conquest. Jews underwent multiple and sometimes radical changes, but they did so always in terms of an ongoing and 'inventing tradition' (for the term, see Sahlins 1999). That is, they articulated changes in their tradition in terms of continuity with the past. This is quite different, for example, when compared to Greeks and Romans: they eventually abandoned their past, as well as their ancestors and divinities, in favor of Judaized counterparts (until partially revived or invented by the nationalists of modern Europe and elsewhere). I am of course talking about gentile Christianity, which we can alternatively understand as a product of a Near Eastern transculturation—transsimilation—in which Syrian, Egyptians, Greeks, Romans and many others gave up their ancestral identities to adopt a new identity articulated in terms of, yet against, Jewish identity. The process of this development is certainly complex, and thus it is doubtful that it emerged though a singular Jesus event. Rather, we should see it in terms of longer processes of cultural interaction that began before Jesus and Christianity. In any case it is difficult in these terms to see Christianity as a parallel development to rabbinic Judaism. The latter, in my terms, is simply a new sectarian Judaism that gains some degree of normative power to promote its own views as normative: yet these are, as even a cursory analysis shows, the same big tradition of Sabbath, dietary laws, temple (now as symbol only), festivals, circumcision and scripture—only now articulated in terms of the new sectarian big tradition.[12] Christianity, by its own self-representation, rejects all of the Jewish big tradition, and instead articulates itself as non-Jews, gentiles, who assume the status of Israel via a singular event. To compare the two, to see rabbinic Judaism as anything but the native continuity of the pre-70 CE traditions, is comprehensible only apart from the data we have and in terms of Christian hegemonic categories.

My goal has been an understanding of Hasmonean origins, expansion and influence outside of its modern, mainly, nineteenth-century context and in terms of some comparative ethnographic models. I have sought to by-pass a particular political and religious present—and a particular theological past—that has been so influential in the (mis-)interpretation of Judaism and Hasmonean origins. As I have noted, this has not meant that I claim to be writing outside of a political-social present. To the contrary, I acknowledge that my own readings are shaped by my fundamental effort to read 'Judaism' outside of Christian hegemonic categories, and within configurations of the interpretation of ancient Judaism in terms of post-colonial and post-Orientalist analysis. This may influence my readings of the data, but certainly no more than other positions influence other scholars—and it certainly does not prevent me from preferring my own readings of the data to that of others.

12. Very much the way Martin Goodman (1983) suggests that rabbinic Judaism achieved gradual hegemony in Galilee.

BETWIXT AND BETWEEN:
THE SAMARITANS IN THE HASMONEAN PERIOD

Lester L. Grabbe

The Samaritan community, with its cult on Mt Gerizim, is one of the most important religious communities in Palestine besides the Jews, not least because it has continued to exist even to the present. To get at the sociology of the community is not a simple matter, and we must begin with the basics: What are the sources? What are the problems with extracting their data? What do they tell us about the history of the community? Only then can we ask sociological questions.

Unless otherwise qualified, the term 'Samaritan(s)' will be used of the community whose religious center was the cult on Mt Gerizim and which produced the community still in existence. How large and extensive that community was, and whether it embraced most of the population in the old region of Samaria, has yet to be determined. This paper makes no *a priori* assumptions about them.

The Sources and their Data

Books of Maccabees

There is nothing in 1 Maccabees which clearly bears on the question of the Samaritans.[1] 2 Maccabees may have been written at a time when relations between Jews and Samaritans were deteriorating. Yet even if this was so, two passages give information not necessarily detrimental to the Samaritans:

1. 1 Macc. 3.10 says that Apollonius 'gathered the Gentiles and a large force from Samaria to fight against Israel'. If Apollonius was governor of Samaria (so Josephus, *Ant.* 12.5.5 [261]; 12.7.1 [287]), he would have had a military force at his disposal, no doubt in part recruited locally. Since this need not imply that the Samaritans as a nation or community sided with Apollonius against the Jews, the incident has no clear bearing on my question.

and he [Antiochus IV] left governors to afflict the people: at Jerusalem, Philip...and at Gerizim, Andronicus; and besides these Menelaus, who lorded it over his fellow citizens worse than the others did (2 Macc. 5.22-23, RSV).

The context and wording indicate that the Samaritans were put under the same restrictions, even religious persecution, which affected the Jews. Another passage supports and supplements this:

Not long after this, the king sent an Athenian senator to compel the Jews to forsake the laws of their fathers...and also to pollute the temple in Jerusalem and call it the temple of Olympian Zeus, and to call the one in Gerizim the temple of Zeus the Friend of Strangers, as did the people who dwelt in that place (2 Macc. 6.1-2, RSV).

What are the implications of this? Did the Samaritans accept the Hellenization of their cult? Some translations suggest that the Samaritans themselves requested that their temple be given a Greek name.[2] The little information in the context does not require that conclusion, but the question will be considered further below.

Statements of Josephus

Josephus is clearly prejudiced against the Samaritans.[3] When he mentions them, he often takes the opportunity to disparage the Samaritan community. Nevertheless, in some instances he may have had useful sources even if he has turned them to his own purposes. (One of these is the alleged letter from the Shechemites to Antiochus IV discussed below.) In one of his more notorious statements (*Ant.* 9.14.3 [291]; translation from LCL 6.153, 155; similarly, 11.8.6 [341]) he claims that

...they alter their attitude according to circumstance and, when they see the Jews prospering, call them their kinsmen, on the ground that they are descended from Joseph and are related to them through their origin from him, but, when they see the Jews in trouble, they say that they have nothing whatever in common with them nor do these have any claim of friendship or race, and they declare themselves to be aliens of another race.

2.   The problem is the final phrase: καθὼς ἐτύγχανον οἱ τὸν τόπον οἰκοῦντες, Διὸς ξενίου. Some take this to refer to the practice of the community, i.e. to be hospitable. Others interpret it to mean that the inhabitants requested that their temple be renamed. The former interpretation seems more likely. See Pummer (1982a: specifically 238-39); Doran (1983).

3.   This seems plain from many passages, despite Egger (1986: esp. 310-13). She may well be right that there are passages where his approach is more neutral, but quite a few simply cannot be explained away.

This may strike one initially as only another expression of prejudice. Undoubtedly, Josephus intended no less, but in fact the statement may describe a genuine state of affairs. Those who have had the experience of sectarian infighting know well that a group may emphasize or disavow resemblances to other groups, depending on the circumstances. It would hardly be surprising if the Samaritans did the same.

Josephus relates another incident on the Samaritans in *Ant.* 12.4.1 (156) (translation from LCL 7.81, 83):

> At this time the Samaritans [Σαμαρεῖς], who were flourishing, did much mischief to the Jews by laying waste their land and carrying off slaves; and this happened in the high priesthood of Onias.

The first question is when this incident took place. It is dated to the time of Ptolemy V Epiphanes (204–180 BCE) and the high priest Onias, son of Simon the Just. This Simon the Just is often identified with Simon II who lived around 200 BCE and is mentioned in Sir. 50.1-24. That would date the event to the early second century. Yet various other episodes in this context, mainly those relating to the Tobiads, are misdated and should be put earlier.[4] Therefore, we cannot be confident that Josephus has correctly placed the incident.

Secondly, who were those doing the enslaving? Although Josephus is not consistent in his terminology, the term *Samareis* is often used generally for the inhabitants of the region of Samaria.[5] We do not know if his source understood the raiders to be members of the community on Mt Gerizim and Josephus does not make this specific identification. They could have been inhabitants of Samaria who had nothing to do with the Gerizim cult, but neither can we rule this possibility out. Therefore, the relevance of this event to the main question is uncertain.

Shechemite Letter to Antiochus IV
Josephus quotes a letter, allegedly written at the time of Antiochus IV, as follows (*Ant.* 12.5.5 [258-61]) (quotation from LCL 7.133, 35):

---

4.   The activities of Joseph Tobiad could have taken place only during Ptolemaic rule over Palestine; therefore, their dating to the reign of Ptolemy V must be mistaken. Ptolemy III (246–221 BCE) is more likely the person intended, though Josephus may have misunderstood his source.

5.   The main study on Josephus terminology is Egger (1986); however, she argues for a theoretical consistency on Josephus's part which is not borne out by the data. See Pummer (1988).

To King Antiochus Theos Epiphanes. A memorial from the Sidonians in Shechem.

Our forefathers because of certain droughts in their country, and following a certain ancient superstition, made it a custom to observe the day which is called the Sabbath by the Jews, and they erected a temple without a name on the mountain called Gerizim, and there offered the appropriate sacrifices. Now you have dealt with the Jews as their wickedness deserves. but the king's officers, in the belief that we follow the same practices as they through kinship with them, are involving us in similar charges, whereas we are Sidonians by origin, as is evident from our state documents. We therefore petition you as our benefactor and saviour to command Apollonius, the governor of the district, and Nicanor, the royal agent, not to molest us in any way by attaching to us the charges of which the Jews are guilty, since we are distinct from them both in race and in customs, and we ask that the temple without a name be known as that of Zeus Hellenios. For if this be done, we shall cease to be molested, and by applying ourselves to our work in security, we shall make your revenues greater.

Antiochus's reply is given as follows (*Ant.* 12.5.5 [262-64]) (quotation from LCL 7.135, 37):

King Antiochus to Nicanor.

The Sidonians in Shechem have submitted a memorial which has been filed. Now since the men sent by them have represented to us sitting in council with our friends that they are in no way concerned in the complaints brought against the Jews, but choose to live in accordance with Greek customs, we acquit them of these charges, and permit their temple to be known as that of Zeus Hellenios, as they have petitioned.

The first question is whether these two documents are authentic. Although the question was widely debated in the past, with eminent names on both sides of the argument, most writers have accepted authenticity since Bickerman's study (Bickerman 1980b; Schalit 1970–71; Egger 1986: 280-81). Both the alleged petition and its reply bear the characteristics expected of Seleucid documents from the period. Just as persuasive is the argument that no clear reason can be found as to why a Jewish forger would have written the documents in their present form (Bickerman 1980b: 129-31). Also in the surrounding context, Josephus makes statements which are contradicted by the documents (e.g. the origin of the Samaritans as colonists from the Medes and Persians). The one difficulty which Bickerman did not deal with is whether we might have original documents which have nevertheless been tampered with in some way (Coggins 1975: 98-99; Alon 1977: 369; Pummer 1982a: 239 n. 94). Such documents are likely to be found elsewhere in Josephus and, despite Bickerman, it seems that this possibility cannot be ruled out here.[6]

If authentic, this letter and the Seleucid response give an important message about the Samaritans, especially when read in the light of 2 Macc. 6.1-2 (see above). Should we conclude, as many have, that the Samaritans gave themselves over to allow their cult to be Hellenized? A closer inspection does not lead to this conclusion.

The actual religious practices of the Jews and Samaritans were very similar: the same Sabbath observance, the same food laws, much the same purity laws, the same requirement of circumcision. The primary distinction between them was the question of God's chosen place for his temple. To an outsider, especially, they must have looked indistinguishable. Antiochus's order suppressing Jewish worship must therefore have delivered the same blow to the Shechemites as to the Jews. The religion to which they adhered with equal fervor was about to be abolished. But they had done nothing to anger Antiochus or to attract this abolition; it was simply a side effect of the Jewish situation. Therefore, it would hardly be surprising if the community of Shechem attempted by diplomacy to have the decree lifted with regard to themselves. But in so doing, they do not deny keeping the Sabbath: instead, they emphasize an origin which might sound rational to a Greek and also appear on a different basis from that of the Jews. This does not suggest they are abandoning the Sabbath but rather are intending to continue observing it. As another means of defense, they could also put stress on an ethnic origin different from the Jews. Although the precise significance of the phrase, 'Sidonians of Shechem', is still not clear, it had a useful function in attempting to distance the community from the Jews.[7]

6.   This is very probably the case with the alleged decree of Claudius in *Ant*. 19.5.2 [280-85]. Although much of the document could well be genuine, the final conclusion is contrary to that of a known decree of Claudius, published in Tcherikover, Fuks and Stern (1957–64: II, 36-55 [text no. 153]).

7.   Bickerman (1980b: 118-22) took the phrase as a synonym for 'Phoenician' which, in turn, was only the Greek term for 'Canaanite'. Schalit (1970–71: 149-56) seems to agree, though his position is not completely clear. But this view is based on assumptions about the origins of the Samaritans which no longer stand up. There is no reason to think that the Samaritans would have any more willingly identified themselves as Canaanites than the Jews. The term 'Sidonians' is known for a group in the Hellenistic Edomite city of Marissa, and it has been proposed that there was a Sidonian colony at Shechem who wrote this letter: Delcor (1962), followed by Pummer (1982b: esp. 184-86), Egger (1986: 266-80), and a number of others. This is unlikely. One can hardly expect a Phoenician colony to be Sabbath keepers, and the explanation that they

None of this suggests an intent to change their cult. On the contrary, it would be a useful means of defending it (Bickerman 1980b: 126-28, 131-35; Bringmann 1983: 142-43).

Other Early Jewish Literature

Various scholars of the past and present have claimed to find anti-Samaritan polemic in a number of early Jewish writings (Pummer 1979: 147-48; 1982a; 1982b). For the most part these do not stand up. Although Genesis 34, with its massacre of the inhabitants of Shechem by Jacob's sons, is treated by several documents, Jubilees and Judith are not clearly anti-Samaritan. The author of *Testament of Levi* 5–7 is plainly polemicizing against the Shechemites of his own time; however, the date and provenance of the Greek writing are disputed.[8]

According to the editor of 4QApocJos[b] (4Q372), this scroll about Joseph also reflects anti-Samaritan views (Schuller 1990). Based primarily on ll. 11-14 which speak of 'building a high place for themselves on a high mountain to arouse the jealousy of Israel', the interpretation may, of course, be correct but is not at all certain.

Similarly, Sir. 50.25-26 derides the 'senseless folk that live at Shechem'.[9] There is some question, however, as to whether these verses were written by Ben Sira himself or were from another source, whether before his time or a later insertion (see Coggins [1975: 83-86]; Pummer [1982a: 232 and n. 45]; Egger [1986: 85-93]). They do not fit well into the context.

---

had picked up some practices from the Samaritan community or were loosely associated with its cult is merely an attempt to explain away a difficulty. Pummer correctly notes (1982b: 184-86) that nothing is said about circumcision, implying that it was being kept; if so, this says little for their being a Sidonian colony but much for the Samaritan community. The best explanation to me is that the Samaritan community itself wrote the letter and that, whatever the origin of the designation, it was trying to distance itself from the Jews.

8. The main debate about the *Testaments of the Twelve Patriarchs* is whether these are Christian documents which make use of Jewish material or are Jewish writings with Christian intervention. Some Aramaic fragments of *T. Levi* are known from the Cairo Genizah and Qumran. One of the Genizah fragments (Cambridge T-S 16.94) seems to contain a version of the story in Gen. 34, though it does not correspond to the extant Greek text of *T. Levi*. See Greenfield and Stone (1979). For discussion of recent scholarship, see Schürer (1973–87: III, 767-81); Collins (1984; 1986: 154-62; 2000: 174-83).

9. NEB. Although the Hebrew and Greek texts differ slightly in these two verses, this phrase is essentially the same.

The sentiment expressed seems clear, but how early it arose is more problematic. Purvis (1968) has attempted to suggest a historical background for the statement, but the evidence offered is extremely scanty.[10] Nevertheless, the statement in Ben Sira is likely to have originated no later than the second century BCE since it is found in the Greek translation of Ben Sira's grandson about 130 BCE.

Samaritan Writings in Greek

Pseudo-Eupolemus is the name given to two passages preserved among the fragmentary Jewish Greek writers.[11] One of these is preserved in the name of Eupolemus, the other as 'anonymous'; the consensus of scholarship is that they are both by an anonymous Samaritan who wrote sometime during the third or second centuries BCE. Among the fragmentary writers is Theodotus, who has also often been identified as a Samaritan, but the weight of evidence seems against it; he is more likely a Jewish writer.[12]

Even with the small amount of preserved text, Pseudo-Eupolemus tells several things. He evidently had a good Greek education, showing that such opportunities were available for Samaritans as well as other Orientals. Pseudo-Eupolemus was quite happy to interpret biblical tradition in the light of Greek mythology. Sometimes this is called 'syncretism' but inaccurately. Pseudo-Eupolemus gives no indication of diluting the Samaritan cult or other aspects of the religion with pagan elements; rather, the biblical tradition is only put in the Greek context, showing how the native tradition fits in with Greek legend and myth. Far from

10. The only data he seems to offer are *Ant.* 12.4.1 [156] and the scholia of the *Megillat Ta'anit*. The first is problematic because its dating is very uncertain, and it does not necessarily have anything to do with Shechem (see the discussion on p. 204 above). His use of the scholia of the *Megillat Ta'anit* is surprising since these are commonly acknowledged to be post-Talmudic in origin, not like the *Megillat Ta'anit* itself which is commonly dated to the first or second centuries CE. (On this writing and the scholia, see Strack and Stemberger [1991: 39-40].) We can have no confidence that the scholia are likely to contain any reliable information for the second or third centuries BCE.

11. For an edition and translation, with a summary of scholarship up to the time of writing, see Holladay (1983: 157-87). One should add to this Collins (1986: 38-39; 2000: 47-50). Doran (1985) suggests the first fragment is from Eupolemus himself.

12. See the summary of the arguments and earlier literature in Holladay (1983: 157-68) and Pummer (1982a: 234-36). Fallon (1985) sees no clear evidence to decide the matter. Mendels (1987: 110-16), however, argues that Theodotus was Samaritan.

engaging in compromise Pseudo-Eupolemus is actually strengthening his people's tradition by showing that the Greeks have a memory of it, if perhaps only a dim and inaccurate one. He is using his Greek knowledge for apologetic purposes, with the aim not of diminishing his own tradition but of defending it.

Pseudo-Eupolemus is thus very much like contemporary Jewish writers in Greek. These, too, made use of Greek knowledge and literary techniques to extend, update, interpret and defend their religious tradition. But to do so required a knowledge of Greek language, literature and culture. This shows that such knowledge was available and that a Samaritan could gain a Greek education but also remain loyal to his native people.

Samaritan Chronicles

The relevant Samaritan Chronicles are Chronicle 2,[13] the Tolidah (Chronicle 3),[14] the Shalshalah (Chronicle 5; see Gaster 1925–28), Abu'l-Fath (Chronicle 6),[15] and the Adler Chronicle (Chronicle 7; see Adler and Seligsohn 1902–1903). The Chronicles are a minefield of problems. On the one hand, they claim to trace the Samaritan religion back to Moses and to give an account of their history independently (at least, in part) of the Old Testament. On the other hand, all the Chronicles are late, some of them from the nineteenth or even twentieth centuries in their present form. Study of them is not far advanced, and Samaritan specialists have reached no consensus on their interrelationship.[16]

Where the Chronicles relate Samaritan history to external events, there is often confusion. In addition, some of the events which Jewish literature recounts with reference to the Jews is claimed for the Samaritans by the Chronicles. For example, where Josephus and other Jewish sources have Alexander the Great doing obeisance to the Jewish high priest, the Chroni-

13. The section on the Hasmonean period has not been published. For a summary of the entire contents, see Macdonald (1971). From his description, the contents sound very similar to Abu'l-Fath.

14. Neubauer 1869 (text and French translation); Heidenheim 1971 (German translation only); Bowman 1954 (text only, using a different manuscript from Neubauer).

15. ET in Stenhouse (1985), though Stenhouse's own critical text of the Arabic original is still unpublished; partial translation in Bowman (1977: 114-213).

16. It seems that each specialist prefers a different Chronicle as the most basic. Bowman (1954) thinks Tolidah is earliest; Stenhouse (1989) concentrates on Abu'l-Fath; Crown (1971–73) argues that the basis of all the Chronicles is the Samaritan book of Joshua (Chronicle 4) and a *Sefer ha-Yamim* (of which the Adler Chronicle and Chronicle 2 are late examples) with the former being incorporated into the latter at some point.

cles (Adler; Tolidah; Abu'l-Faṭḥ; Chronicle 2, *apud* Macdonald 1991) make him do it to the Samaritan high priest (for a discussion of this event, its sources and historicity, see Grabbe 1987). For the Hasmonean period, the only event mentioned is the reign of 'King John', evidently John Hyrcanus though possibly Alexander Janneus.[17] According to their version, however, John destroys Samaria but not Shechem. Eventually, he acknowledges its claim and attempts to go on a pilgrim to Gerizim! The source of this account is uncertain, though it seems remarkably close to that of Josephus; one could argue that it is his version with a deliberate twist.

Another account is more problematic. It concerns a king of the Jews named Simeon and his son Arqiah (Abu'l-Faṭḥ) or Hilqiyah (Adler). This sounds very much like Simon Maccabee and his son (John) Hyrcanus, but the episode is dated to the Persian period, and their reigns are followed by a captivity of the Jews. Simeon is said to have caused great hostility between the Jews and Samaritans because the Jews persecuted the Samaritans and forbade them to worship. Finally, the Samaritans called their Diaspora brethren from Babylon and attacked Jerusalem, destroying it and the temple, though Simeon got away. King Darius heard of this and supported the Jews, whereupon many Samaritans emigrated while those left again had their religion proscribed. Under Arqiah/Hilqiyah a quarrel arose between 'the sons of Ithamar and the sons of Manasseh', which appears to be an inner-Samaritan quarrel. After that 'the nations' besieged Jerusalem and exiled the Jews, allowing the Samaritans to return with thanks and praise to God.

Can anything of historical value be gleaned from these accounts? This seems doubtful in the present state of knowledge. The most one can say is that Josephus's account of the destruction of the Gerizim temple has no memory in the Samaritan sources.[18]

17. The story is found in Abu'l-Faṭḥ (Stenhouse 1985: 140-42; Bowman 1977: 134-35) and apparently also in Chronicle 2 (so Macdonald 1971 in his summary).

18. Bowman (1977) makes the surprising claim that both these events confirm the accounts of Josephus (see the notes to his translation). If the incident relating to 'King John' is borrowed from Josephus, it has no independent value; if not, it specifically denies the destruction of Shechem by Hyrcanus. Similarly, the quarrel between the sons of Ithamar and the sons of Manasseh cannot be dated (is it the Persian period or the time of Hyrcanus?) nor does it make any allusion to the supposed defection of Manasseh, a son of the high priest, to Gerizim. On this last event and its historicity, see Grabbe (1987).

Samaritan Pentateuch

It is widely accepted that the Samaritan Pentateuch is a community (sectarian) recension of a previously existing non-sectarian text-type, sometimes referred to as the proto-Samaritan.[19] If we accept this position, the question remains: When did this sectarian recension take place? Purvis has argued that it followed shortly after Hyrcanus's destruction of Samaria and Shechem in the late second century.[20] This suggestion is plausible, but is there actual evidence? Purvis argues primarily from the script and orthography which he claims indicate an origin in the Hasmonean period. None of his arguments seems to preclude a recension as much as two or three centuries after 100 BCE, however.[21] Indeed, a recension before 100 BCE cannot be excluded, though it is not attested. Thus, the Samaritan scriptures do not provide us with any certain data on when or whether a major break occurred between the Jewish and Samaritan communities.

Archaeology

The archaeology of this period has been on a rollercoaster—or at least archaeological opinion has been. Excavations in the 1950s and 1960s had, it was believed, confirmed the building of the Samaritan temple on Mt Gerizim in the time of Alexander, as Josephus suggests (*Ant.* 11.8.1-6 [304-45]; Bull 1978). Subsequent excavations by Yitzhak Magen led to the questioning of whether there was anything from before the Roman period BCE (see recently Pummer 1989, 1997; Anderson 1991; Magen 1986, 1991–92, 1993). The most recent publications now claim that a temple did indeed exist from the early fifth century BCE, according to the interpretation of the excavator who thinks the temple was founded by the Sanballat of the time of Nehemiah.[22] Not everyone is convinced.[23] We can only await further debate on the question in the light of this new evidence.

19. For a summary of the current consensus with discussion of earlier studies, see Tov (1989; 1992: 80-100).

20. Purvis 1968. I would like to acknowledge a debt to Professor Purvis, who many years ago kindly loaned me a number of books and texts relating to Samaritan studies which were unavailable to me.

21. See, e.g., the doubts expressed by Ben-Hayyim (1971: 255): 'Yet the question which is raised upon the reading of this interesting book is: can one really come to an important historical and social conclusion such as the time of the formation of the Samaritan sect according to the orthographic form and the script of its Holy Writ?'

22. See the articles in *Qadmoniot* 33.2 (2000), the entire fascicle of which is devoted to the question, and especially Magen (2000: 74-118).

23. E.g. Menachem Mor (private communication). My thanks to Professor Mor for

The destruction of Shechem by John Hyrcanus shortly before 100 BCE was also thought to be confirmed archaeologically (*Ant.* 13.9.1 [255-56]; see Wright 1962, 1964; Magen 1991–92, 1993). So far, no new information seems to have been forthcoming. In the light of present data, though, the final destruction of the city could have come during the reign of Alexander Jannaeus rather than of John Hyrcanus.

Analysis of Data

As with so much Samaritan history, we have very little information. There is considerable danger of over interpreting the data that we do have, and it seems to me that this has often been done. The desire to know more is understandable, but we must recognize the fragility of many hypotheses. Indeed, in many cases they are little more than guesses.

The source which seems to give the most information is in many ways also our most problematic one: Josephus. In most passages, if perhaps not in all, he is openly prejudiced against the dwellers of Shechem. This does not mean that he does not give us historical data, but sorting it out of the negative polemic is not easy. Further, his terminology is not always consistent or clear. Sometimes he explicitly refers to the cult on Gerizim and its adherents, but at other times he may have had inhabitants of the entire region of Samaria in mind, and we cannot be sure that they necessarily had anything to do with the Gerizim cult and community. One has to proceed with a good deal of caution and skepticism.

For the origins of the Gerizim cult, Josephus gives two contradictory answers. First, he says that they were foreigners brought in from elsewhere in the ancient Near East (Mesopotamia, Media, Persia). Secondly, he claims they were made up of defected priests and Jews who left the Jerusalem cult for various nefarious reasons. Both claims have a polemical intent: neither is necessary. For my purposes, however, there is no need to settle the matter of origins of the cult and I shall proceed on the basis that the cult was Yahwistic, with no more foreign elements than contemporary Judaism— indeed, that in most respects it was very similar to the worship in Jerusalem at the time.[24]

information about Magen's latest views. In addition, I wish to thank Nadav Na'aman and Oded Lifshitz who also kindly provided information on the question.

24. I am not aware of significant arguments against the idea that the cult was ultimately descended from the Yahwistic worship of the northern kingdom, which would explain its similarity to Second Temple Judaism but would also recognize a

The first and perhaps most difficult area to investigate is that of Jewish and Samaritan relations. The animosity between the Samaritan and Jewish communities has often been taken for granted, though there has been debate over when it began. Yet we do not have to assume a severe breach before the first century CE and perhaps not even then. The episode in which Samaritans scattered bones in the Jerusalem temple (*Ant.* 18.2.2 [30]), the attack on Jewish pilgrims from Galilee and the counter charge of Jewish attacks on Samaritan villages (*War* 2.12.3-6 [232-44]; *Ant.* 20.6.1-3 [118-36]), and the statement in Jn 4.9 all suggest major barriers between Jews and Samaritans. The first example suggests individuals who were hostile to the Jerusalem temple; the second is less clear but could also show religious hostility; the third definitely has differences of worship in mind. But these all relate to the first century CE. Counter to this are many examples showing contact between Jews and individuals from the region of Samaria: Herod's relations (*Ant.* 14.15.3 [408]; 14.15.4 [413]; 14.15.14 [467]; 17.1.3 [70]; 17.4.2 [69]); joint delegation to complain against Archelaus (*Ant.* 17.13.2 [342]); loan to Agrippa from a Samaritan freedman (*Ant.* 18.6.4 [167]); Josephus's Samaritan friends (*Life* 57-59). All of these can be explained away, but they indicate the matter is not straightforward.

If the two religious communities had little to do with each other in the first century, this situation could have had its roots in earlier periods. The enmity between Nehemiah and Sanballat might have been a foreshadow, but the text shows that many Jews did not agree with Nehemiah (Neh. 6.17-19; 13.4-7). The Tobiads, who intermarried with the high-priestly Oniad family, also seem to have had relations with and even relatives in Samaria, whether the city or the region (*Ant.* 12.4.3 [168]). The Samaritan decision to protect their temple by disavowing the Jews may not have helped inter-community relations (see pp. 204-207 above), but it need not have created a permanent breach. Hyrcanus's conquest of Samaria and Shechem could have strained relations seriously—and some scholars see this as the incident which closed the communities off from one another—but we cannot be sure of that. Hyrcanus also forcibly converted the Idumeans, and most of them remained Jewish in their religion according to the later references to them.

The archaeology has yet to be clarified. The latest data still seem to bear

certain independence. Cf. Coggins (1975: 162-65) and the later view of Purvis (1981: specifically 337). Nevertheless, for present purposes it is not necessary to take a position on the question of origins.

up a destruction of the city in the time of Hyrcanus or Janneus (see p. 212 above). If the temple (assuming there was one) and cult were also destroyed at this time, it could have created great hostility. But destruction of the city does not require destruction of the cult. Against the interpretation that Shechem's conquest was the decisive point is the absence of polemic in Jewish literature until the first century. The only probable earlier example is Ben Sira (see pp. 207-208 above). If the Samaritans were the ones to sever relations, Jewish writers as members of the dominant ethnic group may not have been interested in polemicizing against the Samaritans; that is, the Samaritans may not have been of sufficient interest to warrant attention. However, it is not necessary to assume a breach before the first century, and the literature would bear this out. The argument that the Samaritan Penta- teuch shows redaction in the decades after the destruction of Shechem is based on too many uncertainties (see p. 211 above). Neither would such a redaction even require the assumption that the two communities had ceased to communicate.

The question of Hellenization has exercised a number of researchers on the Samaritans, often with unfortunate results. Part of the problem is that the situation in Jerusalem is misunderstood and then a false analogy imported to Shechem. The process of Hellenization was complex, but both the Jews and Samaritans were affected by it the same as other Near Eastern peoples.[25] Therefore, it is hardly surprising to find works in Greek which seem to be by Samaritan authors (see pp. 208-209 above). If the situation in Judea is anything to go by, there was likely a variety of attitudes toward Hellenistic culture within the Gerizim community. Those who propose a 'Hellenistic' party among the Samaritans have plausibility on their side.

Where the misconception lies is assuming a dichotomy of a 'Hellenistic' party on one side versus a 'loyal, pious' group on the other. The authors of the Hellenistic reform in Jerusalem were also loyal, pious individuals— many of them priests—who did not attempt to compromise the traditional temple cult.[26]

25. The question, with supporting data, is discussed at length in Grabbe (1992: 147-70), including interaction with Hengel (1974) and Tcherikover (1959). See also pp. 52-66 of this volume.

26. For a discussion see Grabbe (1992: 221-311). The Jewish cult and religion were, of course, eventually compromised and suppressed at the order of Antiochus IV, and some Jews seem to have had a hand in it. But there is no evidence that the authors of the Hellenistic reform, led by Jason, were involved. When opposition developed, it

Similarly, there is no reason to think that any Hellenistic party in Samaria would have done so there. As has already been noted (see pp. 204-207 above), the evidence available does not indicate that those who wrote to Antiochus IV were seeking a change to their traditional cult. Postulating that this letter was written by a 'Hellenistic party' at Shechem is, therefore, irrelevant to the question.

Conclusions and Social Implications

My investigation has turned up both positive and negative aspects of the question. We must first accept that there is a lot we do not know with regard to Samaritan history in the Hasmonean period. But sometimes even negative conclusions have their positive implications, so both sides of the question will now be considered, with regard to both what we know and what we do not:

1. The origins of the community and cult are still uncertain. The origins according to interpretations of 2 Kings 17 (pagan foreigners brought in) and Josephus (dissident Jerusalem priests) are the product of considerable bias and cannot be taken at face value.

2. Likewise, the ethnic diversity of Samaria is unknown. One could no doubt argue that ethnic outsiders were brought in at various times,[27] producing some ethnic mixing, but whether the older identity was preserved is unknown. But if so, there is little evidence that such mixing had a significant impact on the Samaritan religion. If there were pagan groups in the region of Samaria, this may have created antagonism between them and the Samaritan community, just as between the latter and the Jews. Also, if there were other groups, some of the references to 'Samaritans' or 'Samarians' may have had nothing to do with the Gerizim community.

3. We often do not know precisely who is being referred to when the sources speak of 'Samaritans' and the like.[28] Was it the community with

---

was not against Jason's Hellenistic reform (which had already been aborted by Menelaus) but against the alleged sale of temple vessels (2 Macc. 4.39-50).

27. Thompson (1992: esp. 412-21) argues this. It seems to me that he exaggerates the amount of ethnic mixing since the deportation of peoples often involved a minority of the population. Also, where communities were deported, they frequently kept their identity in their new habitation, sometimes even for centuries. See Grabbe (1998: 81-84).

28. Contra Egger (1986), Josephus does not use his terminology consistently, leaving us uncertain at least some of the time.

worship centered on the Gerizim cult or was it some other group in the region of Samaria, perhaps with no connection to the Samaritan community of concern to us? The problem may even be more acute when no names are used, and we are left guessing from the context (cf. pp. 208-209 above).

4. If, or when, major Samaritan/Jewish hostility arose is uncertain. At least until 100 BCE there was communication between the Jewish and Samaritan communities. Exactly when friction developed between them is unknown, though some friction could go back to an early time, as early as the time of Nehemiah or even pre-exilic times. But the existence of strained relations does not preclude communication and even good relations between some parts of the community. Evidently, these were best between the upper classes, such as the Tobiad family.[29]

5. The Samaritans were evidently as affected by Hellenization as the Jews. As argued elsewhere, the dichotomy of 'Hellenized' versus 'faithful' Jews is a false one. Similarly the idea that the Samaritans were more 'syncretistic' than the Jews is equally a caricature. Hellenization was a cultural phenomenon of the entire ancient Near East. No people was immune to it, though different peoples and different individuals may have responded in different ways. One response was what has been called apologetic historiography, the interpretation of the native history in such a way that it would commend itself to Greek readers.[30] A good example of this is the 'Anonymous Samaritan' or Pseudo-Eupolemus who combines Samaritan tradition with material from Greek mythology.

6. The history of the Samaritan community seems similar to that of Jews but in miniature, since the Gerizim community was apparently smaller than that of the Jews. They had much the same basic customs, with the main difference being the appropriate place for God's temple. They both had a Diaspora population.[31] They both suffered religious suppression or

29. As already noted, Joseph the Tobiad borrowed money from friends in Samaria to fund his initial venture into Ptolemaic politics (*Ant.* 12.4.3 [168]). This transaction may well have been a continuation of contacts going back at least to the time of Nehemiah (Neh. 4.7; 6.1; cf. Mazar 1957).

30. On the concept, see especially Sterling (1992). This was a common phenomenon of nationalism among nations under Greek and then Roman rule: see Mendels (1993: 35-54).

31. For a summary of information on this, see Crown (1989: 195-217). Much of the information on the early history of this Diaspora is, unfortunately, semi-legendary. According to Josephus, Samaritans were taken to Egypt and even held a dispute with Jews there (*Ant.* 12.1.1 [7, 10]; 13.3.4 [74-79]). The Samaritan Chronicles have a

persecution, the Samaritans suffering also at the hands of the Jews and possibly vice versa.

One final point is really little more than speculation, but it has socio-logical implications:

7. There is some small evidence of intermarriage between the Jewish and Samaritan communities. What few data we have concern the upper classes: Joseph Tobiad who had friends in Samaria who loaned him money; Herod, who married a wife from there; perhaps even Josephus himself, who admits to having friends in Samaria. Except for Herod, who may have married for diplomatic reasons, no explicit reference is made to relatives. Yet our sources may have been somewhat coy about admitting actual intermarriage. If there was intermarriage, it illustrates a common sociological phenomenon in which the upper classes have a different standard from those at the bottom end of the scale.

version of this dispute and also refer to a large Diaspora in Babylonia (cf. pp. 209-10 above). Two inscriptions from Delos from the third to the first centuries BCE also seem to be a Samaritan product (see Kraabel 1984). The 'Israelites in Delos' here use the Greek form *Argarizein* for Mt Gerizim which often, though not always, is evidence of Samaritan ethnicity (see Pummer 1987).

BIBLIOGRAPHY

Adler, E.N., and M. Seligsohn
    1902–1903 'Une nouvelle chronique samaritaine', *REJ* 44: 188-222; 45: 70-98, 223-54; 46: 123-46.

Aharoni, Y.
    1975 *Investigations at Lachish: The Sanctuary and the Residency (Lachish V)* (Tel Aviv: Institute of Archaeology, Tel Aviv University).

Alon, C.
    1977 'The Origin of the Samaritans in the Halakhic Tradition', in *idem*, *Jews, Judaism and the Classical World: Studies in Jewish History in the Times of the Second Temple and Talmud* (Jerusalem: Magnes Press): 354-73.

Alt, A.
    1953 'Die Rolle Samarias bei der Entstehung des Judentums', in *idem*, *Kleine Schriften zur Geschichte des Volkes Israel* (Munich: Beck, 2nd edn): 316-37.

Anderson, R.T.
    1991 'The Elusive Samaritan Temple', *BA* 54: 104-107.

Applebaum, S.
    1989 'The Hasmoneans—Logistics, Taxation and the Constitution', in *idem*, *Judea in Hellenistic and Roman Times: Historical and Archaeological Essays* (Leiden: E.J. Brill): 1-24.

Arav, R.
    1989 *Hellenistic Palestine: Settlement Patterns and City Planning, 337–31 BCE* (Oxford: British Archaelogical Reports).

Arhin, K.
    1967 'The Structure of Greater Ashanti (1700–1824)', *Journal of African History* 8.1: 65-85.

Avigad, N.
    1976 *Bullae and Seals from a Post-Exilic Judean Archive* (Qedem, 4; Jerusalem: The Institute of Archaeology of the Hebrew University).

Avi-Yonah, M.
    1966 *The Holy Land: An Historical Geography* (Grand Rapids: Baker Book House).
    1977 'Maresha (Marisa)', in M. Avi-Yonah and E. Stern (eds.), *Encyclopedia of Archaeological Excavations in the Holy Land* (Englewood Cliffs, NJ: Prentice–Hall): III, 782-91.

Baly, D.
    1974 *The Geography of the Bible* (New York: Harper & Row).

Bar-Kochva, B.
    1976 *The Seleucid Army* (Cambridge: Cambridge University Press).

1989	*Judas Maccabaeus: The Jewish Struggle Against the Seleucids* (Cambridge: Cambridge University Press).

Barr, J.

1974–75 'Philo of Byblos and his "Phoenician History"', *BJRL* 57: 17-68.

Bartelmus, R.

1979 *Heroentum in Israel und seiner Umwelt* (ATANT, 65; Zürich: Theologischer Verlag).

Bartlett, J.R.

1979 'From Edomites to Nabataeans: A Study in Continuity', *PEQ* 111: 53-66.

Ben-Hayyim, Z.

1971 Review of Purvis 1968, in *Bib* 52: 253-55.

Bernard, P.

1967 'Aï Khanum on the Oxus: A Hellenistic City in Central Asia', *Proceedings of the British Academy* 53: 71-95.

Bickerman, E.J.

1939 'Sur une inscription grecque de Dison', in *Mélanges syriens offerts à M.R. Dussaud* (Bibliothèque archéologique et historique, 30; Paris: Guethner): I, 91-99.

1979 *The God of the Maccabees* (SJLA, 32; Leiden: E.J. Brill).

1980a 'La charte séleucide de Jérusalem', in *idem*, *Studies in Jewish and Christian History* (3 vols.; AGJU, 9; Leiden: E.J. Brill): I, 44-85.

1980b 'Un document relatif à la persécution d'Antiochos IV Epiphane', in *idem*, *Studies in Jewish and Christian History* (3 vols.; AGJU, 9; Leiden: E.J. Brill): I, 105-35.

Biran, A.

1977 'Tel Dan', *RB* 84: 256-63.

Blenkinsopp, J.

1977 *Prophecy and Canon: A Contribution to the Study of Jewish Origins* (Notre Dame: University of Notre Dame Press).

Bonner, S.F.

1977 *Education in Ancient Rome* (London: Methuen).

Bowersock, G.W.

1983 *Roman Arabia* (Cambridge, MA: Harvard University Press).

Bowman, J.

1954 *Transcript of the Original Text of the Samaritan Chronicle Tolidah* (Leeds: University of Leeds).

1977 *Samaritan Documents Relating to their History, Religion and Life* (Pittsburgh Original Texts and Translations, 2; Pittsburgh: Pickwick Press).

Braun, R.

1973 *Koheleth und die frühhellenistische Popularphilosophie* (BZAW, 130; Berlin: W. de Gruyter).

Briant, P.

1982 *Rois, tributs et paysans* (Annales littéraires de l'Université de Besançon, 269; Paris: Les Belles Lettres).

Bringmann, K.

1983 *Hellenistische Reform und Religionsverfolgung in Judäa* (AAWG, Phil.-hist. Klasse. 3. Folge, Nr. 132; Göttingen: Vandenhoeck & Ruprecht).

Buffière, F.

1956 *Les mythes d'homère et la pensée grecque* (Paris: Les Belles Lettres).

Bull, R.J.
1978   'er-Ras, Tell (Mount Gerizim)', in E. Stern (ed.), *Encyclopedia of Archaeo-logical Excavations in the Holy Land* (4 vols.; Jerusalem: Israel Exploration Society, 1978): IV, 1015-22.
1997   'Ras, Tell, er-', in E.M. Meyers (ed.), *The Oxford Encyclopedia of Archaeology in the Near East* (Oxford: Oxford University Press, 1997), IV: 407-409.
Bull, R.J., and G.E. Wright
1965   'Newly Discovered Temples on Mt. Gerizim in Jordan', *HTR* 58: 234-37.
Butler, E.M.
1935   *The Tyranny of Greece over Germany: A Study of the Influence Exercised by Greek Art and Poetry over the Great German Writers of the Eighteenth, Nineteenth, and Twentieth Century* (Cambridge: Cambridge University Press).
Carney, T.F.
1975   *The Shape of the Past: Models and Antiquity* (Lawrence, KS: Coronado).
Carter, C.E.
1999   *The Emergence of Yehud in the Persian Period: A Social and Demographic Study* (JSOTSup, 294; Sheffield: Sheffield Academic Press).
Cerfaux, L.
1954   'Influence des mystères sur le Judaïsme Alexandrien avant Philon', in *idem, Receuil L. Cerfaux: études d'exégèse religieuse*, II (BETL, 6; Gembloux: Duculot).
Chilton, B.D., and J. Neusner
1995   *Judaism in the New Testament: Practice and Beliefs* (London: Routledge).
Clifford, J.
1988   *The Predicament of Culture* (Cambridge, MA: Harvard University Press).
Coggins R.J.
1975   *Samaritans and Jews: The Origins of Samaritanism Reconsidered* (Growing Points in Theology; Oxford: Basil Blackwell).
Cohen, G.M.
1978   *The Seleucid Colonies: Studies in the Founding, Administration and Organi-zation* (Wiesbaden: Franz Steiner).
Cohen, S.J.D.
1987a   *From the Maccabees to the Mishnah* (LEC, 7; Philadelphia: Westminster Press).
1987b   'Respect for Judaism by Gentiles According to Josephus', *HTR* 80: 409-30.
1989   'Crossing the Boundary and Becoming a Jew', *HTR* 82: 13-34.
1999   *The Beginnings of Jewishness: Boundaries, Varieties, Uncertainties* (Helle-nistic Culture and Society, 31; Berkeley: University of California Press).
Collins, A.Y.
1985   'Aristobulus', *OTP*, II: 831-42.
Collins, J.J.
1984   'Testaments', in M.E. Stone (ed.), *Jewish Writings of the Second Temple Period* (CRINT, 2.2; Assen: Van Gorcum; Philadelphia: Fortress Press): 325-55.
1986   *Between Athens and Jerusalem: Jewish Identity in the Hellenistic Diaspora* (New York: Crossroad).

1989	'Judaism as *Praeparatio Evangelica* in the Work of Martin Hengel', *RSR* 15: 226-28.
2000	*Between Athens and Jerusalem: Jewish Identity in the Hellenistic Diaspora* (Grand Rapids: Eerdmans, 2nd edn).

Collins, J.J. (ed.)

1979	*Apocalypse: The Morphology of a Genre* (Semeia, 14; Atlanta: Scholars Press).

Comaroff, J., and J. Comaroff

1992	'Of Totemism and Ethnicity', in J. Comaroff and J. Comaroff (eds.), *Ethnography and the Historical Imagination* (Boulder, SF: Westview Press): 49-68.

Crenshaw, J.

1985	'Education in Ancient Israel', *JBL* 104: 601-15.

Cross, F.M.

1975	'A Reconstruction of the Judean Restoration', *JBL* 94: 4-18.
1981	'An Aramaic Ostracon of the Third Century B.C.E. from Excavations in Jerusalem', *EI* 15: *67-*69.
1982	'Alphabets and Pots: Reflections on Typological Method in the Dating of Human Artifacts', *Maarav* 3: 121-36.

Crown, A.D.

1971–73	'New Light on the Interrelationships of Samaritan Chronicles from Some Manuscripts in the John Rylands Library', *BJRL* 54: 282-313; 55: 86-111.
1989	'The Samaritan Diaspora', in Crown (ed.) 1989: 195-217.

Crown, A.D. (ed.)

1989	*The Samaritans* (Tübingen: Mohr).

Davies, P.R.

1977	'*Hasidim* in the Maccabean Period', *JJS* 28: 127-40.
1992a	*In Search of 'Ancient Israel': A Study in Biblical Origins* (JSOTSup, 148; Sheffield: JSOT Press).
1992b	'Defending the Boundaries of Israel in the Second Temple Period: 2 Chronicles 20 and the "Salvation Army"', in E. Ulrich, John W. Wright, Philip R. Davies and Robert P. Carroll (eds.), *Priests, Prophets and Scribes: Essays on the Formation and Heritage of Second Temple Judaism in Honour of Joseph Blenkinsopp* (JSOTSup, 149; Sheffield: JSOT Press): 146-54.
1996	'Scenes from the Early History of Judaism', in D. Edelman (ed.), *The Triumph of Elohim* (Grand Rapids, MI: Eerdmans): 145-84.
1998	*Scribes and Schools: The Canonization of the Hebrew Scriptures* (Library of Ancient Israel, Louisville, KY: Westminster/John Knox Press).

Davies, P.R. (ed.)

1991	*Second Temple Studies 1. Persian Period* (JSOTSup, 117; Sheffield: JSOT Press).

Davies, W.D., and L. Finkelstein (eds.)

1984	*The Cambridge History of Judaism. I. Introduction: The Persian Period* (Cambridge: Cambridge University Press).

Delcor, M.

1962	'Vom Sichem der hellenistischen Epoche zum Sychar des Neuen Testamentes', *ZDPV* 78: 34-48.

Delorme, J.
1960   *Gymnasium: Étude sur les monuments consacrés à l'éducation en Grèce* (Paris: Boccard).

Demsky, A.
1983   '*Pelekh* in Nehemiah 3', *IEJ* 33: 242-45.

Dequeker, L.
1985   'The City of David and the Seleucid Acra in Jerusalem', in E. Lipiński (ed.), *The Land of Israel: Crossroads of Civilizations* (Leuven: Peeters): 193-210.

Dever, W.G.
1982   'Monumental Architecture in Ancient Israel in the Period of the United Monarchy', in Tomoo Ishida (ed.), *Studies in the Period of David and Solomon and Other Essays* (Winona Lake, IN: Eisenbrauns): 263-306.

Doran, R.
1983   '2 Maccabees 6:2 and the Samaritan Question', *HTR* 76: 481-85.
1985   'Pseudo-Eupolemus', in *OTP*, II: 873-82.

Dothan, M.
1971   'Ashdod II-III: The Second and Third Seasons of Excavations 1963, 1965', *'Atiqot* 9–10: 1-222.

Doty, L.T.
1980   'The Archive of the Nanâ-Iddin Family from Uruk', *JCS* 30: 65-90.

Duncan, J.S.
1990   *The City as Text: The Politics of Landscape Interpretation in the Kandyan Kingdom* (Cambridge: Cambridge University Press).

Eddy, S.K.
1961   *The King Is Dead* (Lincoln: University of Nebraska).

Efron, J.
1987   'The Hasmonean Revolt in Modern Historiography', in *idem*, *Studies on the Hasmonean Period* (Leiden: E.J. Brill): 1-32.

Egger, R.
1986   *Josephus Flavius und die Samaritaner: Eine terminologische Untersuchung zur Identitätsklärung der Samaritaner* (Freiburg: Universitätsverlag; Göttingen: Vandenhoeck & Ruprecht).

Eister, A.W.
1967   'Toward a Radical Critique of Church-Sect Typology', *JSSR* 6: 85-90.

Elgavish, J.
1976   'Pottery from the Hellenistic Stratum at Shimona', *IEJ* 26: 65-76.

Elliott, J.H.
1986   'Social Scientific Criticism of the New Testament and its Social World', *Semeia* 35: 1-33.

El-Zein, Abdul Hamid
1977   'Beyond Ideology and Theology: The Search for the Anthropology of Islam', *Annual Review of Anthropology* 6: 227-54.

Eskenazi, T.C.
1988   'The Structure of Ezra–Nehemiah and the Integrity of the Book', *JBL* 107: 641-56.

Eskenazi, T.C., and K.H. Richards (eds.)
1994   *Second Temple Studies: 2. Temple Community in the Persian Period* (JSOTSup, 175; Sheffield: JSOT Press).

Ewald, H.
1864   *Geschichte des Volkes Israel* (Göttingen: Dieterichs Buchhandlung).
Fallon, F.
1985   'Theodotus', in *OTP*, II: 785-93.
Feldman, L.H.
1977   'Hengel's *Judaism and Hellenism* in Retrospect', *JBL* 96: 371-82.
1986   'How Much Hellenism in Jewish Palestine?', *HUCA* 57: 83-111.
Figueras, P.
1983   *Decorated Jewish Ossuaries* (Documenta et Monumenta; Orientis Antiqui, 20; Leiden: E.J. Brill).
Finkelstein, I.
1981   'Israelite and Hellenistic Farms in the Foothills and the Yarkon Basin', *EI* 15: 331-48.
1988   'Arabian Trade and Socio-Political Conditions in the Negev in the Twelfth–Eleventh Centuries B.C.E.', *JNES* 474: 241-52.
Fischer, T.
1990   'Hasmoneans and Seleucids: Aspects of War and Policy in the Second and First Centuries B.C.E.', in A. Kasher, U. Rappaport and G. Fuks (eds.), *Greece and Rome in Eretz-Israel* (Jerusalem: Yad Izhak Ben-Zvi, Israel Exploration Society): 3-19.
Forbes, C.A.
1945   'Expanded Uses of the Greek Gymnasium', *Classical Philology* 40: 32-42.
Foucault, M.
1977   *Discipline and Punish: The Birth of the Prison* (trans. Alan Sheridan; London: Allen Lane).
1980   *Power/Knowledge: Selected Interviews and Other Writings 1972–1977* (ed. Colin Gordon; New York: Pantheon Books).
Fraser, P.M.
1972   *Ptolemaic Alexandria* (3 vols.; Oxford: Clarendon Press).
Free, J.
1954   'The Second Season at Dothan', *BASOR* 135: 14-20.
Freyne, S.
1980   *Galilee from Alexander the Great to Hadrian* (Wilmington, DE: Michael Glazier).
1992   'Hellenistic/Roman Galilee', in *ABD*, II: 895-99.
Frick, F.S.
1977   *The City in Ancient Israel* (SBLDS, 36; Missoula, MT: Scholars Press).
Gammie, J.G.
1990   'The Sage in Sirach', in J.G. Gammie and L.G. Perdue (eds.), *The Sage in Israel and the Ancient Near East* (Winona Lake, IN: Eisenbrauns): 355-72.
Gaster, M.
1925–28   'The Chain of Samaritan High Priests', *Studies and Texts* (ET London: Maggs Bros), I: 483-502, III: 131-38.
Geiger, A.
1863   *Sadducäer und Pharisäer* (Breslau).
Geller, M.J.
1983   'More Graeco-Babylonian', *ZA* 73: 114-20.

Geraty, L.T.
1975   'The Khirbet el-Kôm Bilingual Ostracon', *BASOR* 220: 55-61.
Goldstein, J.
1976   *I Maccabees* (AB, 41; Garden City, NY: Doubleday).
1981   'Jewish Acceptance and Rejection of Hellenism', in E.P. Sanders, A.I.
            Baumgarten and Alan Mendelson (eds.), *Jewish and Christian Self-Defini-*
            tion. II. Aspects of Judaism in the Graeco-Roman Period (2 vols.; Philadel-
            phia: Fortress Press): 64-87.
1983   *II Maccabees* (AB, 41A; Garden City, NY: Doubleday).
Goodenough, E.R.
1935   *By Light, Light: The Mystic Gospel of Hellenistic Judaism* (New Haven:
            Yale University Press).
Goodman, M.
1983   *State and Society in Roman Galilee, A.D. 132–212* (Oxford Centre for
            Postgraduate Hebrew Studies; Totowa, NJ: Rowman & Allanheld).
Goodman, M. (ed.)
1998   *Jews in a Graeco-Roman World* (Oxford: Oxford University Press).
Grabbe, L.L.
1987   'Josephus and the Reconstruction of the Judean Restoration', *JBL* 106:
            231-46.
1992   *Judaism from Cyrus to Hadrian: I. The Persian and Greek Periods; II. The*
            Roman Period (2 vols.; Minneapolis: Fortress Press).
1998   '"The Exile" under the Theodolite: Historiography as Triangulation', in
            idem (ed.), *Leading Captivity Captive: 'The Exile' as History and Ideology*
            (JSOTSup, 278; ESHM; 2, Sheffield: Sheffield Academic Press): 80-100.
Graf, D.F.
1984   'Medism: The Origin and Significance of the Term', *JHS* 104: 15-30.
Greenfield J.O., and M.E. Stone
1979   'Remarks on the Aramaic Testament of Levi from the Geniza', *RB* 86:
            214-30.
Gruen, E.S.
1998   *Heritage and Hellenism: The Reinvention of Jewish Tradition* (Hellenistic
            Culture and Society; Berkeley: University of California Press).
Guilick, J.
1976   *The Middle East: An Anthropological Perspective* (Pacific Palisades, CA:
            Goodyear Publishing Co.).
Gunneweg, A.
1983   ''Am ha'arets: a Semantic Revolution', *ZAW* 95: 437-40.
Habicht, C.
1989   'The Seleucids and their Rivals', in *The Cambridge Ancient History* (8 vols.;
            Cambridge: Cambridge University Press, 2nd edn), VIII: 324-87.
Hachlili, R., and A. Killebrew
1983   'Jewish Funerary Customs during the Second Temple Period, in the Light of
            the Excavations at the Jericho Necropolis', *PEQ* 115: 109-39.
Halpern-Silberstein, M.-C.
1989   'The Archaeology of Hellenistic Palestine', in W.D. Davies and L. Finkel-
            stein (eds.), *The Cambridge History of Judaism. II. The Hellenistic Age*
            (Cambridge: Cambridge University Press): 1-34.

Haussoullier, B.
1909   'Inscriptions grècques de Babylone', *Klio* 9: 352-63.
Heidenheim, M.
1971   'Die samaritan: Chronik des Hohenpriesters Elasar', *Vierteljahrsschrift für deutsch- und englisch-theologische Forschung und Kritik* 4: 347-89.
Hengel, M.
1974   *Judaism and Hellenism: Studies in their Encounter in Palestine during the Early Hellenistic Period* (2 vols.; London: SCM Press).
1980   *Jews, Greeks and Barbarians: Aspects of the Hellenization of Judaism in the Pre-Christian Period* (London: SCM Press; Philadelphia: Fortress Press).
1989   *The 'Hellenization' of Judaea in the First Century after Christ* (London: SCM Press; Philadelphia: Trinity Press International).
Herbert, S.
1979   'Tel Anafa 1978: Preliminary Report', *BASOR* 234: 67-83.
Herder, J.G.
1912   *Herders Werke: Auswahl in fünfzehn Teilen Herausgegeben mit Einleitungen und Anmerkungen versehen von Ernst Naumann* (Goldene Klassiker-Bibliothek; Berlin: Deutsches Verlagshaus Bong).
Herzog, Z.
1978   'Israelite City Planning', *Expedition* 20.4: 38-43.
Heschel, S.
1998   'Jewish Studies as Counter History', in D. Biale, M. Galchinsky and S. Heschel (eds.), *Insider/Outsider: American Jews and Multiculturalism* (Berkeley: University of California Press): 101-15.
1999   *Abraham Geiger and the Jewish Jesus* (Chicago: University of Chicago Press).
Hoglund, K.
1990   'The Establishment of a Rural Economy in the Judean Hill Country in the Late Sixth Century BCE', paper read at the ASOR/SBL Southeastern Regional Meeting, Charlotte, NC, USA.
1991   'The Achaemenid Context', in Davies (ed.) 1991: 54-72.
1992   *Achaemenid Imperial Administration in Syria-Palestine and the Missions of Ezra and Nehemiah* (Atlanta: Scholars Press).
Holladay, C.A.
1983   *Fragments from Hellenistic Jewish Authors*. I. *Historians* (Texts and Translations, 70; Pseudepigrapha Series, 10; Atlanta: Scholars Press).
Holmberg, B.
1990   *Sociology and the New Testament: An Appraisal* (Minneapolis: Fortress Press).
Horowitz, G.
1980   'Town Planning of Hellenistic Marisa: A Reappraisal of the Excavations after Eighty Years', *PEQ* 112: 93-111.
Horsley, G.H.R.
1981   *New Documents Illustrating Early Christianity: A Review of the Greek Inscriptions and Papyri Published in 1976* (Ancient History Documentary Research Centre, Sydney: Macquarie University).
Horsley, R.A.
1984   'Popular Messianic Movements around the Time of Jesus', *CBQ* 46: 471-93.

| 1985 | '"Like One of the Prophets of Old": Two Types of Popular Prophets at the Time of Jesus', *CBQ* 47: 435-63. |

1989   *Sociology and the Jesus Movement* (New York: Crossroad).

Hyldahl, N.

1990   'The Maccabean Rebellion and the Question of "Hellenization"', in P. Bilde, T. Engberg-Pederson, L. Hannestad and J. Zahle (eds.), *Religion and Religious Practice in the Seleucid Kingdom* (Aarhus: Aarhus University Press): 188-203.

Ibach, R.

1987   *Archaeological Survey of the Hesban Region: Catalogue of Sites and Characterization of Periods* (Berrien Springs, MI: Institute of Archaeology, Andrews University Press).

Ibrahim, M., J. Sauer and K. Yassine

1976   'The East Jordan Valley Survey, 1975', *BASOR* 222: 41-66.

Kasher, A.

1985   *The Jews in Hellenistic and Roman Egypt* (Tübingen: J.C.B. Mohr).

1988   *Jews, Idumeans, and Ancient Arabs* (Tübingen: J.C.B. Mohr).

Kautsky, J.H.

1982   *The Politics of Aristocratic Empires* (Chapel Hill: University of North Carolina).

Kochavi, M.

1972   *Judaea, Samaria and the Golan: Archeological Survey 1967–68* (Jerusalem: The Survey of Israel).

Kraabel, A.T.

1984   'New Evidence of the Samaritan Diaspora Has Been Found on Delos', *BA* 47: 44-47.

Kraeling, C. (ed.)

1938   *Gerasa: City of the Decapolis* (New Haven: American Schools of Oriental Research).

Kuhnen, H.-P.

1987   *Nordwest Palästina in der griecher-römischer Zeit: Bauten und Gräben* (Weinheim: Humaniora).

1990   *Palästina in griechisch-römischer Zeit* (Handbuch der Archäolgie, 2.2; Munich: C.H. Beck).

Kuhrt, A.

1987   'Berossus' *Babyloniaka* and Seleucid Rule in Babylonia', in Kuhrt and Sherwin-White 1987: 32-56.

Kuhrt, A., and S.M. Sherwin-White (eds.)

1987   *Hellenism in the East: The Interaction of Greek and Non-Greek Civilizations from Syria to Central Asia after Alexandria* (London: Gerald Duckworth, 2nd edn).

La Barre, W.

1971   'Materials for a History of Studies of Crisis Cults: A Bibliographic Essay', *Current Anthropology* 12: 3-44.

Lapp, P.

1961   *Palestinian Ceramic Chronology 200 B.C.–A.D. 70* (New Haven: American Schools of Oriental Research).

1963   'Ptolemaic Stamped Handles from Judah', *BASOR* 172: 22-35.

Launey, M.
　1950　　*Recherches sur les Armées hellénistiques* (2 vols.; Paris: Boccard).
Lee, T.R.
　1986　　*Studies in the Form of Sirach 44–50* (SBLDS, 75; Atlanta: Scholars Press).
Lenski, G.E.
　1966　　*Power and Privilege: A Theory of Social Stratification* (New York: McGraw–Hill).
Levenson, J.
　1993　　*The Hebrew Bible, the Old Testament and Historical Criticism, Jews and Christians in Biblical Studies* (Louisville, KY: Westminster/John Knox Press).
Lipiński, E.
　1989　　' "Celleriers" de la province de Juda', *Transeuphratène* 1: 107-109.
Lloyd, A.B.
　1982　　'Nationalist Propaganda in Ptolemaic Egypt', *Historia* 31: 33-55.
Loretz, O.
　1964　　*Qohelet und der alte Orient* (Freiburg: Herder).
Lowe, M.
　1976　　'Who were the *Ioudaioi*?', *NovT* 18: 101-30.
MacDonald, B.
　1988　　*The Wadi el Hasa Archaeological Survey 1979–1983, West-Central Jordan* (Waterloo: Wilfrid Laurier University Press).
Macdonald, J.
　1969　　*The Samaritan Chronicle No. II* (BZAW, 107; Berlin: W. de Gruyter).
　1971　　'Samaritans', *EncJud* 14: 778-32.
Mack, B.L.
　1985　　*Wisdom and the Hebrew Epic* (Chicago: University of Chicago Press).
Magen, Y.
　1986　　'A Fortified City from the Hellenistic Period on Mount Gerizim', *Qadmoniot* 19: 91-101.
　1991–92　'Mount Gerizim: A Temple-City', *Qadmoniot* 23: 70-96.
　1993　　'Gerizim, Mount', in E. Stern (ed.), *The New Encyclopedia of Excavations in the Holy Land*, II (New York: Simon & Schuster): 484-92.
　2000　　'Mt. Gerizim: A Temple City', *Qadmoniot* 33: 74-118.
Marrou, H.I.
　1956　　*A History of Education in Antiquity* (New York: Sheed & Ward).
Mazar, B.
　1957　　'The Tobiads', *IEJ* 7: 137-45, 229-38.
Mazar, B., T. Dothan and I. Dunayevsky
　1966　　'En-Gedi: The First and Second Seasons of Excavation, 1961–1962', *'Atiqot* 5: 1-100.
Mendels, D.
　1987　　*The Land of Israel as a Political Concept in Hasmonean Literature* (TSAJ, 15; Tübingen: J.C.B. Mohr [Paul Siebeck]).
　1993　　*The Rise and Fall of Jewish Nationalism* (Anchor Reference Library; New York: Doubleday).
Mendelson, A.
　1988　　*Philo's Jewish Identity* (BJS, 161; Atlanta: Scholars Press).

Messenger, J.
1965   'The Role of Proverbs in a Nigerian Judicial System', in A. Dundes (ed.),
            The Study of Folklore (Englewood Cliffs, NJ: Prentice–Hall): 299-307.
Meyer, E.
1921–23   *Ursprung und Anfänge des Christentums* (3 vols.; Stuttgart: J.G. Cotta).
Meyers, E., J. Strange and D. Groh
1978   'The Meiron Excavation Project: Archaeological Survey in Galilee and
            Golan, 1976', *BASOR* 230: 1-24.
Milik, J.T.
1976   *The Books of Enoch: Aramaic Fragments of Qumran Cave 4* (Oxford:
            Clarendon Press).
Millar, F.
1978   'The Background to the Maccabean Revolution: Reflections on Martin
            Hengel's "Judaism and Hellenism"', *JJS* 29: 1-21.
1983   'The Phoenician Cities: A Case-Study of Hellenisation', *Proceedings of the
            Cambridge Philological Association* 209: 55-71.
1987a   'The Problem of Hellenistic Syria', in Kuhrt and Sherwin-White 1987:
            110-33.
1987b   'Empire, Community and Culture in the Roman Near East: Greeks, Syrians,
            Jews and Arabs', *JJS* 38: 143-64.
1993   'Hagar, Ishmael, Josephus, and the Origins of Islam', *JJS* 44: 23-45.
Miller, S.G.
1979   *Arete: Ancient Writers, Papyri, and Inscriptions on the History and Ideals of
            Greek Athletics and Games* (Chicago: Ares).
Momigliano, A.
1970   Review of M. Hengel, *Judaism and Hellenism*, in *JTS* 21: 149-53 (repr. in
            H.A. Fischel [ed.], *Essays in Greco-Roman and Related Talmudic Literature*
            [Library of Biblical Studies; New York: Ktav, 1977]: 495-99).
1975   *Alien Wisdom: The Limits of Hellenization* (Cambridge: Cambridge
            University Press).
1981   'Greek Culture and the Jews', in M.I. Finley (ed.), *The Legacy of Greece: A
            New Appraisal* (Oxford: Clarendon Press): 325-46.
Moore, G.F.
1921   'Christian Writers on Judaism', *HTR* 14: 197-254.
1927–30   *Judaism in the First Centuries of the Christian Era: The Age of the Tannaim*
            (3 vols.; Cambridge, MA: Harvard University Press).
Mørkholm, O.
1965   'The Municipal Coinages with Portrait of Antiochus IV of Syria', in
            Congresso Internazionale di Numismatica (2 vols.; Rome: Istituto Italiano di
            Numismatica): 67ff.
1983   'The Ptolemaic Coinage in Phoenicia and the Fifth War with Syria', in
            E. van't Dack, P. van Dessel and W. van Gucht (eds.), *Egypt and the Helle-
            nistic World* (Studia Hellenistica, 27; Leuven: Imprimerie Orientaliste): 241-
            51.
Morrison, C.M.K.
1982   *Ethnicity and Political Integration: The Case of the Ashanti Ghana* (Syracuse,
            NY: Maxwell School of Citizenship and Public Affairs).

Naveh, J.
1986   'A Medical Fragment or a Writing Exercise? The So-called 4Q Therapeia', *IEJ* 36: 52-55.

Ne'eman, Y.
1990   Map of Ma'anit (54) 15-20 (Jerusalem: The Israel Antiquities Authority, Archaeological Survey of Israel).

Neubauer, A.
1869   'Chronique samaritaine, suivie d'un appendice contenant de courtes notices sur quelques autres ouvrages samaritains', *JA* 14: 385-470.

Neusner, J.
1985   'Was Rabbinic Judaism Really "Ethnic"?', *CBQ* 57: 281-305.
1987   *Self-Fulfilling Prophecy: Exile and Return in the History of Judaism* (Boston: Beacon Press).

Neyrey, J.H. (ed.)
1991   *The Social World of Luke–Acts* (Peabody, MA: Hendrickson).

Nickelsburg, G.W.E.
1977   'Apocalyptic and Myth in 1 Enoch 6-11', *JBL* 96: 383-405.

Nock, A.D.
1933   *Conversion: The Old and the New in Religion from Alexander the Great to Augustine of Hippo* (Oxford: Clarendon Press).

Noth, M.
1960   *The History of Israel* (trans. P. Ackroyd; New York: Harper & Brothers, 2nd edn).

Pasto, J.
1998   '"Islam's Strange Secret Sharer": Orientalism, Judaism, and the Jewish Question', *CSSH* 44.3: 437-74.
1999a   'Who Owns the Jewish Past: Judaism, Judaisms, and the Construction of Jewish History' (PhD dissertation, Cornell University).
1999b   'When the End is the Beginning? Or When the Biblical Past is the Political Present: Some Thoughts on Ancient Israel, "Post-Exilic Judaism", and the Politics of Biblical Scholarship', *SJOT* 12: 157-202.
2002   'W.M.L. De Wette and the Invention of Post-Exilic Judaism: Political Historiography and Christian Allegory in Nineteenth Century German Biblical Scholarship', in D. Martin and H. Lapin (eds.), *Jews, Antiquity, and the 19th-Century Imagination* (Meyerhoff Series in Jewish Studies; Bethesda: University Press of Maryland, forthcoming).

Peel, J.D.Y.
1982   'Making History: The Past in the Ijesha Present', *Man* NS 19: 111-32.

Pélékidis, C.
1962   *Histoire de l'éphébie attique des origines à 31 avant Jésus-Christ* (Paris: Boccard).

Peremans, W.
1978   'Les révolutions égyptiennes sous les Lagides', in H. Maehler and V.M. Strocka (eds.), *Das ptolemaische Agypten: Akten des Internationalen Symposions 27.–29. September 1976 in Berlin* (Mainz: Zabern): 39-50.

Peters, J., and H. Thiersch
1905   *Painted Tombs in the Necropolis of Marissa (Mareshah)* (London: Palestine Exploration Fund).

Pfeiffer, R.
1968   *History of Classical Scholarship* (Oxford: Clarendon Press).
Polk, T.
1983   'Paradigms, Parables and *Mešalim*: On Reading the *Mašal* in Scripture',
          CBQ 45: 564-83.
Porter, F.C.
1927   'Judaism in New Testament Times', *JR* 8: 30-62.
Prakash G. (ed.)
1995   *After Colonialism: Imperial Histories and Postcolonial Displacements*
          (Princeton, NJ: Princeton University Press).
Pritchard, J.
1985   *Tell es-Sa'idiyeh: Excavations on the Tell, 1964–1966* (Philadelphia:
          University Museum, University of Pennsylvania).
Pugliese Carratelli, G., and G. Garbini
1964   *A Bilingual Graeco-Aramaic Edict by Asoka: The First Greek Inscription
          Discovered in Afghanistan* (Serie Orientale Roma, 29; Rome: Istituto
          Italiano per il Medio ed Estremo Oriente).
Pummer, R.
1979   'The *Book of Jubilees* and the Samaritans', *Eglise et Théologie* 10: 147-78.
1982a   'Antisamaritanische Polemik in jüdischen Schriften aus der intertestamen-
          tarischen Zeit', *BZ* 26: 224-42.
1982b   'Genesis 34 in Jewish Writings of the Hellenistic and Roman Periods', *HTR*
          76: 177-88.
1987   'Αργαριζιν: A Criterion for Samaritan Provenance?', *JSJ* 18: 18-25.
1988   Review of Egger 1986, in *JBL* 107: 768-72.
1989   'Samaritan Material Remains and Archaeology', in Crown (ed.) 1989:
          166-75.
1997   'Samaritans', in Eric M. Meyers (ed.), *The Oxford Encyclopedia of Archae-
          ology in the Near East*, IV (Oxford: Oxford University Press): 469-72.
Purvis, J.D.
1968   *The Samaritan Pentateuch and the Origin of the Samaritan Sect* (HSM, 2;
          Cambridge, MA: Harvard University Press).
1981   'The Samaritan Problem: A Case Study in Jewish Sectarianism in the Roman
          Era', in B. Halpern and J.D. Levenson (eds.), *Traditions in Transformation:
          Turning Points in Biblical Faith* (Winona Lake, IN: Eisenbrauns): 323-50.
Raban, A.
1982   Nahalal Map (28) 16-23 (Jerusalem: The Archaeological Survey of Israel).
Rajak, T.
1984   'Was There a Roman Charter for the Jews?', *JRS* 74: 107-123.
1990   'The Hasmoneans and the Uses of Hellenism', in P.R. Davies and R.T.
          White (eds.), *A Tribute to Geza Vermes: Essays on Jewish and Christian
          Literature and History* (JSOTSup, 100; Sheffield: JSOT Press): 261-80.
Rappaport, U.
1967   'Hellenistic Cities and the Judaization of Palestine in the Hasmonean Age',
          in S. Perlman and B. Shimron (eds.), *Doron: Studies in Classical Culture
          Presented to B.Z. Katz Benshalom* (Tel Aviv: Mif'al ha-Shikhpul, 1967):
          214-30.
1969   'Les Iduméns en Egypte', *Revue de Philologie* 43: 73-82.

1984 'Numismatics', in Davies and Finkelstein 1984: 25-59.

1991 'The Material Culture of the Jews in the Hellenistic-Roman Period', in S. Talmon (ed.), *Jewish Civilization in the Hellenistic-Roman Period* (JSPSup, 10; Sheffield: Sheffield Academic Press): 44-49.

Redford, R., and M.B. Singer

1954–55 'The Cultural Role of Cities', *Economic Development and Cultural Change* 3: 53-73.

Reviv, H.

1989 *The Elders in Ancient Israel: A Study of a Biblical Institution* (trans. Lucy Plitmann; Jerusalem: Magnes Press).

Richardson, P.

1996 *Herod: King of the Jews and Friend of the Romans* (Columbia, SC: University of South Carolina Press).

Robertson, R.G.

1985 'Ezekiel the Tragedian', in *OTP*, II: 803-19.

Roesch, P.

1971 'Une loi fédérale béotienne sur la preparation militaire', in *Acta of the Fifth International Congress of Greek and Latin Epigraphy, Cambridge, 1967* (Oxford: Basil Blackwell): 81-88.

Rogerson, J.W.

1992 *W.M.L. de Wette: Founder of Modern Biblical Criticism* (JSOTSup, 126; Sheffield: JSOT Press).

Roller, D.

1980 'Hellenistic Pottery from Caesarea Maritima: A Preliminary Study', *BASOR* 238: 35-42.

1982 'The Northern Plain of Sharon in the Hellenistic Period', *BASOR* 247: 43-52.

Ross, W.D. (ed.)

1928 *The Works of Plato* (Oxford: Clarendon Press).

Rostovtzeff, M.

1932 'Seleucid Babylonia: Bullae and Seals of Clay with Greek Inscriptions', *YCS* 3: 1-114.

1939 'Some Remarks on the Monetary and Commercial Policy of the Seleucids and Attalids', in W.M. Calder and J. Keil (eds.), *Anatolian Studies Presented to W.H. Buckler* (Manchester: Manchester University Press): 277-98.

1941 *The Social and Economic History of the Hellenistic World* (3 vols.; Oxford: Clarendon Press).

Roueché, C., and S.M. Sherwin-White

1985 'Some Aspects of the Seleucid Empire: The Greek Inscriptions from Failaka, in the Arabian Gulf', *Chiron* 15: 1-39.

Sahlins, M.

1981 *Historical Metaphors and Mythical Realities: Structure in the Early History of the Sandwich Islands Kingdom* (ASAO Special Publications, 1; Ann Arbor: University of Michigan Press).

1999 'Two or Three Things I Know about Culture', *Journal of the Royal Anthropological Institute* NS 5: 399-421.

Saldarini, A.J.

1988 *Pharisees, Scribes, and Sadducees in Palestinian Society* (Wilmington, DE: Michael Glazier).

Samuel, A.E.
1983   *From Athens to Alexandria: Hellenism and Social Goals in Ptolemaic Egypt*
            (Studia Hellenistica, 26; Louvain: Imprimerie Orientaliste).
Sanders. J.T.
1983   *Ben Sira and Demotic Wisdom* (Chico, CA: Scholars Press).
Sangreen, P.S.
1984   'Great Tradition and Little Traditions Reconsidered: The Question of
            Cultural Integration in China', *Journal of Chinese Studies* 1: 1-24.
Sarkisian, G.K.
1974   'Greek Personal Names in Uruk and the *Graeco-Babyloniaca* Problem', *Acta
            Antiqua* 22: 495-503.
Schäfer, P.
1977   'The Hellenistic and Maccabean Periods', in J.H. Hayes and J.M. Miller
            (eds.), *Israelite and Judean History* (London: SCM Press; Philadelphia:
            Westminster Press): 539-604.
Schalit, A.
1970–71   'Die Denkschrift der Samaritaner an König Antiochos Epiphanes zu
            Beginn der Großen Verfolgung der jüdischen Religion im Jahre 167 v. Chr.
            (Josephus, *AJ* XII, §258-64)', *ASTI* 5: 131-83.
Schmidt, F.
2001   *How the Temple Thinks: Identity and Social Cohesion in Ancient Judaism*
            (trans. J. Edward Crowley; BibSem, 78; Sheffield: Sheffield Academic
            Press).
Schuller, E.M.
1990   '4Q372 1: A Text about Joseph', *RevQ* 14.55: 349-76.
Schürer, E.
1973–87   *The Jewish People in the Age of Jesus Christ* (3 vols.; rev. G. Vermes *et al.*;
            Edinburgh: T. & T. Clark).
Schwartz, S.
1991   'Israel and the Nations Roundabout: 1 Maccabees and the Hasmonean
            Expansion', *JJS* 42: 16-38.
1993   'A Note on the Social Type and Political Ideology of the Hasmonean
            Family', *JBL* 112: 305-17.
Scott, J.C.
1977   'Protest and Profanation: Agrarian Revolt and the Little Tradition, Part I',
            Theory and Society 4: 1-38.
Sellers, O.
1933   *The Citadel of Beth-zur* (Philadelphia: Westminster Press).
Shatzman, I.
1991   *The Armies of the Hasmoneans and Herod* (Tübingen: J.C.B. Mohr).
Sherwin-White, S.M.
1982   'A Greek Ostrakon from Babylon of the Early Third Century B.C.', *ZPE* 47:
            51-70.
1983   'Ritual for a Seleucid King at Babylon?', *JHS* 103: 156-59.
1987   'Seleucid Babylonia: A Case Study for the Installation and Development of
            Greek Rule', in Kuhrt and Sherwin-White 1987: 1-31.
Sherwin-White, S.M., and A. Kuhrt
1993   *From Samarkhand to Sardis: A New Approach to the Seleucid Empire*
            (London: Gerald Duckworth).

Shiloh, Y.
    1978   'Elements in the Development of Town Planning in the Israelite City', *IEJ* 28: 36-51.
Sievers, J.
    1990   *The Hasmoneans and their Supporters: From Mattathias to the Death of John Hyrcanus I* (Atlanta: Scholars Press).
Skehan, P.W., and A.A. Di Lella
    1987   *The Wisdom of Ben Sira* (AB, 39; Garden City, NY: Doubleday).
Smith, J.Z.
    1978   *Map is Not Territory* (Leiden: E.J. Brill).
Smith, M.
    1971   *Palestinian Parties and Politics that Shaped the Old Testament* (New York: Columbia University Press).
Smith, R.
    1987   'Trade in the Life of Pella of the Decapolis', in A. Hadidi (ed.), *Studies in the History and Archaeology of Jordan III* (London: Routledge & Kegan Paul): 53-58.
    1990   'The Southern Levant in the Hellenistic Period', *Levant* 22: 123-30.
Spek, R.J. van der
    1987   'The Babylonian City', in Kuhrt and Sherwin-White 1987: 57-74.
Stadelmann, H.
    1980   *Ben Sira als Schriftgelehrter* (Tubingen: J.C.B. Mohr).
Stemberger, G.
    1996   *Introduction to the Talmud and Midrash* (Edinburgh: T. & T. Clark; Minneapolis: Fortress Press, 2nd edn).
Stenhouse, P.
    1985   *The Kitâb al-Tarîkh of Abū 'l-Fath, Translated into English with Notes* (Mandelbaum Studies in Judaica; Sydney: Sydney University Press).
    1989   'Samaritan Chronicles', in Crown (ed.) 1989: 218-65.
Sterling, G.E.
    1992   *Historiography and Self-Definition: Josephus, Luke–Acts and Apologetic Historiography* (NovTSup, 24; Leiden: E.J. Brill).
Stern, E.
    1977   'Yehud: The Vision and the Reality', *Cathedra* 4: 13-25.
    1978   *Excavations at Tel Mevorakh (1973–1976). Part One: From the Iron Age to the Roman Period* (Qedem, 9; Jerusalem: Institute of Archaeology, The Hebrew University of Jerusalem).
    1982   *Material Culture of the Land of the Bible in the Persian Period 538–332 B.C.* (Warminster: Aris and Phillips).
    1985   'The Excavations at Tel Dor', in E. Lipiński (ed.), *The Land of Israel: Cross-roads of Civilizations* (Leuven: Peeters): 169-92.
Stern, E. (ed.)
    1974–84   *Greek and Latin Authors on Jews and Judaism* (3 vols.; Jerusalem: Israel Academy of Sciences and Humanities).
Stone, M.E.
    1976   'Lists of Revealed Things in Apocalyptic Literature', in F.M. Cross, W.E. Lemke and P.D. Miller (eds.), *Magnalia Dei: The Mighty Acts of God* (Garden City, NY: Doubleday): 414-52.

Strack, H.L., and G. Stemberger
    1991   *Introduction to the Talmud and Midrash* (Minneapolis: Fortress Press; London: SCM Press).
Strange, J.
    1989   'Architecture and Theology', *SEÅ* 54: 199-206.
Tadmor, H.
    1992   'The Aramaization of Assyria: Aspects of Western Impact', in H.-J. Nissen and J. Renger (eds.), *Mesopotamien und Seine Nachbarn: Politische und kulturelle Wechselpeziehungen im Alten Vorderasien vom 4. bis 1. Jahrtausend v. Chr.* (Berlin: Reimer): 449-70.
Tarn, W.W., and G.T. Griffith
    1952   *Hellenistic Civilisation* (London: Edward Arnold, 3rd edn).
Taylor, J.
    1979   'Seleucid Rule in Palestine' (PhD dissertation, Duke University, Durham, NC).
Tcherikover, V.A.
    1959   *Hellenistic Civilization and the Jews* (repr.; New York: Atheneum).
Tcherikover, V.A., A. Fuks and M. Stern
    1957–64   *Corpus Papyrorum Judaicarum* (3 vols.; Cambridge, MA: Harvard University Press; Jerusalem: Magnes Press).
Teske, R.H.C., and B.H. Nelson
    1974   'Acculturation and Assimilation: A Clarification', *American Ethnologist* 1.1: 21-33.
Theissen, G.
    1978   *The Sociology of Early Palestinian Christianity* (Philadelphia: Fortress Press).
    1985   *The Miracle Stories of the Early Christian Tradition* (Philadelphia: Fortress Press).
Thompson, T.L.
    1992   *Early History of the Israelite People from the Written and Archaeological Sources* (Studies in the History of the Ancient Near East, 4; Leiden: E.J. Brill).
    1999   *The Mythic Past: Biblical Archaeology and the Myth of Israel* (New York: Basic Books).
    2000   'Lester Grabbe and Historiography: An Apologia', *SJOT* 14: 140-61.
Tomson, P.J.
    1986   'The Names Israel and Jew in Ancient Judaism and the New Testament', *Bijdragen, Tijdschrift voor filosofie en theologie* 47: 120-40, 266-89.
Tov, E.
    1989   'Proto-Samaritan Texts and the Samaritan Pentateuch', in Crown (ed.) 1989: 397-407.
    1992   *Textual Criticism of the Hebrew Bible* (Assen: Van Gorcum; Minneapolis: Fortress Press [2nd edn, 2001]).
Trebilco, P.
    1991   *Jewish Communities in Asia Minor* (Cambridge: Cambridge University Press).
VanderKam, J.C.
    1984   *Enoch and the Growth of an Apocalyptic Tradition* (CBQMS, 16; Washington: Catholic Biblical Association).

Vermes, G.
1997   *The Complete Dead Sea Scrolls in English* (New York: Allen Lane).
Vogel, E.K.
1971   'Bibliography of Holy Land Sites: Part I', *HUCA* 42: 1-96.
1981   'Bibliography of Holy Land Sites: Part II', *HUCA* 52: 1-92.
1987   'Bibliography of Holy Land Sites: Part III, 1981-1987', *HUCA* 58: 1-63.
Weinberg, J.
1973   'Probleme der Sozialokonomischen Struktur Judaas vom 6. Jahrhundert v.u.z. bis zum 1. Jahrhundert u.z.', *Jahrbuch fur Wirtschaftsgeschichte* 1: 237-51.
1992   *The Citizen–Temple Community* (trans. Daniel L. Smith-Christopher; JSOTSup, 151; Sheffield: JSOT Press).
Wellhausen, J.
1874   *Die Pharisäer und Sadducäer* (Greifswald).
1905   'Über den geschichtlichen Wert des zweiten Makkabäerbuches im Verhältnis zum ersten', *Nachbericht von der Gesellschaft der Wissenschaft zu Göttingen, Phil.-hist. Klasse*: 117-63.
Wilk, R.R.
1985   'The Ancient Maya and the Political Present', *JAR* 41: 307-26.
Wilks, I.
1975   *Asante in the Nineteenth Century: The Structure and Evolution of a Political Order* (Cambridge: Cambridge University Press).
Williams, M.H.
1997   'The Meaning and Function of *Ioudaios* in Graeco-Roman Inscriptions', *ZPE* 116: 249-57.
Worsley, P.
1957   *The Trumpet Shall Sound: A Study of 'Cargo' Cults in Melanesia* (London: Macgibbon & Kee).
Wright, G.E.
1962   'The Samaritans at Shechem', *HTR* 55: 357-66.
1964   *Shechem: The Biography of a Biblical City* (New York: McGraw–Hill).
Wright, J.W.
1990   'Guarding the Gates: 1 Chronicles 26.1-19 and the Roles of Gatekeepers in Chronicles', *JSOT* 48: 69-81.
Wycherley, R.E.
1962   Review of Delorme 1960, in *JHS* 82: 201.
Yavetz, Z.
1993   'Judeophobia in Classical Antiquity: A Different Approach', *JJS* 44: 1-22.
Zeitlin, S.
1974   *Solomon Zeitlin's Studies in the Early History of Judaism* (2 vols.; New York: Ktav).
Zenner, W.P.
1972   'Aqiili Agha: The Strongman in the Ethnic Relations of the Ottoman Galilee', *CSSH* 14: 169-88.
Zeron, A.
1980   'The Swansong of Edom', *JJS* 3: 190-98.

Zertal, A.
    1990   'The *Pahwah* of Samaria (Northern Israel) during the Persian Period: Types of Settlement, Economy, History and New Discoveries', *Transeuphratène* 3: 9-30.

Zori, N.
    1977   *The Land of Issachar: Archaeological Survey* (Jerusalem: Israel Exploration Society).

INDEXES

INDEX OF REFERENCES

OLD TESTAMENT

APOCRYPHA

INDEX OF AUTHORS